Praise for

"Here is a collection of superb essays speaking to one of the most pressing moral and civil issues of our time. Religious freedom, once taken for granted in our culture, is increasingly under threat today, at home as well as abroad. *Set Free* is a welcomed resource in a struggle all persons of conscience must embrace—for eternal vigilance is still the price for religious liberty."

— Timothy George, Beeson Divinity School of Samford University, general editor of the Reformation Commentary on Scripture

"Religious freedom is under assault to various degrees throughout the world and this timely book, with contributions by leading experts, explains the principles, reasoning, and laws that underpin America's unique understanding of religious freedom. It explains why religious freedom is the foundation of our free society; how it is not limited to the confines of one's home or the four walls of a building; and the significance of "reasonable accommodation" for religious practice in a religiously pluralistic society like our own. *Set Free* offers an important primer for defending the precious right of religious freedom for all Americans."

— Nina Shea, Director, Hudson Institute's Center for Religious Freedom, Former Commissioner, U.S. Commission on International Religious Freedom

"Many Americans treat political, economic, and religious freedom separate, and separable, things. Some defend political and economic freedom while ignoring religious freedom. Some ardent religious believers are dismissive of economic freedom. And even some Christians believe the idea of religious freedom is the product of the secular enlightenment. This important book shows why these ways of thinking are deeply mistaken and ultimately self-destructive. Religious freedom is our first freedom, and it is deeply rooted in Scripture and Christian history. No society that ignores it can long enjoy freedom in the political and economic spheres."

—Jay Richards, Research Assistant,
Professor in the Busch School of Business
at the Catholic University of America
Senior Fellow at the Discovery Institute

"Religious freedom is more than America's first freedom, it is God's gift to humanity, a beacon of hope, and a blessing for all faiths in every corner of the world. People that care about preserving and protecting religious freedom domestically and abroad should read this book and become more than articulate about its history, its Biblical foundations, its importance to all other freedoms, and the looming dangers of losing it."

—David Nammo, Executive Director and CEO, Christian Legal Society

"In a world of increasing incivility in the public square, it is essential that people of goodwill embrace religious liberty. After all, no one has the ability to force another human being to believe anything that he or she does not believe. The liberty of conscience is in desperate need of affirmation in our day. Toward this end, *Set Free* is an important read. The book grapples with the relevant issues and should help the reader engage others in a thoughtful and civil manner."

—Paul A. Cleveland, PhD Professor of Economics and Finance, Department of Business, Birmingham-Southern College

"*Set Free* is a must-read for those who care about the linkage between religious freedom and human flourishing. It is refreshing to see an outstanding group of scholars use Biblical principles, history, ethics, and empirical analysis to examine the role of religious freedom and its importance as a source of personal liberty, sound institutions, and human progress."

—James Gwartney, Professor of Economics, Florida State University

"Religious liberty is the root of every other human right and duty. Without soul freedom, there can be no freedom at all worthy of the name. This First Freedom is grounded in the *imago Dei* reflected in every human being and in the gospel of Jesus Christ itself. *Set Free* guides the reader through the importance of religious liberty with an eye to developments in the culture around us. This book is worthy of deep reflection and conscientious consideration."

—Russell Moore, President, The Ethics & Religious Liberty Commission of the Southern Baptist Convention

"With a diverse cast of powerhouse contributors, *Set Free* makes a stirring biblical, historical, and practical case for defending religious freedom for all. Every Christian who cares about religious freedom will learn from this valuable book."

—Luke Goodrich, Vice President and Senior Counsel at the Becket Fund for Religious Liberty and author of *Free to Believe: The Battle over Religious Liberty in America*

SET FREE

SET FREE

RESTORING

RELIGIOUS FREEDOM
---
for ALL

ART LINDSLEY & ANNE R. BRADLEY

EDITORS

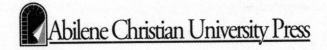
Abilene Christian University Press

ACU
PRESS

Contents

Contents

The Relationship between Religious, Economic, and Political Freedom

Why Is Religious Freedom at Risk in Today's Culture and What Can Be Done about It?

Acknowledgments

Set Free: Restoring Religious Freedom for All was produced by the Institute for Faith, Work & Economics (IFWE) in collaboration with the John Templeton Foundation and made possible through a grant in the funding area of Individual Freedom and Free Markets. IFWE is grateful for its partnership with the John Templeton Foundation on the project, Religious Freedom: Communicating the Moral Foundations of Freedom and Human Flourishing that provided the content for this book.

About the Institute For Faith, Work & Economics

The Institute for Faith, Work & Economics™ (IFWE) is a nonprofit, 501(c)(3) Christian research organization committed to promoting biblical and economic principles that help individuals find fulfillment in their work and contribute to a free and flourishing society.

IFWE's research starts with the belief that the Bible, as the inerrant Word of God, provides the authoritative and intellectual foundation for a proper understanding of work and economic truths that, when properly followed, can help individuals, companies, communities, and nations flourish.

IFWE's research is based on three core principles:

1. Each person is created in God's image and, like him, has a desire to be creative and to find **fulfillment** using their God-given talents through work.
2. All work, whether paid or volunteer, matters to God, and we as Christians are called to pursue excellence throughout the week—not just on Sundays—stewarding all that we've been given for God's glory and for the **flourishing** of society.
3. Therefore, we as citizens must promote an economic environment that not only provides us the **freedom** to pursue our callings and flourish in our work but also reflects the inherent dignity of every human being.

Our desire is to help Christians view their work within the bigger picture of what God is doing in the world. Not only do we help Christians find personal fulfillment, but we also help them understand how to better alleviate poverty, address greed, and view possessions properly. With a biblical view of work and economics, we can partner together to be meaningful participants in God's plan to restore the world to the way he intended it to be.

Introduction

Art Lindsley

Religious freedom is what the founding fathers called the first freedom, and it is one of the most important things the U.S. experiment gave the world. Legal scholars throughout this nation's history have believed that the First Amendment of the U.S. Constitution recognized one's right to lead life according to faith and religious moral code, not only in our churches but also in our homes, in our places of work, and in the public square. In recent years, however, that belief has been challenged.

We view any attack on religious freedom as alarming because it threatens to negate the guarantee of individual liberty afforded to every person, regardless of faith. Left unchecked, attacks on religious freedom threaten the culture of freedom upon which our system of republican government was founded. The Institute for Faith, Work & Economics (IFWE) sees our nation at a critical point in its history; what we do in the near future will have significant impact on what kind of country we will leave to our children. This is why we think that the work on religious freedom represented in this book is so important.

Unfortunately, an overwhelming majority of the U.S. population—and especially its more than eighty million Evangelical Christians—seem to have little regard for the topic of religious freedom. Many in this population have forgotten not only the importance of this core freedom but also its roots in biblical principles.

Most Evangelical Christians in the United States are either unaware of or do not understand why it is important. They also do not know that they are called to champion religious freedom for all, as their Christian forefathers did over the last four centuries in the cultures and eras where they lived and worked. These Evangelical Christians have even mistakenly opted out of parts of civil life—for example, almost half did not vote in the last three presidential elections.

At IFWE, we engage, educate, and activate Christians and help them apply biblical principles to all of life—work, home, church, community, and nation. We do this by focusing on three core concepts: freedom, fulfillment, and flourishing. We believe that these three values are moral and grounded in Scripture.

You can see this visually in the chart below (contrasted with consequences, if these values are missing).

Moral	Immoral
Freedom	Slavery and bondage
Fulfillment	Frustration
Flourishing	Poverty

We believe that if there is economic, political, and religious freedom, people (made in the image of God) will be free to use their creativity to unfold the potential of the creation around them (Gen. 1:26–28). When people are free to use their creative gifts, there is fulfillment as they see and enjoy the fruits of their own labor (Mic. 4:4). When millions of people are free to use their creative gifts and cooperate with others in society, there is flourishing.

Without freedom, there is bondage or slavery (in whole or in part). In the political sphere, governments can seek to be increasingly involved in every aspect of our lives. In the extreme, it can become totalitarianism or government by a ruling elite. We believe that government should remain small, both in its reach and spending, in proportion to the economy, and it should allow citizens the freedom to live out their lives in peace (see Chapter Nine by Jennifer Marshall Patterson).

The primary role of government is to restrain and punish those who do evil (Rom. 13:1–7). First, government is "established by God" (Rom. 13:1). Second, government is designated as a "minister of God" twice in Romans 13:4 and a "servant of God" in Romans 13:6. Third, government does not "bear the sword" in vain and is entrusted with "punishment of the evildoer." In 2 Peter 2:13–14, it says that rulers are given the role of "punishment of evildoers and the praise of those who do right." Government's primary role is a negative one (punishment of evil) rather than a positive one (providing goods and services). Fourth, note that government should give "praise to those who do right," meaning that it can acknowledge and uphold as a positive role model those in the culture who are doing good things. Fifth, we are to pray for those in government, that we "may live a tranquil and quiet life in all godliness and dignity" (1 Tim. 2:1–2), emphasizing the place of rule of law: giving safety to those it serves.

Economic freedom means having the ability to buy and sell without undue restrictions. This involves minimizing regulations and resisting ever-increasing taxes, making it relatively easy to start small- and medium-sized businesses (SMEs) (see Section 3). Without economic freedom, there is bondage or slavery (in whole or in part) to government restrictions on the economy. People become frustrated as they have increasing obstacles to do business and live their lives freely.

Religious-based moral values are imperative for the economy. Without religious freedom, individuals would not be able to believe and practice their faith as they wish (or choose not to practice any faith). These religiously based moral values need to be applied by people in the public arena. Most people make their moral judgments based upon their faith. Otherwise, they lack sufficient basis to decide the difference between a good law and a bad law. Without these values, they also lack an adequate foundation for educating people to form good character and godly conscience. An economy is dependent on the character of its citizens. If there is not fundamental honesty and trust, an economic system slowly grinds to a halt or proceeds in a halting fashion. If there are many breeches of contract, the courts become clogged and people become reluctant to make agreements.

In the United States, as we shall see in the upcoming chapters, freedom, in the general sense, requires virtue; virtue requires faith; and faith requires freedom.[1] I once hosted a major general from the Soviet air force who had been second in command in the KGB. He was traveling around the United States (after the wall came down) because he saw the need for a restored moral foundation in the former USSR and wanted to understand (as an atheist) what faith in Christ could provide for his nation. He believed that this moral foundation was especially important for the economy to grow and flourish; and, as mentioned earlier, where there is not flourishing, there is poverty.

This book deals with the topic of religious freedom from many angles. In Chapter One, Os Guinness provides a sweeping survey of the present situation and what is at stake if we fail to address the threats to religious freedom.

In Chapters Two through Chapter Four, we look at religious freedom in the Old and New Testaments, focusing on key biblical concepts such as the image of God, the importance of freedom and responsibility, the place of conscience, and the way these biblical concepts influenced the debate on religious freedom at key points in history. John Redd, Barrett Duke, and Hugh Whelchel approach this topic from various directions.

Greg Wallace shows in Chapter Five how the idea of religious freedom developed from the period of the early church through the Reformation. In Chapter Six, Daniel Dreisbach explores the origins of religious freedom in

---

[1] Os Guinness, *A Free People's Suicide: Sustainable Freedom and the American Future* (Downers Grove, IL: IVP, 2012), 99.

America. It is important to note here that religious freedom arises from a biblical foundation and not from secular sources. Then in Chapter Seven, I note how the biblical view of freedom underlies political, economic, and religious freedom in the United States today.

In Chapter Eight, Anne Bradley and Joe Connors further explore the relationship between political, economic, and political freedom. They provide data that show the importance of religious freedom in allowing opportunities for voluntary associations—the building blocks of an emerging society. If this cultivated soil is present, economic freedom can flourish.

In Chapters Nine through Eleven, we look at our current situation along with the issues we are facing now or will likely face in the near future. Jennifer Marshall Patterson surveys the impact of sex and gender issues; Mark David Hall gives us a helpful survey of the way that religious accommodations have been addressed by America's founders and, later, many legislators and jurists; and finally, Stanley Carlson-Thies demonstrates the significant contributions that faith-based organizations have made to our society. If these organizations are unreasonably driven out of business by being forced to do things that they cannot, in good conscience, do, society will be much, much poorer.

What we don't address explicitly in this book is the current international situation regarding religious freedom. We are aware of religious hostilities or restrictions on religion in a majority of countries throughout the world. This is a massive subset of the discussion around religious freedom that is worthy of attention. Numerous organizations exist to shed light on religious persecution or issues related to restricted religious freedom internationally. In this volume, however, we focus on religious freedom in the United States.

What we aim to do in this book is to make the case for *religious freedom for all,* regardless of religion and geographic location. Often, the temptation of Christians is to spend time documenting and defending real or attempted assaults on *their* religious freedom. This effort certainly has its place. But Christians have a vested interest in protecting religious freedom for all, and the reasons for this defense are found in scripture itself. God graciously allows us to choose to follow him, and people of other faiths or no faith must be free to make this choice as well. Christians believe in the truth of the Bible and that it is our guide to faith and practice—we want freedom to live this out, but we want freedom for those who don't believe this to be able to live out their faith as well. Our belief in the truth of the Bible does not mean we want to force it on others.

The authors of this book strongly maintain that religious belief cannot and should not be coerced. Religious belief cannot be coerced, because such coercion would only produce a hypocritical faith and not a true faith. Faith should not be coerced because forcing any person to act against their own conscience is wrong. Whatever is not of faith is sin (Rom. 14:23). Any such coercion also goes against the First Amendment, which states, "Congress shall make no law respecting the establishment of religion nor prohibiting the free exercise thereof."

Christians should be at the forefront of the battle for religious freedom even for people with whom we deeply disagree. The best way to retain our rights is to be defenders of others' rights.

We hope that this book will provoke thought and stir discussions in churches, colleges, and seminaries and that many would take seriously this issue of religious freedom. We want not only to be better informed but also to be advocates on the issue of religious freedom. What we need is not "freedom from" religion but "freedom of" religion in personal and public life.

Religious Freedom Overview

Chapter 1

First Freedom First: Christian Advocacy for Freedom of Religion and Conscience

Os Guinness
Author and Social Critic, Washington, DC

"Congress shall make no law respecting an establishment of religion, or prohibiting the free exercise thereof."
—First Amendment of the U.S. Constitution, 1791

"Everyone has the right to freedom of thought, conscience and religion; this right includes freedom to change his religion or belief, and freedom, either alone or in community with others and in public or private, to manifest his religion or belief in teaching, practice, worship, and observance."
—Article 18, Universal Declaration of Human Rights, 1948

"Son, we're in trouble. Chiang Kai-shek has just flown to Taiwan with his family and his money."

Those words from my father in January 1949, when I was seven, were my introduction to an early crash course on the importance of freedom of religion and conscience. We were living in what was then Nanking, the capital of the Western-supported National Republic of China. Following the generalissimo's flight, it was only a matter of weeks before the Red Army captured the city, Mao moved the capital of China back to Beijing, and his Communist regime began its reign of terror, including the vicious persecution of Christians. Earlier, as a small boy, I had been bored to death as I endured church services and sermons, which were growing longer and longer each week, only to be told that the pastors were planning for the dire persecution that lay ahead. They were laying down all the foundational teaching they could in order to prepare their people for whatever was coming. And come it did. It was one of the most vicious, brutal, and systematic persecutions in the history of the Christian church, yet one in which the faith of the Christians prevailed gloriously and the church in China grew exponentially—as it will again, despite the brutality-cum-sophistication of the current persecution under Xi Jinping.

From that day on, the lesson has been branded on my heart: freedom of religion and conscience is a precious, foundational, and indispensable right, and we must never take it for granted. It is no casual matter. It is not merely an abstract principle or parchment right. Lying at the heart of the freedom to be human and to be faithful, it is ultimately a matter of life and death for millions of people in our world—and not only for Christians but for people of almost every faith. Truly, we can declare with a ringing conviction that freedom of religion and conscience is the "first freedom" and a foundational human right, a principle and a protection that every lover of freedom and justice, and certainly every follower of Jesus, should understand, promote, and defend as critical and priceless.[1]

Weighing the Stakes

Humanity now faces one of the most extraordinary moments we have ever encountered in the long story of our existence on planet earth. For today, we humans stand "post-Auschwitz," "post-Hiroshima," and "pre-Singularity," and we must answer to ourselves what we mean when we call ourselves "human."

"Post-Auschwitz" means that we have to answer the question, "What does it say of us that those who carried out these monstrous crimes against humanity were the same species we are?" "Post-Hiroshima" and the later nuclear defense of the doctrine of Mutually Assured Destruction (MAD for short) means that we have to ask ourselves, "What does it say of us that our safest defense against the threats of a menacing Other is a counterthreat to destroy them entirely and even to destroy many of our fellow humans and much of the earth that is our home?" And "pre-Singularity" means that we have to explore the question, "What has brought us to the point where we pursue progress and seek salvation through technology, even though the price of this salvation and progress is a vision of humanity that would be unrecognizable, if not repellent to almost all human beings up until now?"

These are titanic questions, but the basic challenge facing our generation is simple: in the words of the great Jewish leader, Rabbi Lord Jonathan Sacks, the former chief rabbi of Great Britain, "Can we make, on earth, a social order not based on the transactions of power but on respect for the human person—each person—as 'the image of God'?"[2] And, I would add, as we attempt to do that in

---

[1] William Lee Miller, *The First Liberty: Religion and the American Republic* (New York: Alfred A. Knopf, 1987).

[2] Jonathan Sacks, *The Jonathan Sacks Haggadah* (New Milford, CT: Maggid Books, 2013), 6.

today's advanced modern world, can we transform people long enervated by ancient and modern forms of deference, passivity, dependency, and victimhood into members of society and citizens of nations with a capacity for freedom, responsibility, initiative, enterprise, and justice?

That prospect is easy to state but hard to bring about. There is no question that a thicket of questions and controversy now surrounds each of the ideas just mentioned—human dignity, freedom, responsibility, equality, justice, peace, and stability. But no issue is more crucial to them all and to the human future than the human understanding of humanity, and no principle is more critical to this issue than freedom of religion and conscience. Hence this book, setting out the importance of this principle, and my privilege in introducing it.

Needless to say, the issue of freedom of religion and conscience is huge and complex, beyond the scope of any single book, let alone an introduction. But let me highlight its basic significance through some foundational points that others will expand on in later chapters. I am writing for anyone dedicated to freedom, but above all, for Christians who desire to defend freedom of religion and conscience, and especially for Evangelicals who have an immense stake in the issue today.

With Gratitude but Humility

First, we must start with the reminder that we who call ourselves Christians and followers of Jesus have a mixed record over the issue of freedom of religion and conscience. We must therefore acknowledge both the best and worst of the past, showing genuine humility over the church's worst failures, even if they do not come from our own particular tradition, while still standing with real gratitude and pride over the magnificent contributions of other Christians. For the truth is that Christians have been the *pioneers* of religious freedom as well as *perpetrators* of some of the most egregious offences against religious freedom, and today we are the most *persecuted* faith on the earth.

As Christians, we proudly stand as pioneers of religious freedom. The Genesis declaration that humans are made in the image and likeness of God has been described as the Magna Carta of humanity. It can properly be argued that human freedom itself is rooted in the Bible's view of creation—especially the Hebrew notion of freedom that lies at the heart of the first two books, Genesis and Exodus. But the first specific mention of religious freedom in history was by Tertullian in the second century. He used the term "religious liberty" (*libertatem religionis*) in his *Apology*.[3] He was soon followed by Lactantius who, as tutor to the son of the Emperor Constantine, may well have been behind the Edict of Milan in AD 313. This was the first official document to set out the notion of religious freedom and distinguish it from mere tolerance. In the view of these early Christians, God, in his sovereign freedom, requires from his creatures a response of free trust, free worship, and free allegiance. Coercion is therefore absolutely antithetical and contradictory to Jewish and Christian faith, which should be entirely voluntary, based solely on the dictates of each person's conscience.

Yet sadly, Christians have also been perpetrators of some of the worst violations of conscience. During the Middle Ages, for example, the church's power became both corrupt and oppressive, and Christians violated religious freedom in countless egregious ways—through such evils as the forced conversion of the Jews, the appalling notion that "error has no rights," and the Inquisition. In Hebrew, these "converts" were the *anusim*, "the coerced," and in Spanish, they were the contemptuous word *marranos*, "the swine." Such acts were vile in themselves, and their consequences have been long-lasting. As a result, a major reason for the rise of modern secularism and secularity was the massive revulsion against the corruptions and repressions of the established churches in Europe. Church and state, throne and altar were in collusion, corrupt and oppressive, so those who desired freedom believed they had to overthrow both of them. (Take, for example, Diderot's maxim, which became the cry of the French revolutionaries: "We shall never be free until the last king is strangled with the guts of the last priest.")

Following Vatican II, the Catholic Church reversed its position on religious freedom and now stands as a worldwide champion of what it once opposed. But centuries before that, the Reformation came to reassert the early Christian stance on religious freedom, and Vatican II launched a radical reversal of the medieval position, with Pope John Paul II publicly confessing the medieval sins more than sixty times. Christians are not the persecutors now; rather, they are the most persecuted faith in the world. Many other religions are savagely persecuted too—for example, the Bahai in Iran and the Muslim Uighurs in China. But wherever people are persecuted, Christians are persecuted too.

The first two of these three points pull in opposite directions. But the facts are an unavoidable, if regrettable, part of Christian history, and the damage has been done. There is a practical reason why we must never forget the problem: fairly or not, our critics and enemies will commonly point out our worst and forget our best. They will cite the fires and thumbscrews of the Inquisition,

---

[3] See Timothy Samuel Shah and Allen D. Hertzke, ed., *Christianity and Freedom* (Cambridge: Cambridge University Press, 2016), 52–54, 62–66.

though not the fact that freedom of conscience owes everything to the Reformation and such early modern Christian pioneers as Roger Williams, William Penn, Isaac Backus, and John Leland. Contrary to what many critics imagine, freedom of religion and conscience owes little to the Enlightenment, and recent scholarship has actually shown the incontrovertible link between the Enlightenment and such evils as racism, anti-Semitism, coercion, and violence.[4]

More Urgent than Ever Before

Second, we must understand why the issue of freedom of religion and conscience has become so urgent in our day. Three factors have converged to make freedom of religion and conscience an absolute necessity. If "freedom for the good of all" is to have any chance of being established widely, we must recognize why this is urgent. As Madison urged in his famous "Memorial & Remonstrance" in 1785, "it is proper to take alarm at the first experiment on our liberties. We hold this prudent jealousy to be the first duty of Citizens."[5]

First, the last generation has witnessed an expansion of diversity on an unprecedented scale. Previous periods with rich social diversity, such as that of the Roman Empire during the time the church was born and prospered, were profound but comparatively restricted in area—to countries bordering on the Mediterranean. Today, thanks to such obvious modern factors as travel, the media, scholarship, and, above all, migration and the mass movement of peoples, diversity has increasingly become a global phenomenon. "Everyone is now everywhere," it is said with only a little exaggeration. Naturally, this explosion of diversity raises a basic social and political question: How are we to live with our deepest differences, especially when those deep differences are religious and ideological? And this question, of course, underscores the necessity for freedom of religion and conscience.

Evangelicals, in particular, need to define their terms and respond with care over this issue. "Diversity," or "pluralism," is a social fact, and it holds no more fear for us than it did for the early church. "Relativism" and "multiculturalism," however, are different. One is a philosophical conclusion with which we disagree strongly, and the other is a political policy that we need to weigh wisely, sizing up its pros and cons as a matter of prudential judgment. Too many

---

[4] See John Ralston Saul, *Voltaire's Bastards: The Dictatorship of Reason in the West* (New York: Simon & Schuster, 1992).

[5] James Madison, *The American Republic: Primary Sources*, Bruce Frohnen, ed. (Indianapolis: Liberty Fund, 2002), 328.

Evangelicals now fear "pluralism" as if it were the same as "relativism," and in doing so, they look as if they are blind to an inescapable fact of modern life that all modern people have to live with.

Second, the explosion of diversity has called into question many of the earlier national "settlements," the social and political arrangements by which different nations handled the issues of religion and public life. These settlements usually reflected decisive historical moments in the affairs of each nation—for the French, for example, 1789 and the French Revolution led to a radical separation of church and state that they call *laicite* (remember the Jacobin slogan); whereas for Americans, 1791 and the First Amendment represented a bold separation of church and state but, importantly, *not* a separation of faith and public life.

There is no question that the U.S. settlement does far greater justice to religious freedom than the French settlement. But regardless of such comparisons, what matters is that the current explosion of diversity has called *all* the settlements into question—the American no less than the French. No one can have failed to notice how disputes over religion and public life have been a key feature of fifty years of U.S. culture warring. The traditional U.S. settlement has been called into question and, in effect, is now being transformed—badly. The whole world now needs to stand back and reconsider how to do justice to religious freedom for all and for the good of all under current conditions.

Third, the notion of the "public square" has morphed into a powerful new dimension: the virtual. The notion of the public square has been prized in Europe for centuries. It is the place where citizens come together to debate and decide the issues of their common life. As such, it goes back to Athens and the *agora,* which was the civic center down below the Acropolis. Importantly, it began as a physical place—the *agora* in Athens, the Forum in Rome, the Houses of Parliament at Westminster, and the U.S. Congress on Capitol Hill. Later, the notion expanded from the physical to the metaphorical. The public square could be anywhere that citizens debated issues of common public life—such as the op-ed pages of a newspaper or a television talk show.

Thanks to the Internet and the power of social media, the notion of the public square has now expanded again and become virtual. Think of the responses to Salman Rushdie's novel *Satanic Verses*, to the Danish cartoons of the Prophet Muhammad, or to Pope Benedict's speech at the University of Regensburg. The lesson is simple: today, even when we are not talking to the world, we can be heard by the world—and the world can instantly organize a response, even a violent response. In short, the age of the Internet and social media has led to the emergence of a real, though very rudimentary and as yet highly uncivil, "global public square." As with the two other factors, the emergence of the virtual public square underscores the urgency of the need for a proper understanding of freedom of religion and conscience.

Why First?

Third, we must understand and be able to articulate and defend why freedom of religion and conscience is so foundational and important. Once self-evident to most Americans, these reasons now need to be argued both within the United States and around the world. Three reasons are, I believe, the most important.

First, freedom of religion and conscience has rightly been called the "first liberty." It has long been argued that religious freedom is the first freedom, both logically and historically, and the freedom that "secures the rest" (Lord Acton).[6] But what matters is the underlying reason why this is so: freedom of religion and conscience affirms the dignity, worth, and agency of every human by freeing us to align "who we understand ourselves to be" with "what we believe actually is," and then to think, speak, and act in line with these convictions. As such, freedom of religion and conscience is an expression of the heart of our humanity. Through freedom of thought, conscience, religion, and belief, we are guaranteed the right to the deepest self-understanding and self-constitution. Roger Williams captured this indispensable and foundational role of freedom of religion and conscience in his famous term "soul liberty."[7]

Conscience is the inner forum of an individual person, in which we each settle the grand debates about reality and unreality, truth and falsehood, right and wrong. We believe whatever we come to believe to be "true," "good," and "right" because we are convinced of it. So long as we remain convinced, we simply cannot believe otherwise. It is impossible to believe one thing and its opposite at the same time, which is why no one should be forced to believe what they do not believe. This means that what the freedom of the public square is to a city-state or a nation, freedom of conscience is to a person. Respect and protect the freedom of these twin forums together, one the outer forum and the other the inner forum, and do so for all faiths, and you create a just, free, and truly human community.

What true liberal or freedom-loving conservative can argue with each person's right to think and to order their lives in accordance with what they believe

---

[6] Roland Hill, *Lord Acton* (New Haven, CT: Yale University Press, 2000), 377.
[7] John M. Barry, *Roger Williams and the Creation of the American Soul* (New York: Viking Penguin, 2012).

to be true, based on the dictates of their conscience? In the powerful words of Timothy Shah, "When people lose their religious freedom, they lose more than their freedom to be religious. They lose their freedom to be human."[8]

Needless to say, this defense of freedom of religion and conscience as the essential expression of human dignity depends on the underlying appreciation of human dignity itself. Not long ago, its advocates claimed that the human rights revolution was sweeping the world, and they commonly praised the Universal Declaration of Human Rights in terms such as "the Bible of the modern world." That is no longer the case. Human rights are now routinely dismissed as philosophically ungrounded, Western-centric, and "the last utopianism."[9] Marxists and Muslims have long assaulted the Universal Declaration, but human rights are now seriously questioned within the West itself. We are, in fact, moving to a world that is not only "post-truth" but increasingly "post-rights." This challenge to the basis of human rights is neither a surprise nor a problem for Jews and Christians, for the rejection of the Bible means the rejection of the only sound basis for human rights. As I said, the Genesis declaration that humans are made in "the image and likeness of God" has been called the Magna Carta of humanity (Gen. 1:26–27). But with the deepening crisis of human rights, their defense, including freedom of religion and conscience, becomes both more urgent and more difficult.

Second, freedom of religion and conscience is important because it is a vital key to a healthy civil society and helps to form what is now called "social capital." A society or nation is healthy, it is said, if, between its citizens and its government, there is a thick layering of voluntary associations in which individuals can participate and give money and time in order to pursue their visions of one kind or another—charitable, reformative, educational, or whatever. Contrary to Christopher Hitchens's repeated jibe that "religion poisons everything," the truth is that many of the most beneficial movements in Western history were inspired by faith. Philanthropic outreach, the emergence of the university, the rise of modern science, the abolition of slavery, and the growth of human rights themselves are some of the most obvious.

But regardless of the past, all who appreciate Edmund Burke's "little platoons," Peter Berger and Richard John Neuhaus's "mediating structures," and Robert Putnam's "social capital" know well that faith and faith-based

---

[8] Timothy Shah, *Religious Freedom: Why Now? Defending an Embattled Human Right* (Princeton, NJ: Task Force on International Religious Freedom of the Witherspoon Institute, 2012), 28.

[9] Samuel Moyn, *The Last Utopia: Human Rights in History* (Cambridge, MA: Belknap Press, 2012).

communities have a unique and unrivaled role to play in nongovernmental initiatives around the world.[10] That is, of course, if they are free to play that part. There are strong links between a civil society and a free market of ideas. Freedom of religion and conscience is basic to both. It is therefore vital not only to religion but also to economic development, technological advances, democratic politics, and artistic creativity.

Third, freedom of religion and conscience is important because it provides a vital secret to achieving social harmony both within and between societies. Chinese President Hu Jintao used to speak proudly of his vision of China as a "harmonious society," but the fraudulence of the Communist solution has become even clearer under his successor Xi Jinping. China has remarkable diversity within its overall harmony, but at a steep price—oppressive coercion. Xi Jinping's "re-education camps" for Muslims and his destruction of Christian churches by the hundreds tells the real story. The Communist Party brooks no alternative to its authority. The price of Chinese harmony is silence or death for those who differ from the regime. Such diversity without liberty is routine for authoritarian regimes, but humans should never be slaves to governments or ideologies, whether Marxism in China, Islam in Iran, or pansexualism in the West. Under the advanced modern conditions of the global era, the challenge of our time is to match diversity with liberty and still create harmony—a feat that is possible only if there is respect for freedom of religion and conscience for all. No society is worthy to call itself free unless it has truly widened the spheres of liberty for all. To do that requires freedom of religion and conscience.

A Sea Change in Twenty Years

Fourth, Americans must come to terms with the great sea change in attitudes toward freedom of religion and conscience that has occurred in the last generation. No nation has had a greater commitment to religious freedom than the United States, and no nation has had a more original and constructive understanding of the relationship of religion and public life. From the very beginning, "civil and religious liberty" were the twin elements of freedom in U.S. history. Again and again, George Washington and citizens at all levels cited them as the two main reasons why people came to the United States and why U.S. citizens fought for their freedom in the revolution. For a foreign observer such as Alexis de Tocqueville, religious freedom is what made the United States

---

[10] Peter L. Berger and Richard Neuhaus, *To Empower People* (Washington, DC: American Enterprise Institute for Public Policy, 1977).

startlingly different from Europe. In most of the old world, religion and politics were at loggerheads, but in America they were blood brothers. "Religion in America takes no direct part in the government of society, but it must be regarded as the first of their political institutions."[11]

That is not to say that the full logic of the First Amendment was understood at once or that the American settlement was flawless. At different times, there were vile outbreaks of nativism, religious prejudice, and discrimination against Jews, Catholics, and Mormons—such as the raw Protestant prejudice and murderous assaults on Roman Catholics (fifty-four deaths in New York City in one day—on July 12, 1871), the Know Nothing movement in the 1850s, and the only European-style pogrom in U.S. history (in Atlanta in August 1915). Yet the overall trend was always toward expansion of religious freedom for people of all faiths. And always, too, the contrast with most of the rest of the world remained strong and encouraging. The U.S. way, therefore, stood out as distinctive, and it beckoned toward a better way for the entire world—or so it appeared. Yet troublingly, that has all changed, and the challenge has come not from the rest of the world but from within the United States itself.

Two recent events are taken as the high-water mark of general U.S. acceptance of freedom of religion and conscience. One was the publishing of the Williamsburg Charter in 1988, a bicentennial celebration of the First Amendment, which was signed by two presidents, two Supreme Court chief justices, and a wide array of leaders across national life, including Muslims. The other was the passing of the Religious Freedom Restoration Act in 1993, which was signed into law by President Clinton, approved almost unanimously by the U.S. Congress, and supported even by the ACLU.

But that was then. What has caused the sea change in the mere twenty years since? A simple way to describe the deterioration is to see the impact of what might be called the three dark *Rs*. First, there has been a growth in the *Reducers,* those who shrink freedom of religion and conscience from "free exercise" to "freedom of worship." In 1776, in Virginia's landmark Bill of Rights that preceded the First Amendment by fifteen years, the young, twenty-five-year-old "Jemmy" Madison succeeded in striking out George Mason's word "toleration" and inserting the words "free exercise." His move represented an immense leap forward in the understanding and protection of religious freedom.

Every dictator worthy of the name, and most totalitarian regimes, have guaranteed "freedom of worship"—in theory. The Chinese claim to do so today,

---

[11] Alexis de Tocqueville, *Democracy in America*, trans. Henry Reeve, ed. Francis Bowen, vol. 1 (1838, repr., Cambridge: Sever and Francis, 1876), 390.

even as Xi Jinping orders the destruction of churches, imprisons and tortures Christians, and rounds up Muslims for his concentration camps. In other words, freedom of worship is reduced to what a person believes between his two ears when his mouth is firmly shut, and he stays at home. Such freedom of worship means nothing. Freedom of religion and conscience, in contrast, is robust and comprehensive—the right to adopt, to practice, to share, and to change one's ultimate belief, based solely on the dictates of conscience. The religious liberty clauses, the first sixteen words of the First Amendment, guarantee such "free exercise," and Article 18 of the Universal Declaration of Human Rights spells out the freedom in even greater detail.

Therefore, more than a matter of ignorance, it was a witting or unwitting flouting of the genius of U.S. history when President Obama and Secretary of State Hillary Clinton began, for a considerable time, to refer to freedom of religion and conscience as mere "freedom of worship."

Second, there has also been a significant growth in the *Removers*, those who would like to remove religion from public life altogether. There has long been an American tradition of understanding the separation of church and state in a strict way. Rather than viewing the religious liberty clauses of the First Amendment together, seeing them as a double protection for religious freedom, separationists emphasize the "no establishment" clause at the expense of the "free exercise" clause. They support their strict separationist view of a "high and impregnable wall" between church and state by citing Thomas Jefferson's notion of a "wall of separation," but they apply the principle in a manner that is quite different and far more extreme than "Mr. J" did.

This long-held separationist view received a massive boost from the impact of 9/11. New atheists such as Richard Dawkins have been candid about the way the terrorist strike opened their eyes to the lethal danger of religion. If such carnage was the price to be paid for religion in public life, religion should be excluded from public life altogether. After all, in the words of the subtitle of Christopher Hitchens' famous book *God Is Not Great,* history is all about "How religion poisons everything."

The net effect of these and other arguments by the Removers is both devastating and ironic. U.S. religious freedom has been upended and stood on its head. Freedom of religion and conscience is no longer freedom *for* religion, or ultimate beliefs; it has become freedom *from* religion. Worse, the strict separation of religion from public life is closer to the French-style *laicite* than to the distinctive understanding that has been the unique hallmark of the U.S. settlement. Most importantly of all, the Removers' denial of freedom of religion and conscience is one more instance of how ideas and ideals that owe everything to

1789 and the French Revolution are slowly replacing ideas and ideals whose roots go back to 1776 and the American Revolution.

Third, a new trend has developed among those who might be called the *Rebranders,* those who have turned the notion of freedom of religion and conscience upside down and inside out, and then attacked it as a form of power play that is dangerous and should be abolished. At the moment, the most prominent Rebranders are the activists who work on behalf of the sexual revolution, who wield the notion of "discrimination" that they hijacked from the 1960s civil rights movement. They now brandish the term to attack all who disagree with them and rebrand religious freedom as an exercise in discrimination, prejudice, bigotry, and hate. For example, Martin Castro, Obama's chairman of the U.S. Commission on Civil Rights, wrote that "The phrases 'religious liberty' and 'religious freedom' will stand for nothing so long as they remain code words for discrimination, intolerance, racism, sexism, homophobia, Islamophobia, Christian supremacy, or any form of intolerance. . . . Present day 'religious liberty' efforts are aimed against the LGBTQ community."[12]

Fortunately, there are distinguished supporters of LGBTQ rights who also strongly affirm the importance of freedom of religion and conscience. They reject the idea that disagreement is automatically discrimination. That blanket charge is a blunder of historic proportions, with grave implications for freedom that are highly illiberal. To characterize ("demonize") all disagreement as "discrimination," simply by definition and without investigation into real cases, is a subversion of liberty. In the end, such illiberalism undermines such precious liberal freedoms as the right to dissent and the right to conscientious objection.

But the damage is done. Following the great sea change, freedom of religion and conscience is no longer self-evidently positive in America as it has been for more than three hundred years. It has been rebranded, pronounced to be "weaponized," and caught up in the clash and din of the ongoing culture wars. For all who love freedom, the scorched-earth, totalitarian overtones of the Rebranders is deeply troubling. All dissent is to be crushed as discrimination, all conscientious objection is to be ripped away as a fig leaf to cover bigotry, and all civil disobedience is to be rejected as hateful. Will the legal firepower of the Progressive Left soon be trained on religious advocacy in public life, on religious nonprofit activity and status, against religious speech that is deemed incorrect, and even against churches, synagogues, and mosques? In the chilling

---

[12] Joe Davidson, "Civil Rights or Religious Liberty—What's on Top?" *Washington Post,* September 9, 2016.

words of a New Mexico Supreme Court ruling against religious freedom, compulsion is "the price of citizenship."[13] Jean-Jacques Rousseau's infamous idea that citizens should be "forced to be free" is on the march again.

Which Model Best Serves Freedom for All?

Fifth, which model of religion and public life serves freedom best? This question lies at the heart of the issue of freedom and religion today, and it deserves far greater attention than it has been given—and urgent attention by Christians in the United States. Quite extraordinarily, apart from the Williamsburg Charter and a tiny number of books, Evangelicals have given almost no attention to what is an urgent, practical matter. They prefer to protest violations rather than promote solutions. But the fact is that the present stage of the culture warring cannot last. The former U.S. settlement has broken down, perhaps irremediably, and one or another of the competing views is bound to replace it before long. But which? Will it be one that serves the gospel well, and serves America and freedom for the good of all, or will it be one that restricts all three? Americans would do well to step back from the immediacy of the battles and to weigh up the pros and cons of each option with care.

There are three major models on offer in today's world, the first two being the dominant models in most countries at the present moment. The first common model is that of the *sacred public square*. This is a vision of public life in which one particular religion is preferred, formally established, or a monopoly. The sacred public square was, of course, the traditional settlement for most of Europe's history until the French Revolution. Hence, the place of the Roman Catholic Church in France, Spain, or Italy; the Anglican Church in England; the Presbyterian Church in Scotland; the Lutheran Church in Sweden; and so on. Today there is still a wide range of countries with a sacred public square. Some versions are mild and weak—the Church of England, as its critics quip, is now fit only for "hatching, matching, and dispatching" (baptizing, marrying, and burying). Other versions are far more severe. All too often, for example, to be a Bahai in Iran or a Christian in Pakistan and Saudi Arabia can be life-threatening.

In other words, the "sacred public square" model does not protect freedom and justice for those who do not subscribe to the religion that is preferred, established, or a monopoly. Indeed, they who do not share the faith are always second-class citizens in some way, and at any moment, they may find

---

[13] Elane Photography, *LLC v. Willock*, 309 P.3d 53 (N.M. 2013).

themselves in serious danger. As such, the model of the sacred public square does not provide freedom and justice for all, so it cannot be advanced as the best model for the global world.

The second model is that of the *naked public square*.[14] This is Richard John Neuhaus's term for a vision of public life in which all religions—whether considered irrelevant, unnecessary, divisive, dangerous, or false—are rigorously excluded. Once again, there are mild versions of the naked public square, such as the French *laicite,* but there are also draconian versions, such as those in China, North Korea, and Cuba. What matters, however, is that this second model does not serve the interests of "freedom and justice for all" any better than the first model. The plain fact is that more than 80 percent of the world identifies itself as religious in some way. So the "naked public square" excludes the great majority of the world's peoples, and in the process, it often establishes secularism as the official ideology. (Centuries ago, Leibnitz predicted, "The last sect in Christendom and in general in the world will be atheism."[15]) In short, the "naked public square" is the mirror image of the "sacred public square," but it takes a secularist rather than a religious direction. Neither model does justice to freedom for all or demonstrates what is required for it to be a model worthy of the global world.

The third model is that of the *civil public square.* This is a vision of public life in which citizens of all faiths are free to enter and engage in public affairs on the basis of their faith, as a matter of freedom of religion and conscience, but—and this is critical—within an agreed framework of what is understood and respected to be just and free for people of all other faiths too, and thus beneficial for the common good. The vision of a civil public square is "utopian" in the sense that it is not yet operative anywhere (*u-topia* being the Greek for "no place"), but it is the natural development of the twin imperatives of freedom and diversity, and in many ways it is the logical development of what used to be the U.S. settlement at its best.

It is important to say that the framework of the civil public square is political and not religious. In John Courtney Murray's apt description, it is a matter of "articles of peace" rather than "articles of faith." As such, it has to be agreed upon, affirmed, and then handed down from generation to generation, through civic education, until it truly becomes the "habits of the heart" for the citizenry. At its core are the three *Rs* of freedom of thought and conscience: *rights, responsibilities,* and *respect*. A right for one person is a right for another person, and it

---

[14] Richard John Neuhaus, *The Naked Public Square* (Grand Rapids, MI: Eerdmans, 1984).

[15] Emil Brunner, *Christianity and Civilization* (London: Nisbet, 1947), 163.

is a responsibility for both—and for everyone. Freedom of religion and conscience therefore means that there are no special rights, no favored faiths, and especially no protected beliefs. It is the conscience of believers, not the content of beliefs, that is protected.

The civil public square is the political embodiment of the Golden Rule: treat others with the respect you would like to be treated with, and protect for others the rights you would like protected for yourself. Thus, a right for a Christian is automatically a right for a Jew, an atheist, a Muslim, a Buddhist, a Mormon, a Hindu, a Scientologist, and every believer in every faith under the sun. All human rights are the rights of all human beings. They are to be protected for each person and for the good of all. Persuasion, not coercion, is the language of civility.

The United States is in the throes of the culture wars, when detachment and objectivity are in extremely short supply. At such a time, it will take an extraordinary level of leadership or a remarkable stand by some group of citizens to assess where the nation is now and to persuade the citizens of where it needs to go. It is therefore essential to decide wisely which model of religion and public life is best for freedom.

Realistic or Utopian?

Sixth, is there any realistic solution to the challenges of religious diversity today, or is that hope forlorn? The notion of a civil public square sounds good on paper, but can it solve the levels of rancor and incivility that have broken out in the public square, especially through social media? There are certainly solid reasons why civility is widely scorned today, and the vision of the civil public square is not taken as seriously as it should be.

First, civility is confused with niceness and dismissed as a wimp word. At best, civility is viewed as displaying manners and etiquette, using a mild tone of voice, or feeling a refined distaste for the messiness of differences. Such ideas are nonsense. Civility is a tough-minded, classical virtue and duty that enables citizens to take their public differences seriously, debate them robustly, and negotiate and decide them peacefully rather than violently. To be sure, there is always the sober reminder that needs emphasizing today: when words break down, violence is never far away, and the possibility of scapegoating and assassination is at the door.

Second, civility is confused with the search for a lowest-common-denominator unity, along the lines of an interfaith dialogue. The concern, then, is that civility means a necessary compromise of truth or principle, and thus unfaithfulness. Not at all. The ultimate goal is never ecumenical unity. The

23

differences between the ultimate beliefs are irreducible. As stressed earlier, the framework for political discourse is a matter of "articles of peace" and not "articles of faith."

Conclusion

There is no question that this Introduction is sketchy. It is, after all, only an introduction, and the chapters that follow are what matter. But let me emphasize three things in conclusion. First, I am not suggesting that there is any one-size-fits-all solution for the problems of freedom of religion and conscience around the world. Each nation has its own history and its own values. But what we should argue for is that, across the many natural differences between nations, there should be a common core of rights and responsibilities that all rights-respecting nations should guarantee and guard for all their citizens.

Also, we should acknowledge with humility that any vision and settlement that we advocate and achieve is only the best *so far*. None of us is omnipotent and none of us is omniscient. We still "see through a glass darkly." So our best and highest solutions will be incomplete and imperfect. Yet we still offer them, knowing they will be superseded in their turn; at least then it might be known that the firm and unashamed commitment we held in our time, based on things as we saw them, was to strive for freedom and justice and the good of all.

Third, allow me to close this Introduction with a personal plea. As I wrote at the beginning, I have had a passion for the importance of freedom of religion and conscience ever since I was a boy, when I had firsthand experience with the horror of persecution. Upon coming to the United States, that urgency lay behind my proposal for the Williamsburg Charter (1988) and, later, both the Global Charter of Conscience (2012) and the American Charter of Freedom of Religion and Conscience (2018). But I would have to say with sorrow that most of my fellow Evangelicals have not been stirred to join such initiatives except when the issue touched their own circles.

That may now be changing, as Christians in the West find themselves more in the firing line, and this book itself is an encouraging sign of deeper concern and commitment. Yet my hope is that Christians are inspired not only by the importance of religious freedom for the church, but also by a vision of religious freedom for the world and for humanity. One of humanity's most urgent questions in the global era is this: How do we live with our deepest differences, especially when those differences are religious and ideological? Created "in the image and likeness of God," we humans display both universality and uniqueness. We have commonalities, and we have distinctions and differences. Such differences are positive as well as negative (sometimes called "the dignity of difference" as well as the "divisiveness of difference"). If we humans were completely identical, we probably would not need to communicate. And if we were completely different, we might not be able to communicate.

Human differences, therefore, matter crucially, and respect for freedom of religion and conscience is essential to negotiating those differences well. May each of you who read this book and reflect on its overall message join the ranks of those who strive for greater human dignity, greater freedom, greater justice, and greater peace and stability in the world of tomorrow. The double challenge of today's complex, crazy world is first to understand it and then to do something about it. We Christians differ radically with Karl Marx on many points, but on one point we agree: "Philosophers have only interpreted the world in various ways. The point, however, is to change it."[16]

The life of faith is not a call to drop out, settle back, or withdraw from the heat and din of what Teddy Roosevelt called "the arena." The life of faith is an ongoing journey toward the restoration and renewal of the world. We are God's partners in this grand enterprise, and what a time to be alive. Read on. Think hard. Stand firm. Speak out. So help us, Lord.

---

[16] Karl Marx, "Theses on Feuerbach," trans. Cyril Smith and Don Cuckson, Marxists Internet Archive, 2002, www.marxists.org/.

Chapter 2

The Earth Is the Lord's: A Biblical Theology of Religious Liberty

John S. Redd Jr.
President and Associate Professor, Reformed Theological Seminary

"We look upon our epoch as a time of troubles, an age of anxiety. The grounds of our civilization, of our certitude, are breaking up under our feet, and familiar ideas and institutions vanish as we reach for them, like shadows in the failing dusk."

—Arthur M. Schlesinger Jr.

Schlesinger's mid-century observation rings as true today as it did in its own time, the only difference being that the dissolution of traditional societal institutions seemed altogether new and terrifying then, whereas now the same dissolution seems mature, developed, and inevitable. At the time of Schlesinger's musing, religion was slowly, perhaps unbelievably, moving out of a position of priority in U.S. life. Post-war Europe saw that decline much more rapidly, but the secular prophets in the United States anticipated a similar trajectory in America's future. Now, after seven decades of epochal shift, the anxiety persists, the vanishing "familiar ideas and institutions," once of the brick-and-mortar variety, are now more basic to the human endeavor. The former cultural consensus on issues as far-ranging as sexuality, freedom of speech, and religious liberty seems to have been degraded to something closer to a loose coalition, soon to be a quaint antique.

In the midst of this epoch of uncertainty, Christians do well to return to Scripture to determine just which ideas and institutions deserve our preservation efforts. The Scriptures speak to a vast diversity of human experience to help us understand what the Westminster Shorter Catechism describes as "what man should believe concerning God and what duty God requires of man." The question that this paper will address is whether the Scriptures affirm explicitly or implicitly the notion of religious liberty in any of its forms.

The question of religious liberty, or of the liberty of religious belief and practice apart from infringement by the state, is not one that is assumed in the ancient context of biblical literature, but that does not mean the underpinnings of such a doctrine are not present in the ancient text. But what are these underpinnings? Do they point directly to religious liberty as a practice or do they generally affirm notions like religious liberty in ways that can be further worked out in trial and error? Such an endeavor will require a nuanced discussion that may frustrate partisan exigencies, but nuanced discussion is a spiritual discipline. In developing an argument for religious liberty from the Scriptures, readers should be careful not to fall into the bad intellectual habits of proof-texting, which confirms anachronistic political bias by way of superficial engagement with the text; rather, we should look for the broad themes and reoccurring motifs that can be traced through the whole of redemptive history.

This chapter will argue that the theological framework expressed the Old and New Testaments assumes a commitment to religious liberty. It will also consider several biblical commitments such as the doctrine of divine kingship, the nature of personal faith, and the call to love one's neighbor. Divine kingship reminds us that the world is created and sustained by the God of justice, and that creation is interwoven with his character, to which humans, made in his image, are called to respond with wisdom and faith. Such a response requires the liberty of personal belief and commitment. Furthermore, true faith is always represented as sincere and heartfelt rather than as nominal or a result of the threat of force. God calls his people to genuinely love him with their whole hearts, not merely in response to external pressure. Such sincere faith finds expression in one's care of the oppressed and love of neighbors that leads to a concern for their own liberty of conscience. What we desire for ourselves, we ought to desire for others.

When surveyed from the perspective of progressive revelation and the development of the history of salvation, these doctrines formulate the basic contours of a biblical doctrine of religious liberty.

Divine Kingship and the Image of God

For the Christian, every question of human ethics begins, in one way or another, with the character of God, before flowing inevitably to the beliefs and behaviors of humanity, which has been made in the image of God (Gen. 1:26, 5:1–2; 1 Cor. 11:7; Col. 1:15). What we believe concerning God necessarily forms our understanding of the duties he requires of us. The doctrine of *Imago Dei* is intensive and extensive at once, in that it says something about the whole of the human and the whole of humanity. It speaks to more than one human faculty, such as reason (contra the rationalist) or creativity (contra the aesthete) or language (contra the sophist), by speaking to all that is human. What is the image of God? It is what the human is. Whenever we consider the unique qualities of humanity, we are recognizing aspects of the image of God that find expression in his image. As such, we can acknowledge the human's sense of meaning and purpose as being derived from the human's status as a creature that bears the image of the creator.

The creation account in Genesis 1 retells the origin of the cosmos as if it were an ancient Near Eastern building program.[1] Depicted as a king constructing his throne room, God completes the two-part construction of the heavens and the earth, with each domain in good order and properly populated and furnished. The final phase of the program is to place his *tselem*, "image," in the sanctuary, much as a representation of the deity would have been placed in sanctuary complexes around the ancient world.[2] Like their creator God, in whose image they are made, man and woman are commissioned to have dominion over the world as stewards of the cosmos and to continue furnishing creation with other images of the creator (Gen. 1:28; Ps. 8:3–9). In this way, it is the responsibility of the image of God to continue in the work of the divine creator and sustainer, filling out the throne room in a way that is fitting for the king. The totality of the command to fill and subdue the earth gets at what it means to be image of God; that is, to be human.

There are two significant implications for our focus here. First, the dignity and the responsibility of humanity as being the image of God are necessarily derived from the creator, meaning that they do not reside in humanity itself but reside in the God whom humanity images. Second, it follows that humanity's status as being the image of God is irrevocable. The image of God is part of God's creation, which he has declared "very good," and he has not rescinded that judgment (Gen. 1:31). Even the condemnation of the Fall of humanity does not turn back the quality of humanity as images.

---

[1] See G. K. Beale, *The Temple and the Church's Mission: A Biblical Theology of the Dwelling Place of God* (Downers Grove, IL: IVP, 2004), 29–80.

[2] See the Israelite tabernacle and temple designed around the Holy of Holies and the ark of the covenant. Bruce K. Waltke, *An Old Testament Theology: An Exegetical, Canonical, and Thematic Approach* (Grand Rapids, MI: Zondervan, 2007), 741–42. Roland De Vaux, "Le lieu que Yahvé a choisi pour y établir son nom," in *Das Ferne und nahe Wort*, ed. Festschrift L. Rost (BZAW 10, Berlin: Töpelmann, 1967), 219–28. K. A. Kitchen, "The Tabernacle—A Late Bronze Age Artefact," *Eretz Israel* 24 (1993), 119–29.

For Calvin, the derivational quality of the image meant that whenever human dignity or industry were honored or acknowledged, God himself was being glorified.[3] Likewise, the persistence of the image of God after the Fall meant that all humans, even the ardent atheist or the antagonistic apostate, were deserving of the dignity and honor of being in the image of God:

> We are not to consider that men merit of themselves but to look upon the image of God in all men, to which we owe all honor and love. . . . Say that [a man] does not deserve even your least effort for his sake; but the image of God, which recommends him to you, is worthy of your giving yourself and all your possessions.[4]

One striking element about the history of redemption as it is recounted in Scripture is that, in spite of the clear distinction between the redeemed and the condemned, all humans are images of God and deserving of dignity. For Bavinck, a person does not bear the image of God but merely *is* the image of God:

> In our treatment of the doctrine of the image of God, then, we must highlight, in accordance with Scripture and the Reformed confession, the idea that a human being does not bear or have the image of God but that he or she is the image of God. As a human being a man is the son, the likeness, or offspring of God.[5]

This is what it means to be human. When humans desire a thing, their desire has meaning. When they yearn, when they pursue, when they choose one thing over another, such actions also have meaning and speak to a broader truth. We should not be surprised that humans of all animals are the only ones to erect monuments to meaning, whether in the form of a hero, an accomplishment, or an abstract idea. The human world is a haunted world, inhabited by the spirit of progression, purpose, goal-reaching, sublimity, and horror. Humans alone speak of things being evil or being wondrous, and the biblical authors reject any notion that such categories can be merely understandable in the "immanent frame." For the biblical authors, human activity is understood to be subject to divine agency (Gen. 15:20; Prov. 16:9, 16:33; Acts 17:28), and yet the character of that agency

---

[3] Calvin argued, however, that "the chief seat of the Divine image was in his mind and heart," though this limitation to the noncorporeal elements of the human is not supported biblically. John Calvin, *Commentaries on the First Book of Moses Called Genesis*, trans. J. King (Grand Rapids, MI: Baker, 1979), 1:95.

[4] John Calvin, *Institutes of the Christian Religion*, 3:7.6.

[5] Herman Bavinck, *Reformed Dogmatics*, 2:554.

defies human understanding. While we might understand certain beliefs and behaviors to derive from certain biological processes or solidarity with the species, these sources cannot be the origination of the belief or behavior; rather, they are "secondary causes," contingencies ultimately put into play by primary divine cause. While they may explain the feelings that attend to such a sense of meaning, they can do so only in the local sense. In the biblical perspective, each secondary cause reflects the transcendent character of God that is known in some capacity or another by all humans who are made in his image.

While the notion of the image of God does not speak directly to religious freedom, it does shed light on the value of human reason, volition, and agency. If the human is understood as just another animal, devoid of the dignity and purpose derived from the creator, then the discussion of religious liberty becomes as arbitrary as a debate over whether one ought to dress up his poodle in a polka-dot sweater. The dog's taste doesn't really matter.

The doctrine of the image of God also ensures that an ethical system does not veer into the direction of anarchy. The human made in the image of God has the quality of agency, but such agency is not radical. Freedom in the biblical sense is never a radical existential freedom in which all options are equally accessible. Rather, the human, as creature, is dependent upon his or her circumstances. Such circumstances may include their impulses, desires, wants, loves, fears, and their physical and perspectival limitations. Every human—every creature, for that matter—is limited in the sense that they are constrained by the will of the creator. This doctrine, called the doctrine of divine aseity or simplicity (Ps. 94:8–11; Isa. 40:18; Dan. 4:34–35; Acts 17:25; Rom. 11:33–34; Rev. 4:11), speaks to the lack of complexity or contingency within the character of God. As such, we can say that all humans are free, and yet no human is merely free.

We find, perhaps, no more vivid example of human agency and human constraint than in the account of humanity in the Garden of Eden. The man and the woman are free to eat of every fruit in the garden. They are morally constrained, however, by the will of God, not to eat of the fruit of the tree of the knowledge of good and evil. Here we have both human freedom and divine lordship over all creation. The reality of religious liberty should not exclude the more transcendent reality that God has applied righteous, holy, and wise stipulations to the human race. Humans may have the agency to choose what they should do, but their actions are not ignored by the living God who has created them and who constrains them (Ps. 1:6).

The image of God cannot be properly understood apart from the doctrine of divine lordship. Humans image God, to be sure, but they image God as a divine king and creator, and this bestows on them a royal dignity and responsibility derived from the Divine King himself. Every individual human and every governmental entity derives its authority from the God who bestows all authority (Rom. 13). In the Old Testament, this doctrine of derived authority is inchoate and emergent, but it is developed in the Apostle Paul's writings in the New Testament. It finds expression in Augustine and in various other places throughout church history, perhaps most strongly in the Reformed tradition. It reminds us that while humans ought to enjoy a certain modicum a freedom in their belief systems, no human is free from the lordship of the God who made humanity.

Creation Theology and the General Revelation

Over the last fifty years, there has been a reaffirmation of the connection between creation and the work of redemption in the Bible.[6] McConville represents the recent consensus when he says, "Creation is not in one category while history, politics, and salvation are in another. Rather salvation is restoration to how things ought to be."[7] This return of creation theology should be distinguished from certain "natural law" approaches that hold that the natural order should be equated with moral or social order. Creation theology describes a cosmos in which God's character, usually represented by the terms *tsedeq* or *tsedaqah* (loosely translated as "justice" and "righteousness"), is interwoven into creation, accessible to the human, and revelatory of the character of God.[8]

---

[6] The return of creation theology is reflected in two books by Gerhard von Rad: "The Theological Problem of the Old Testament Doctrine of Creation" in *The Problem of the Hexateuch,* trans. E. W. Trueman Dicken (London: SCM Press, 1984), 131–43 and *Wisdom in Israel* (Nashville: Abingdon, 1972), 144–76, 191. For a short history of this development, see Walter Brueggemann, *Theology of the Old Testament: Testimony, Dispute, Advocacy* (Minneapolis: Fortress, 1997), 159–64. See also H. H. Schmid, "Creation Righteousness and Salvation: 'Creation Theology' as the Broad Horizon of Biblical Theology," in *Creation in the Old Testament,* ed. B. W. Anderson (Philadelphia: Fortress, 1984), 102–17.

[7] J. G. McConville, *God and Earthly Power: An Old Testament Political Theology* (New York: T & T Clark, 2006), 32.

[8] The systematic theologian Herman Bavinck anticipated this connection between creation theology and the redemptive program set forth in Scripture when he argued for the reciprocity between the two:

[G]eneral revelation maintains the unity of nature and grace, of the world and the kingdom of God, of the natural order and the moral order, of creation and re-creation, of φύσις and ethos, of virtue and happiness, of holiness and blessedness, and in all these things the unity of the divine being. It is one and the same God who in general revelation does not leave himself without a witness to anyone and who in special revelation makes himself known as a God of grace. Hence general and special revelation interact with each other. (Herman Bavinck, *Reformed Dogmatics: Prolegomena* [Baker Academic, 2003], I: 321–22)

The personification of God's wisdom tells us that she was present at creation and rejoiced in it (Prov. 8:22–31) and that, as a result, the learner can gain wisdom from creation (the industrious ant, Prov. 6:6; the ubiquitous lizard, Prov. 30:28). Job's inquiry about the nature of God and human suffering is directed toward the vastness of creation (Job 38:1–40:2, 40:7–41:34). The Qoheleth begins his search for satisfaction in this life by observing meteorological phenomenon and the water cycle (Eccles. 1:5–8).

Creation theology flows from the lordship of God who, as the creator of the cosmos, has left his personal mark on it. The command to "go to the ant, you sluggard" does not involve an arbitrary word-picture; rather the wisdom teacher knows that wisdom is present in creation and can be found there by the learner. Such a reliance on observations of creation is common throughout wisdom literature and the ancient world, but the tendency toward a pagan view of deity as continuous with nature is offset in the Scripture by the priority placed on "the fear of the Lord" (Prov. 1:6, 9:10). The world is made in a way that favors and responds well to wise and skillful living. That is why the father encourages his son to pursue joy, satisfaction, and even harmony with creation by living in a way that is commensurate with the character of the creator.

Wisdom does not offer a series of "lifehacks." Instead, wisdom offers a range of skills for living rooted in the first foundational premise, "the fear of the Lord," a disposition that includes the spiritual and emotional dimensions of the person.[9]

Approaching the question of religious liberty in light of creation theology provides us with some promising ways forward. For instance, the testimony of creation or the general revelation about the character of God supports wisdom's instruction, but the power of wisdom training is found in the persuasive nature of wisdom's argument. It is easy to miss the presupposition of freedom in the teacher's instruction, but note that the son is invited to choose, desire, and pursue wisdom while rejecting, hating, and avoiding folly. The teacher strives for persuasion, using vivid images like Lady Folly's house of horrors (Prov. 7:24–27) and Lady Wisdom's bountiful feast (9:1–6). The teacher and Lady Wisdom alike make their pleas to those who are labeled only as "the simple" (8:5, 9:4) meaning those who have not yet chosen the wisdom or folly.[10] The foolish and the wise are depicted as having made their decisions, indicating that the wisdom

---

[9] In Psalm 119, the fear of the Lord is poetically compared to other attributes such as a love of the law and the pursuit of the Lord's character (vv. 7–9).
[10] Bruce K. Waltke, *The Book of Proverbs: Chapters 1–15* (Grand Rapids, MI: Eerdmans, 2004), 111–12.

program assumes a process of teaching, experience, and persuasion through which the simple may grow to love wisdom with sincerity or reject it. The father knows that he cannot force his son to leave the ways of the simpleton and walk the path of wisdom, but he can lead the son to appreciate wisdom through persuasive argumentation, compelling examples, and wise aphorism. While this process of persuasion occurs against the backdrop a divine sovereignty (Prov. 16:9, 33), it assumes that true wisdom cannot be forced upon someone by any human agent. Wisdom must be given by God and sincerely embraced by the learner.[11]

If creation bears the marks of the creator's character, then it does not fall to the wisdom teacher to ensure that wisdom endures in society. Creation will continue to reflect the wisdom of God, whether the simpleton is convinced or not. As mentioned above, even the reality of sin in the world does not negate the goodness of creation (Gen. 1:31). As a result, humans can be assured the creation will bear witness to the character of the creator (Ps. 19:1; Isa. 40:26; Rom. 1:20). Because God's creation bears witness to his righteousness and his wisdom, humans can be assured that evil will not stand forever. Such confidence is usually understood to be true in an eschatological sense. As the Apostle Paul writes,

> For the creation waits with earnest expectation for the revelation of the sons of God. For the creation was subjected to futility, not voluntarily, but because of the one who subjected it, in hope that the creation itself will be set free from its slavery to destruction and gain the freedom of the glory of the children of God. (Rom. 8:19–21)

That creation is currently groaning under the effects of the curse is indicative of the good end that is coming. The groaning adumbrates the time that is to come when the groaning will come to an end.

Any fulsome biblical case for religious liberty must account for the fact that the discussion about liberty necessarily occurs within the context of creation and of the righteous, holy, and wise God who created. Creation gives expression to the invisible attributes of the Godhead in the present, and it will not cease in its groanings until righteousness and justice prevail on the earth. As such, there is a constant and pervasive witness of the righteousness of God, regardless of the actions of man.

---

[11] See the depiction of the wise life as one that is marked by the love of wisdom and not simply by a duty to behave in a certain way (Prov. 4:6, 8:17, 21, 9:8; and the contrary point, 8:36).

Final Judgment

The biblical teaching about the divine lordship, image of God, and creation theology inevitably lead to discussion about the teaching of the final judgment. Having created the world and declaring that it was good, making certain that his wisdom and his character were interwoven into it in such a way that creation becomes a witness to his character and a proponent of his redemptive work, God ensured that the redemptive project would be successful and that divine justice would ultimately prevail. Of course, justice has been at work in the world from the beginning, being meted out over the course of human history, during which time the wicked are punished and the righteous are blessed. The Old Testament accounts in the so-called Deuteronomistic history (Joshua through Kings, excepting Ruth) provide a careful retelling of God's justice in response to human activity in Israel. At times, it seemed as if injustice prevailed, as in the case of the exile, when the cruel and oppressive Babylonian regime conquered and exploited Judah, but even in these cases God was clear that his justice was still at work in the arc of history. Babylon had a purpose, but the empire would be judged by God for its oppressive behavior (Isa. 46:1–2, 2:8). The solution to the problem of how to reconcile the suffering of the people and God's ultimate redemptive aims is not always scrutable, even to inspired prophets (Isa. 55:19; Rom. 11:33–34), but its inscrutability does not mean that God is not just and holy in that situation. It merely points to the nature of the creator and the creature.

Just as divine justice is at work in the present, it is at work in the future. The story of redemptive history progresses to a moment when God's justice will be applied to all of humanity in a final and complete way (Matt. 25:31–46; John 5:27–29; Rom. 2:5–11; Heb. 9:27, 10:27; 2 Pet. 3:7; Rev. 20:11–15). This future moment represents, in a sense, the end of history, or at least the end of conflict between good and evil. At last, all of creation will stand under the judgment of God, creation will be freed from the bondage of the curse of sin, and all humanity will receive its just desserts. All things will be set aright, and the goodness of creation will be restored and augmented to reflect the presence of God that will fill it. In human terms, this renewal and augmentation will be manifested in the resurrection and final judgment.

Of significance for the present question, God's judgment of unbelief is established and will be completed, and this will be an act of divine fiat, not agency. The eschatological role of judge that God and Christ will initiate at the Second Coming need not be hastened or enacted ahead of time by human governments. Such an act would be as ineffective as it is inappropriate, because only God has the power, presence, and authority to judge the human heart (Matt. 10:28; James 4:12, 5:9). For the Christian, the idea of religious liberty is corroborated by the assurance that God alone judges the human heart, a teaching that is at once consoling and challenging: "It is a terrible thing to fall into the hands of a living God" (Heb. 10:31).

Sincere Faith and Love of Neighbors

The previously discussed biblical themes—divine lordship, image of God, creation theology, and final judgment—provide the foundation upon which we can approach the call for true faith and a wholehearted love of God. Because of divine lordship, we know that a personal God has created this world for his glory and that the course of human history is inevitably moving toward that end. Because of the notion of the image of God, we know that humans reflect the character and glory of the creator who made them in his image. As such, human identity, beliefs, and behaviors are meaningful and point to the transcendent nature of the Godhead in a unique way. Because of creation theology, we know that the cosmos also reflect the character of God in a way that encourages wisdom and faithfulness and yearns for justice and restoration. Because of the final judgment, we know that divine lordship will play out to the end. Our beliefs and commitments are not arbitrary, and God does not rely on human government to ensure that ultimate justice will come to bear in human history. In other words, it is precisely because of our connection to him as his image, and because of divine lordship, creation theology, and final judgment, that sincere faith is both possible and desirable. Otherwise, faith would be a guess in the dark. Even if it were the correct guess at a given time, what assurance does the believer have that the situation could not change and my faith be misplaced? Who is to say the Lord is God if the forces of chaos, or Baal, or humanity itself are constantly threatening his control of the cosmos?

After the Lord redeemed Israel out of Egypt and moved them securely through the desert for the forty years of wandering, he met with them on the steppes of Moab where he gave what would become the core command of the Mosaic covenant and perhaps even the Bible:

Hear, O Israel: The Lord is our God. The Lord is one.

You shall love the Lord your God with all your heart, with all your soul, and with all your strength. (Deut. 6:4–5)

As I have argued elsewhere, this command establishes an ethical command to love from a theological principle about the character of God as covenantal and singular.[12] Because God has willingly bound himself to his people by way of covenant ("the Lord is your God"), and he is not a divided, local deity with limited jurisdiction and power ("the Lord is one"), the people of God ought to respond in a covenantally appropriate way ("you shall love") that corresponds to God's character ("with all of your heart, self, and strength"). God is not interested in partial or merely outward expressions of faith; he is interested in genuine personal belief.

Long before this command is given, we encounter Cain and Abel as they offer two different kinds of sacrifices to the Lord. Abel offers the best of his flocks, while Cain offers "from some" of his produce (Gen. 4:3–4). Later, Abraham personally believes in God, and it is "reckoned to him as righteousness" (Gen. 15:1). After the Exodus and conquest of the land, Kings Saul and David provide a pair of case studies in faithfulness. Saul is depicted as a man of shallow belief, who carefully tends to perceptions to maintain his reputation with the people (1 Sam. 15:30). David is present as a flawed character who nevertheless has a heart for the Lord (1 Sam. 16:7; cf. 1 Sam. 13:14). Much later in Israelite history, the prophets condemn the religious and political leaders of their day for insincere, nominal faith that covers over inner corruption (Isa. 28:7–8; Ezek. 8:8–12, passim). In the New Testament, Jesus Christ reserves his strongest condemnation for the hypocrites and false believers—"white-washed tombs for dead men's bones"—indicating that their inner unbelief has corrupted their outward displays of faithfulness (Matt. 23:27–28). The Apostle Paul warns church members against taking the Lord's Supper in a way that is inappropriate, without personally "discerning the body" (1 Cor. 11:29), and how they are suffering as a result of such nondiscernment.

In no part of Scripture is nominal or merely outward faith tolerated, much less encouraged. One common analogy for faith in the Scriptures suggests that the only way that true faith can be recognized is when it bears fruit during a drought (i.e., when no external circumstances can suggest another cause than true faith) (Ps. 1; Jer. 17:7–8). In other words, the importance of authentic faith implies that the best context for such faith to take root is in the context of the liberty to believe or not to believe. Otherwise, the context is encouraging a false expression of faith.

---

[12] John S. Redd Jr., *Wholehearted: A Biblical Look at the Greatest Commandment and Personal Wealth* (McLean, VA: Institute for Faith, Work & Economics, 2016).

The historic reality of the persecuted church reminds us that sincere faith can certainly exist and even thrive during times of religious restriction, but the fact of God's faithfulness during those times does not mean the church ought to actively desire persecution. Instead, Christians ought to encourage and advance the cause of peace, social order, and freedom that creates a context in which sincere faith can thrive. We should pray "for kings and those with authority, that we may live tranquil and quiet lives in all piety and dignity" (1 Tim 2:2). Such a prayer is completely in keeping with the biblical themes introduced above.

Religious liberty cannot be applied only to Christian belief; if it were, it would not be true liberty. Sincere faith means that the believer was free of coercion by the state. The love principle found in the Scriptures offers another clear example of how religious liberty must be broadly available across religious boundaries. Jesus affirms the belief that the love of God must find expression in love of one's neighbor (Matt. 22:49; Mark 12:31; Luke 10:27 [citing Lev. 19:18]), a belief that would have been common in the Second Temple Jewish context of his ministry. Following this line of thought, Paul argues that the love of one's neighbor summarizes the old covenant law concerning human interactions (Rom 13:9; Gal 5:14; cf. James 2:8). This ethic of reciprocity generates a variety of conclusions about human interaction and the sociopolitical order, not the least of which involve the issue of religious liberty. We should note that, when asked who exactly qualifies as a neighbor, Jesus tells a story about a religious outsider, a citizen of Samaria (Luke 10:25–37) and an adherent to a corrupted form of the Israelite Pentateuchal religion who worshipped at a sanctuary located outside of Jerusalem. The parable is meant to stretch the moral imaginations of his audience, as even the Samaritan is to be loved and treated in the way an observant Jewish believer would want to be treated. One need not stretch the imagination much further to see how the Golden Rule applies to the case of religious liberty.

The Case of Old Testament Israel

A common critique of the biblical case for religious liberty is the theocratic statecraft of ancient Israel in the area of personal belief. If idol worship and other forms of unbelief or apostasy were punishable by law in the one political system explicitly established and ordained by God, how can we rule out other forms of religious mandates in modern political theory?

The Israelite theocracy was a unique arrangement even in the Old Testament. Even Abraham, the father of the nation, is called to keep himself and his household faithful, but operating in a pluralistic society, he enters alliances with foreign leaders regardless of their personal beliefs (Gen. 12:10–14:24). Later in Israelite history, the descendants of Abraham, during their wandering in the wilderness, are commanded to first sue for peace when engaging other nations (Deut. 2:27). The command for *cherem* warfare, or the ban, is often mentioned as a problem for any positive case for religious liberty, but the circumstances surrounding the conquest of the Levant is the only period in history when any literal *cherem* ban is considered a just act in God's eyes (Gen. 15:16; Deut. 7:24–26; note the Amalekites as an object of a *cherem* ban in Deut. 25:17). Otherwise, Israel is expected to operate diplomatically as a good neighbor (Deut. 20:1–15). Once the Israelites are exiled in Babylon, they are expected to seek benefit for the city, to seek its *shalom*, a word that refers to welfare and flourishing (Jer. 29:4–9).

So is theocratic Israel merely an outlier of mainstream Old Testament theology, or is something else at work? While it has some unique characteristics, Israel as a nation-state should be understood by the role it plays in redemptive history. Old Testament Israel gives one expression of God's creative and redemptive work, which began in the garden and will be completed in the new heavens and the new earth. From the beginning, this work involved a land, or theater, in which God's purposes would be worked out; a people or offspring whom the work would be completed for and through; and a king who would provide order and justice. In creation, the land theme is found in the earth and the garden. Later, it was the tabernacle, the temple, and the land. All of these spaces serve as sanctuary, to be formed and filled to God's glory ("fill the *earth*" [Gen. 1:28]; Noah [Gen. 9:1], Abraham [Gen. 12:1, 15:7], and Moses ["land" Exod. 3:8; Deut. 1:21, passim; "many nations" Deut. 4:5–8, 15:6; war with other nations Deut. 20:1–15]). The people/offspring theme is also returned to in the Old Testament epochs ("*fill* the earth" [Gen. 1:28, 3:15]; Noah [Gen. 9:1], Abraham [Gen. 15:5], and Moses ["no barrenness" Deut. 7:14]). Finally, the king is an integral part of God's redemptive program ("subdue the earth/have dominion" [Gen. 1:28], Noah [9:1–7], Abraham [Gen. 17:6], Moses [Deut. 17:14–20; Judg. 17:6, 21:25], and David [2 Sam. 7:1–17]).

Just as in the case of the Temple and the sacrificial system, Israel as a nation-state provided a pattern, or typology, through which God's people could understand his redemptive work that would culminate in the person and work of Jesus Christ (Heb. 8:3–6). The New Testament authors use superlative language to describe Christ's role as a fulfillment of Israel's roles and responsibilities, though he is more than a fulfillment of the type; he is the faithful Israelite whom the law calls for. Jesus is Christ/Messiah in the line of David (Matt. 22:42–46, 25:31–34); he claims that his "kingdom is not of this world" (John 18:36; Acts 2:32–36); he is depicted as a creator who exerts command over the cosmos (John 1:1; Mark 4:35–41); and he claims "all rule, and authority and power and dominion" (Eph. 1:20–21); Jesus even claims that he is the True Israel, the faithful Israelite who has lived in accordance with the law (John 15). In this way, Christ's two natures are on display in his authority and rule: he is king of Israel and lord of the cosmos in one person.

Christ's kingdom is advanced not by any policy of human government, but by the proclamation and publication of the gospel, the account of Christ's victories over Satan, sin, and death (Matt. 28:18–20). On the side of the recipient, belief and salvation comes by way of hearing the gospel, professing with one's mouth, and believing with one's heart (Rom. 10:8–15). According to this typological arrangement, the nation-state of Old Testament Israel corresponds to the New Testament people of God who have been brought in through their union with Jesus Christ by faith. What is true of the garden, the temple, the land, and Israel is true now of the church united with Christ. Indeed, Jesus's "words and deeds pointed back toward the goodness of the original garden, even as he also pointed ahead to the future feast of shared shalom."[13] If the religious policies of the nation-state of Israel have relevance for the world today, it is in the government of the people of God gathered to proclaim his kingdom's coming. The Apostle Paul authorizes this approach to the old covenant when he applies passages regarding capital offenses in the Old Testament to excommunication from the church (1 Cor. 5:1; cf. Deut. 13:5, 17:7, 12, 21:21, 22:21, 22, 24; Judg. 20:13). Likewise, many would accept the notion that church membership is reserved for Christian believers and their children, as citizenship in Israel was reserved for believing Israelites, Gentiles, and their offspring.[14]

Conclusion

In 212 AD, the Christian apologist Tertullian wrote to the proconsul of Africa that "it is a fundamental human right, a privilege of nature, that every man should worship according to his own convictions: one man's religion neither harms nor helps another man. It is assuredly no part of religion to compel

---

[13] Kelly Kapic, "Anthropology," in *Christian Dogmatics: Reformed Theology for the Church Catholic*, ed. M. Allen and S. Swain (Grand Rapids, MI: Baker, 2016), 192.

[14] For an extended discussion of Israel in biblical theology and its implications for the church from a Reformed perspective, see O. Palmer Robertson, *The Israel of God: Yesterday, Today, and Tomorrow* (Phillipsburg: P & R, 2000).

religion—to which free-will and not force should lead us."[15] His argument follows somewhat closely the case laid out here regarding divine lordship and the need for sincere faith, though he relies much more on common grace, whereas the case above focuses on the image of God and creation theology. Given the trajectory of redemptive history, however, we should not be surprised to find such a sentiment expressed by a Christian so shortly after the apostolic period. We should also be encouraged in the face of Schlesinger's anxieties expressed at the opening of this essay. The notion of religious liberty is neither an outworking of the Western Enlightenment nor a recent trend with little success outside of a democratic context. Ideas such as sincere love, hypocrisy, and oppression have remarkable traction across cultures and history.

While the idea of religious liberty is not explicitly taught in Scripture, the idea comes into focus as larger themes and structures of God's creative and redemptive designs are recognized and explored. Because God is Lord and we are not, we are free from the impulse to demand or force belief. Because we are made in his image, our sense of the divine is not arbitrary or without meaning, even if it is corrupted by sin. Because the world reflects the character of the creator, we can trust in its stable witness of the Godhead. Because God is judge of all of humanity, we know that his purposes will come to fruition in this world, either through the punishment of sin in the final judgment or for his people on the cross of Christ. Because he requires true and sincere faith, we know that any efforts to force or legislate faith will likely result in false belief and therefore undermine our purpose. Because we are citizens of Christ's kingdom, we know that our identity is in his name, our mission is the proclamation of his kingdom, and our power is in his spirit. In other words, not only is the idea of religious liberty fair; it is beneficial to the kingdom of Christ.

---

[15] Tertullian, "Ad Scapulam," in *Ante-Nicene Fathers*, ed. Alexander Roberts, James Donaldson, and A. Cleveland Coxe, trans. S. Thelwall (Buffalo, NY: Christian Literature Publishing, 1885), III:105.

Chapter 3

The Bible and the Three Spheres of Religious Freedom

Barrett Duke

Executive Director and Treasurer, Montana Southern Baptist Convention

While the Bible teaches us many truths, the unbroken thread that winds its way through the entire book, from Genesis to Revelation, is the unfolding story of God's redemption of humanity. It isn't about the human pursuit of God; rather, it's about God's relentless pursuit of humans. From the beginning, the reader sees the constant struggle between people and God, as people seek to make their way without God and God continually brings them back into encounter with him.

Humans were actually created for relationship with God. They are the only creature in all of the Bible said to be created in God's image. They alone are tasked with the responsibility of overseeing God's creation, of exercising delegated authority to act as God's vice regents on earth. In the garden, we see God giving the first people the task of populating the earth and tending to his creation (Gen. 1:26–28); however, it was not God's intention for humans to exercise this godlike activity apart from relationship with him. Scripture even describes God "walking in the garden in the cool of the day" looking for the man and the woman (Gen. 3:8).

This relationship was not automatic, however. The first humans were free to determine the nature of their relationship with God. The book of Genesis reveals this freedom when it describes the way in which the first man and woman disobeyed God's command not to eat from the tree of the knowledge of good and evil and then hid from God when he came looking for them (Gen. 3:1–10). This is religious freedom in its simplest description. The Oxford Dictionary defines religion as "the belief in and worship of a superhuman controlling power, especially a personal God or gods."[1] Religious freedom, then, is the freedom of people to decide what they believe about a superhuman

---

[1] "Religion," Oxford Living Dictionary, accessed January 31, 2019, https://en.oxforddictionaries.com/definition/religion.

controlling power and the manner and activities in which they feel compelled to engage as expressions of worship of that power, without external interference.[2]

This freedom is under intense pressure around the world. In its 2018 report on the status of religious freedom, the United States Commission on International Religious Freedom (USCIRF) began by stating the following:

> Religious freedom conditions continued to deteriorate in countries across the globe in 2017. This ongoing downward trend often intersected with authoritarian practices characterized by hostility toward dissent, pluralism, independent media, and active civil society, or took place under the guise of protecting national security or countering terrorism. In the 28 nations addressed in this report, governments and nonstate actors targeted religious minorities, dissenting members of majority communities, and nonreligious persons. The most severe abuses included genocide and other mass atrocities, killings, enslavement, rape, imprisonment, forced displacement, forced conversions, intimidation, harassment, property destruction, the marginalization of women, and bans on children participating in religious activities or education.[3]

The countries addressed in the USCIRF report aren't the only places where religious freedom is under assault. In other countries, majority religions use the power of the state to limit and persecute minority faiths. Even in the United States, the religious freedom protections afforded by the First Amendment are being questioned by some, as they seek to limit the ability of people of faith to live out their religiously informed beliefs in public.[4]

With this current environment as the backdrop, it is necessary to be reminded of the origin of religious freedom and the extent to which people should be free in matters of religion. In this chapter, I glean from the Bible what it reveals about religious freedom as it tells the history of God's efforts to redeem

---

[2] Of course, even religious freedom has its limits. Generally speaking, the freedom a person has to pursue relationship with the divine ends at the point at which a person causes harm to another.

[3] United States Commission on International Religious Freedom, *2018 Annual Report*, 1, https://www.uscirf.gov/sites/default/files/2018USCIRFAR.pdf (accessed January 31, 2019).

[4] A prime example of this form of limitation are recent efforts to force Christian bakers and photographers to produce artistic messaging that condones same-sex marriage, which is contrary to their personal religious beliefs.

humanity. As with many theological doctrines, the Bible doesn't set out to teach its readers about religious freedom. The Bible assumes that people have freedom in matters of religion. Readers simply encounter this freedom as they read their Bibles. If they want to understand this freedom, they must mine the text for it.

It would be much easier to discern the Bible's emphases if it were written like a theological treatise or academic textbook, but that is not generally what we get when we open our Bibles. Instead, we are treated to various literary genres, which require us to discern the truths expressed in them. For example, often, biblical truth is embodied in a story. It is incumbent on the reader to identify or describe the truth that one encounters there. This is the case with practically any other effort to understand foundational truths in Scripture. We often see truths acted out only when we read our Bibles. It is generally up to us to identify or describe them.[5]

This is the space in which we find ourselves when we seek to understand what the Bible teaches about religious freedom. There is no Bible passage that declares that God granted religious freedom to people or that details what such freedom entails. We must read the Bible's stories and other literary genres and piece together what they reveal about it. This is what I attempt to do in this chapter. I will demonstrate that the Bible's various genres produce a picture of religious freedom that is normative for people today—not only adherents to the great Judeo-Christian faiths, but people of all faiths. I will also describe some ways in which this picture applies to some of the contemporary religious-freedom challenges people are facing today.

In examining the biblical material, I believe it is possible to describe religious freedom as operating in three spheres: the individual, the ecclesial, and the civil. Because the Bible is written from the perspective of the Judeo-Christian experience, the picture that will emerge will be based on that context. It should not be assumed, however, that the principles are not normative for all faiths. I believe the universal nature of religious freedom will be evident as I describe it in its Judeo-Christian setting. To the degree that it is possible, I will raise additional arguments, from the particular to the general, in the conclusion.[6]

---

[5] We must engage in a hermeneutical process to develop a biblical view of many subjects. Just to mention a few, one must be a very careful reader to understand the Bible's teaching about the triune nature of God, the sanctity of human life, and gambling, to name a few.

[6] None of the arguments here are new. For greater insight into this crucially important subject, refer to such past stalwarts of religious freedom as Roger Williams, William Penn, Isaac Bacchus, and John Leland; these men are only a few who recognized these truths and expressed them with much more passion and at significant personal risk.

Religious Freedom and the Individual Sphere

Religious freedom is God's gift to humanity. He holds human choice in matters of religion inviolable. This truth serves as bookends for all of the Bible. When we read of God's initial interaction with the first people, we see a surprising respect for human free will as he relates to them. In chapters 2 and 3 of Genesis, we find the first people being placed in the Garden of Eden and given access to all the garden had to offer, including access to the tree of the knowledge of good and evil. They were merely told not to eat from that tree. This is remarkable considering what was at stake, which was nothing less than the current and eternal fate of humanity. Our first ancestors ate from the tree anyway and brought a terrible fate on themselves and all their progeny. The Fall ushered human tragedy into this world as humans separated themselves from God and were left to make their own halting way through life. It also set the eternal spiritual destiny of billions of people.

As tragic as the Fall was, it resulted precisely from the freedom God granted to people. He gave us the freedom to make choices, including whether we will obey him. In this instance, that freedom to choose affected all of humanity's relationship with God. While the text doesn't tell us exactly what it means to gain the knowledge of good and evil, the consequences God spelled out for disobeying his command were dire. Through their disobedience, our first parents were separated from God and doomed all of their progeny to the same fate.

It shouldn't escape our attention that, throughout this tragedy, Adam and Eve acted under God's watchful eye. He knew the stakes better than they, and yet he chose not to intervene. He could have easily appeared at that crucial moment or commanded the angels to come to their aid and prevent impending disaster, but he left these two individuals to decide whether they would be obedient to the command he had issued. Clearly, God was respecting an aspect of human will that he had purposely granted to humans: the freedom to make choices about matters that affected relationship with him. In other words, Adam and Eve were exercising religious freedom.

On the other end of the Bible, we see God continuing to respect human freedom to choose in matters of great spiritual consequence. In the book of Revelation, Jesus delivered messages to seven churches in the Roman Empire. In each instance, he revealed the freedom the church members possessed to decide whether they would respond to him and, if so, to what extent. He concluded each message with the words, "He who has an ear, let him hear what the Spirit says to the churches" (Rev. 2:7). Notice the individual nature of the call. It is extended to each person, not to the group. Each person stands or falls on his or her own in relationship to God.[7]

Jesus's call constitutes an invitation to obey. Granted, repercussions are spelled out clearly if they choose not to obey, but that makes the call that much more striking. In these messages, Jesus is speaking to real people and calling on them to make decisions that can have significant repercussions. Whether they respond properly or adequately is left entirely up to each of them.

This is best illustrated in the Lord's call to the church at Laodicea (Rev. 3:14–22). In addition to the standard call to make a choice, Jesus included a further invitation: "Here I am! I stand at the door and knock. If anyone hears my voice and opens the door, I will come in and eat with him, and he with me" (v. 20). Consider the stakes here. Jesus has warned this church that they are in danger of being spewed out by him if they don't make appropriate adjustments in the practice of their faith. While we don't know all that Jesus was threatening, it is obvious that the situation was consequential. Nevertheless, Jesus left it to the people of this church to decide whether they would make the requisite adjustments in their spiritual comportment.[8]

This divine respect for human free will in spiritual matters doesn't occur only at the beginning and end of the Bible; we encounter it throughout Scripture. The most poignant places we find it are often on the lips of Jesus himself. A couple examples will have to suffice. Scripture records that Jesus stood overlooking the city of Jerusalem and pronounced, "O Jerusalem, Jerusalem . . . how often I have longed to gather your children together . . . but you were not willing" (Matt. 23:37). This moment is astonishing. The Lord of creation was grieving over the city because the people refused to turn to him. Surely, we would all agree that Scripture tells us Jesus had the power to create in these people an irresistible desire to repent, yet he restrained himself from compelling the response he desired. Craig Blomberg notes that "Jesus' words betray great tenderness and employ maternal imagery" as he reveals His longing to love,

---

[7] There is still a community component, though. Jesus is speaking to the churches in each of these locations. It seems that our individual actions affect the community. We'll see this more clearly when we look at the ecclesial sphere of religious freedom.

[8] David Aune, *Revelation 1–5*, Word Biblical Commentary (Grand Rapids, MI: Zondervan, 1997), 251, provides an extensive discussion of Revelation. 3:20, demonstrating that commentators are deeply divided over what Jesus is asking the readers to open themselves up to. He, nevertheless, concurs with the point I'm making here: "The speaker is a deity who begs admission to the home of the worshiper." The God of creation is asking the reader to respond to him.

protect, and nurture the people. Despite this desire, he notes that "God never imposes his love by overriding human will."[9]

One other incident should be enough to drive this point home. In Matt. 11:28, Jesus said, "Come to me, all you who are weary and burdened, and I will give you rest." In this passage, Jesus invited people to come to him.[10] Giving people rest from their spiritual burden is largely what Jesus's incarnation was about. He took on human flesh in order to bring people into right relationship with God. Leon Morris remarks, "Those who take Christ's yoke on them have rest, rest now, and eternal rest in the hereafter."[11] Nothing less than salvation was at issue here. Yet, rather than compelling the response that would lead to salvation and ensuring the greatest possible success in his mission, Jesus left it to the people he came to save to decide whether they would avail themselves of his offer.

Religious freedom doesn't stop with the decision of whether or not to come to Jesus for salvation. It also applies to worship. People are free to decide how they will worship God. We come back to the beginning of the Bible to pick up this truth. The book of Genesis tells us that on a particular day, Cain and Abel both made their offerings to God (Gen. 4:1–16). We're told God accepted Abel's offering and rejected Cain's. The Genesis account doesn't tell us precisely how these two men knew what was expected of them, but it seems clear that they knew. For some clarity, we must look to the writer of Hebrews. In Hebrews 11:4, he tells us faith was involved: "By faith, Abel offered to God a better sacrifice than Cain did." To help us understand the role of faith in this incident, the writer defined it as "being sure of what we hope for and certain of what we do not see" (Heb. 11:1). According to the writer, God reveals his will to people in such an impressionable way that they simply know what

---

[9] Craig Blomberg, *Matthew*, New American Commentary (Nashville: Broadman Press, 1992), 350; Robert Stein, *Luke*, NAC (Nashville: Broadman Press, 1992), 384, notes the contrasting Greek that shows the choice made by the people: "I (Jesus) willed" ("*ēthelēsa*"), "but you (Jerusalem) did not will" ("*ouk ēthelēsate*"). Donald Hagner, *Matthew 14–28*, Word Biblical Commentary (Dallas: Word Books, 1995), 680, sums up the situation: "Despite the invitation to receive what Jesus was bringing, the Jews refused it."

[10] Henry Alford, *The Four Gospels, The Greek Testament* (Chicago: Moody Press, 1958), 1:123, notes that the Greek "*deûte*" ("come") is a command, but by it, Jesus is issuing an invitation. Blomberg, *Matthew*, 350, comments that response to Jesus's call would be determined by volition rather than intellect. It wasn't a question of whether people knew what they needed to do but of whether they would choose to.

[11] Leon Morris, *The Gospel According to Matthew*, Pillar New Testament Commentary (Grand Rapids, MI: Eerdmans, 1992), 297.

is expected of them.[12] Faith is the certainty that what you know is correct or true. There is no guesswork. It is absolute certainty. Abel was absolutely certain he was making the correct offering because God had revealed this to him. The text of Genesis reveals Cain had the same knowledge when it tells us that God counseled Cain some time after he had rejected his offering to "do what is right" (Gen. 4:7).

The writer of Hebrews tells us that, by faith, Abel offered what he knew beyond doubt God had required. On the other hand, Cain decided he would offer to God what he wanted to offer and then expect God to accept it. Kenneth Gangel and Stephen Bramer conclude, "The contrast then is not primarily about faith, although faith is absolutely required, but between offering what the Lord had declared was acceptable and what Cain decided was admissible."[13]

As we know, it did not go well for Cain. God rejected his offering. As God did with Adam and Eve, here again, we see an instance when God let someone make a decision about a matter of great consequence without intervening to prevent it. He had revealed his will in a way that was unmistakable, and then he left these people to decide whether they would obey.

Our schooling about religious freedom continues with these two men. As Cain stewed over God's rejection of his offering, his jealousy toward Abel began to consume him. Out of a genuine desire to help Cain avoid a tragic decision, the Lord confronted him and counseled him to "do what is right" (Gen. 4:7). It seems, God was giving Cain an opportunity to get it right. He even warned him that sin was crouching at the door ready to take over and lead him to destruction if he chose to continue down the path he was on. It should not be lost on us that this is the God of the universe, fully aware of what was at stake and fully capable of stepping in to prevent looming catastrophe, who was counseling Cain to do the right thing. But that was the extent of

---

[12] After sorting through the various explanations scholars have given about the meaning of Hebrews 11:1, David Allen, *Hebrews*, New American Commentary (Nashville: Broadman Press, 2010), 543, sides with those who recognize an objective sense in the writer's definition of faith. He comments that "it is best to take the clause ('what we hope for') to have an objective sense with the meaning 'faith gives substance to what is hoped for,' and not a subjective sense that faith is the assurance that what is hoped for will come to pass." He notes further that "such faith springs from a personal encounter with God." The Greek scholar B. F. Westcott, *The Epistle to the Hebrews*, repr. ed. (Grand Rapids, MI: Eerdmans, 1990), 351, drew a similar conclusion: "Abel recognized the natural obligations of man to God generally." Simon Kistemaker, *Hebrews*, New Testament Commentary (Grand Rapids, MI: Baker Book House, 1984), 311, concludes that, in faith, "the believer is convinced that the things he is unable to see are real."

[13] Kenneth Gangel and Stephen Bramer, *Genesis*, Holman Old Testament Commentary (Nashville: B&H, 2002), 57.

God's involvement. God chose to let Cain make his own decision, knowing the terrible price that would be paid if he persisted in his rebellion. Kenneth Mathews studied this passage closely in his commentary on Genesis and concluded, "Cain is urged to repent lest he be consumed; he cannot claim helplessness nor ignorance, for he has divine counsel."[14] Ultimately, it was Cain's decision to make. This episode shows us that God allows people to be in error regarding his will. He reveals what he wants humans to do, but then he lets them decide whether they will obey. There may be consequences afterward, but we are masters of our fate.

God not only allows people to choose how they will worship him; he also allows them to engage in entirely false worship. This point is pretty much self-evident, since false religions exist today and existed in the past without God intervening to eradicate them, but this in itself is instructive for our understanding of the extent of the freedom God has given us in matters of religion.

To understand the full implications of this point, we need to be reminded that the Bible tells us "the heavens declare the glory of God" (Ps. 19:1). In other words, it is possible to look at creation and perceive that God exists. Paul assures us that creation tells us not only that God exists but also something about what he is like. He says that "what may be known about God is plain" to people. God's "eternal power and divine nature" have been "clearly seen" since the creation of the world (Rom. 1:19–20). According to John Murray, this passage reveals that "a clear apprehension of God's perfections may be gained from his observable handiwork."[15] Even in their fallen spiritual state, people can perceive of the existence and nature of God through general revelation.

Despite the efficacious power of general revelation, it is evident that most people fail to respond appropriately to it. Instead, as Paul noted, people "exchanged the glory of the immortal God for images made to look like mortal man and birds and animals and reptiles" (Rom. 1:23). Instead of worshipping the God they perceive through natural revelation to exist, many people worship creation instead. This choice brings serious consequences. God abandons those who engage in false worship to demeaning and degrading activities (Rom. 1:28).

This is no small thing when we think about religious freedom. Rather than intervening to prevent all of the consequences that result from idol worship, God lets us make these choices and suffer the results. All sorts of errant

---

[14] Kenneth Mathews, *Genesis 1–11:26*, New American Commentary (Nashville: Broadman Press, 1996), 271.

[15] John Murray, *The Epistle to the Romans*, NICNT (Grand Rapids, MI: Eerdmans, 1968), 40.

religions have been formed as people have sought to respond to their knowledge of God's existence, and yet God does not prevent them. Indeed, the number of adherents to the worship of a deity or deities other than the God who has revealed himself in the person of Jesus and Scripture is proof of God's tolerant attitude toward false religion. Not only does God allow false religions to exist; it seems he allows them to thrive. This is astonishing when one considers what is at stake. Few human activities in the Bible draw the level of ire from God as idol worship.

If God, who deserves and expects the worship of all humanity, allows people to get it wrong in their actual worship, we should not imagine that we fellow humans possess the authority to restrict or persecute those who engage in false religion. I think the parable of the tares and wheat is applicable here. In that parable, Jesus told the story of a man who sowed good seed in his field. But, during the night, his enemy came and sowed weed seeds among the wheat. Eventually, the weeds were living right alongside the wheat. Jesus said the landowner's servants asked him if he wanted them to go out and pull up the weeds. The landowner told them to leave the weeds alone. Everything would be sorted out at the harvest (Matt. 13:24–30).

Jesus used this parable to illustrate something about the growth of the kingdom of God. The wheat represented true believers, and the weeds were unbelievers. Jesus instructed his disciples to let those in error and rebellion live alongside the true believers. God would sort it out in the end. This is a clear instruction to the church, or anyone interested in protecting the church, to allow people to persist in their error if they choose to. Of course, Scripture is clear that believers should attempt to persuade people of their error. Paul tells us God desires that all be saved and come to the knowledge of the truth (1 Tim. 2:4), and James says, "Whoever turns a sinner from the error of his way will save him from death and cover over a multitude of sins" (James 5:20); but that persuasion stops at the point of intrusive coercion (i.e., don't pull up the weeds).[16]

---

[16] The freedom to act on religious impulses is not absolute, however. In their treatise on religious freedom, the Witherspoon Institute's Task Force on International Religious Freedom provides helpful clarification: "The right to religious freedom is not a legal right to act on whatever beliefs we fancy about the transcendent, however manifestly evil, illogical, or absurd they may be. Nor does it constitute a right to autonomy of action in a radical sense." The Task Force on International Religious Freedom, "Religious Freedom: Why Now?" (Princeton: Witherspoon Institute, 2012), 17. The freedom of one person to make decisions regarding his religious choices ends where another person's well-being or personal decisions regarding religious belief or practice begins. In other words, religious freedom is not absolute freedom.

In our current environment, this biblical teaching contradicts efforts by those who are attempting to use the power of the state to prevent the expression of religious views that undermine their religion. When I was working at the Southern Baptist Ethics & Religious Liberty Commission, we expended considerable effort, including direct intervention at the U.N. headquarters in New York City, to prevent passage of what had become known as antidefamation resolutions. Some nations were attempting to get these resolutions passed in order to justify their own efforts to silence religious views that competed with or contradicted their state religion. A principal ally in this effort was the Becket Fund for Religious Liberty. In a document titled "Defamation of Religions," the Becket Fund argued, "Defamation of religious resolutions at the UN operate as international anti-blasphemy laws and provide international cover for domestic anti-blasphemy laws, which in practice empower ruling majorities against weak minorities and dissenters."[17] Under these defamation resolutions, countries sought U.N. sanction for government actions against everything from proselytizing to the distribution of literature that contradicted the majority religion. We don't find God calling for such actions in Scripture.

Religious Freedom and the Ecclesial Sphere

The freedom to live according to the dictates of one's conscience is not limited to personal understandings of God's unique will for each of our lives; it extends to aspects of our shared experience as a faith community. Scripture provides a couple helpful examples. First, God allows people to decide for themselves the level of involvement they want to have in helping to fulfill the church's mission. A prime example is found in Paul's instructions to the church at Corinth, in which he counseled the church in how to go about working to advance its mission. He told them there are helpful ways that produce lasting results and there are other ways that contribute nothing lasting. In Paul's language, one can build on the foundation of the church with wood, hay, and straw, or with gold, silver, and precious stones (1 Cor. 3:10–15). I'm sure Paul had a preference for each of his readers, but he just presented the facts and let them decide which kind of church member they wanted to be.

This passage illustrates the Bible's distinction between those who are in healthy relationship with God and those who are not. It is possible to be in true relationship with God but fail to serve him in ways that bring reward in the life

---

[17] Becket Fund for Religious Liberty, "Defamation of Religions," July 2, 2008, https://web.archive.org/web/20090206220325/http://www.becketfund.org/files/73099.pdf.

to come. This is an important point since God has chosen to work through his people to accomplish much of his work of advancing the church in the world. People can be genuine believers but not conduct themselves in a way that God will reward. While this failure results in the loss of reward at the judgment of believers, it does not result in eternal rejection. Paul wanted the church to understand this. He said if anyone's work does not survive God's scrutiny, he will suffer loss but "he himself will be saved, but only as one escaping through the fames" (1 Cor. 3:15). In C. K. Barrett's terminology, the "rotten superstructure" these workers are building will perish, but they "will not be excluded from salvation."[18]

Notice that Paul indicated that God is the one who sorts this out. It might be very obvious to someone that a fellow believer is not contributing anything meaningful to the advancement of the church, but he is not required to intervene and force that errant believer to become more effective. I don't think this means that we should not try to help a fellow believer see the error of his ways. For example, equipping church members for ministry and correcting them when they stray is part of the role of the pastor, but there are appropriate and inappropriate ways to do this. So, Paul instructed Timothy not to rebuke an older man but to "exhort him as if he were your father" (1 Tim. 5:1). In correcting fellow believers, we must be sure we are not assuming God's work of guiding his people. This reminds me of the saying that we are to work for God but not do God's work. Paul reinforced this when he reminded the Corinthian believers, "If anyone destroys God's temple, God will destroy him" (1 Cor. 3:17). We should be careful about when and how we correct someone in error. Just because people don't measure up to our standards doesn't mean we have God's permission to set them straight.

Second, God allows us to be in error about certain practices within the church. For example, look at Paul's counsel to Christians struggling over what to do about eating meat offered to idols (1 Cor. 8:1–13). Paul explained that there were some true worshippers who believed that eating meat offered to idols was equivalent to engaging in the act of idol worship itself. Other true worshippers, however, including himself, did not believe the two were connected (i.e., one can eat meat offered to idols with a clear conscience because there really are no false gods [1 Cor. 8:4]). Yet, rather than attempting to correct those among this spiritual family who were in error, Paul instructed those who knew the meat was not spiritually tainted to refrain from eating it.

---

[18] C. K. Barrett, *The First Epistle to the Corinthians* (San Francisco: Harper and Row, 1968), 89.

This is extraordinary guidance. Paul acknowledged that the people who refused to eat the meat offered to idols were in error in their beliefs, yet rather than telling them to change their views, he called on those who knew the truth about this meat to refrain from eating it in order to protect the conscience of those in error. Incredibly, Paul told the church to adjust to the error of their fellow members. In the words of William Orr and James Walther, Paul's "sense of liberty in Christ is everlastingly circumscribed by the weakness of others."[19] This is hardly the guidance of someone who believed the church must be exacting toward all its members in all things. Apparently, it is acceptable for true worshippers to hold to different beliefs about some matters of a theological nature without breaking fellowship with one another.[20]

Of course, there is a limit to what God and the church can tolerate in the community of faith. When the early church began pooling its resources, a couple named Ananias and Sapphira lied about the amount of money they had made off the sale of a piece of property when they donated the money to the church (Acts 5:1–11). Apparently, they told the church they donated the full amount from the sale of the property, when, in reality, they held back some of the proceeds. They were not judged for holding back some of the money; Peter acknowledged it was theirs to do with as they pleased (v. 4). What brought the judgment of God was the fact that they lied about the amount they gave. God took this matter into his own hands and struck the couple dead for lying to the Holy Spirit. It was not the church's job to mete out punishment for this attempted deception. That was God's job.

---

[19] William F. Orr and James Arthur Walther (in *1 Corinthians*, The Anchor Bible [Garden City: Doubleday, 1976], 235) comment that the principle here is "remarkably like the idea set forth in Matthew 25:45."

[20] This freedom has its limitations. Some matters are too important for believers to disagree about. Paul raised this point with the church in Galatia. He let it be known that there is only one true gospel. Anything that undermined that gospel was to be rejected (Gal. 1:6–9). It is appropriate, then, to talk about negotiables and non-negotiables of the faith. If one's differences in belief do not impinge on matters of eternal destiny, grace is to be extended. If they touch on matters that can endanger eternal destiny, there is no room for error within the body. For example, it is hard to imagine that a church could condone different opinions about the sinless life of Jesus and still be able to share a common life together. Scripture makes it clear that the sinless life of Jesus is the very reason that he was able to take on the sins of humanity. He had no sin of his own for which to be held accountable (2 Cor. 5:21). On the other hand, it is quite possible for members of the same congregation to disagree about the moment of the rapture of the church and still enjoy close fellowship. While the doctrine of the rapture is clearly taught in Scripture and is a point of varying degrees of encouragement about the future, opinions about it have no real bearing on spiritual destiny or the faithful life.

On the other hand, there are instances in which the church is expected to act, but even in these cases, the range of response is limited. The Apostle Paul provides a good example to guide the church in such instances. In the same letter in which he instructed the church to accommodate the errant views of fellow believers regarding eating meat sacrificed to idols, Paul excoriated the church for its failure to discipline a man who was living in some form of open immoral behavior (1 Cor. 5:1–13). This behavior had scandalized the church in Corinth to the point that Paul instructed them to "expel the wicked man from among you" (1 Cor. 5:13) (i.e., deny him access to the fellowship of the church). Denying the man fellowship with the church was a significant judgment, but nothing like the judgment God meted out to the couple for lying. Exclusion was an appropriate action for the church to take; anything more than that was not.

What we are seeing in these passages is a high regard for individual conscience, even in the church. Except for instances where the teaching of Scripture is indisputable, no human has the authority to tell another what God's will is for his life. The church has worked out its understanding of this over the millennia. Today, this is referred to as the "priesthood of the believer." It is the individual, free spiritual standing of every believer to follow what he understands is God's leading in his life. Every believer is free to live before God according to her understanding of what God requires and the extent to which she will live in obedience to that understanding.

Importantly, the above passages demonstrate that the priesthood of the believer does not give a member of a faith community the right to believe or do anything he chooses. If a person's beliefs or practices take him too far outside the pale of the beliefs or practices of his faith community, the community can take action. In such instances, the community has three tools available. The first tool is instruction. The faith community may instruct the person in its beliefs and practices to help restore him. The book of Acts offers a helpful example of how instruction might work to help an errant person. Luke records that Priscilla and Aquila took aside Apollos, the great future leader of the church, to instruct him more fully in the faith. The result bore great fruit for the church (Acts 18:24–28).

If instruction does not accomplish its goal or if other factors are involved, the faith community may exclude the errant member from certain aspects of community life, such as in leadership roles, or it may remove the person from membership entirely. I have already mentioned the instance in 1 Corinthians where Paul instructed the church to exclude a man from its fellowship because of his immoral lifestyle (1 Cor. 5:1–13). Additionally, the church may find it necessary to report a member to the civil authority. When a member of the faith community's actions result in harm to another (e.g., in cases of sexual abuse or assault), the church must report this to the civil authority so that the civil authority can wield its God-ordained sword of justice. Religious freedom may not be used as a covering for violation of another's civil liberties. No one surrenders their civil liberty and civil protections because they become a member of a faith community. But, take note, this sword belongs to the civil authority, not to the faith community. If more is required than these three remedies, God will mete it out in his own way and time.[21]

Religious Freedom and the Civil Sphere

The church does not exist in a void. It worships and works within society. As a result, there can be a strong impulse for the church to look to the civil authority to assist it in its mission. One such type of assistance the church might look for is help with sorting out disagreements. The church must resist this impulse. There is no evidence in Scripture that shows the church looking to the civil authority to resolve its differences.

In one instance, Paul wrote to the church at Corinth and chided them for involving people outside of the church in disputes among themselves. Apparently, they were involving the civil courts in their interpersonal disputes. Paul told them it would be better for them to be wronged by a fellow believer than to take their disputes before unbelievers (1 Cor. 6:1–11). To be sure, Paul did not instruct those who felt they had a legitimate complaint against another believer to just lie down and take it. Instead, he suggested they find a "wise person" among them to "arbitrate." Regardless, he did not want them to take their disputes outside of the church to be settled.

Additionally, as I noted earlier, the church is empowered to remove people from its fellowship, but it is not empowered to utilize the power of the state to enforce its standards. Perhaps the best example of this is found in Paul's guidance to the church of Corinth in dealing with a couple living in what was likely an incestuous relationship. All Paul instructed the church to do was to

---

[21] Much of what I am describing in these paragraphs is known as church discipline. Church discipline is the practice by a congregation of holding its members accountable to one another. For a fuller understanding of the purpose and practice of church discipline, refer to Jonathan Leeman's volume *Church Discipline: How the Church Protects the Name of Jesus* (Wheaton, IL: Crossway, 2012).

dis-fellowship the couple, not to resort to acts of physical harm, either by the church or the civil authority (1 Cor. 5:1–13).

God did not intend for the church to use the authority of the state to impose its will on anyone. The church is the custodian of truth, but not its enforcer. We've seen in history what has happened whenever the church sought to use the power of the sword to impose spiritual fidelity. It has always ended badly. When presented with the opportunity to use the power of the sword, Jesus declared that his kingdom is not of this world. Using the sword to advance the mission of the church is contrary to God's design for the church (John 18:36).

This claim leads immediately to the question of ancient Israel. Members of that community of faith certainly depended on the sword of the civil authority to maintain the community's spiritual fidelity. Biblical Israel was a theocratic state established by God, a designation that included the authority to eliminate threats to the religious fidelity of the people. The question is whether any modern state can claim to be a legitimate theocracy, sanctioned by God in the same way as ancient Israel, to use the power of the sword to enforce fidelity to that state's official or preferred religion. After all, the argument would go, if ancient Israel were a legitimate theocratic state, that would leave open the possibility that others could be as well. The simple response to that claim would be, no, it does not.

No one should assume that the Israel of the Bible serves as a model for any modern state. No other nation can demonstrate that God has entered into covenant with it in the way he did with ancient Israel. Some faith groups have sought to conduct themselves as religious states. They have even pledged themselves to be faithful to the teachings of the Bible, but that doesn't mean God has obligated himself to them in the same way he obligated himself to Israel. Any people can make promises to God and pledge to uphold them through civil power. The question is whether God has committed to the covenantal relationship to which these people have committed themselves.

If God doesn't demonstrate in unmistakable ways that he has entered into a political covenant with a group of people, there is no reason to believe those people enjoy the same relationship with God as ancient Israel did. Absent that affirmation by God, there is also no reason to believe that the state bears the same responsibility that ancient Israel bore to ensure the religious fidelity of its citizens through the power of the sword.

On the other hand, there are plenty of reasons to reject all claims that a nation, or any community, is in covenant relationship with God in the same way that biblical Israel was. Here are a few: First, no other people have experienced the manifest presence of God in its founding like Israel did. Second, no other group of people has had its governing documents delivered to them like ancient Israel did. A third point even addresses modern Israel: no group of people can claim they are in political covenant with God unless they acknowledge the lordship of Jesus Christ. Jesus declared, "Whoever rejects me rejects him who sent me" (Luke 10:16). Religious states that reject the lordship of Jesus are, by that very rejection, not in political covenant with God. Any people can choose to create a geopolitical entity and pledge allegiance to it, but that is much different from actually possessing divine authority to regulate the religious activity of its citizens through the power of the sword. No modern state possesses that right.

Another danger to people of faith as they work within society is that the civil authority may decide to try to limit their ability to live out the requirements of their faith in the public arena. Religion is not only about adherence to a set of theological beliefs. It is also about what people understand those beliefs require them to do in public. These activities come in the form of acts of commission and acts of omission. For example, the Bible regularly shows Jesus and his disciples engaged in acts of compassion toward others, both inside and outside the church. Jesus sent out his disciples to heal the sick in their communities (Luke 10:1–23). He gave money to the poor (John 13:29). Peter was involved in the healing of a man near the temple (Acts 3:1–10). There are also multiple examples of Christians speaking to others about their faith and attempting to gain converts (e.g., Acts 2:1–41, 8:26–40).[22] On the other side of the church's life in the public arena, there are times when Christians must refuse to accommodate the practices of the culture in which they live. We see an example of this in Peter's guidance to the church to persist in a life of spiritual fidelity despite public pressure (1 Pet. 4:1–6).

The public expression of faith is an indispensable part of faith. James said, "I will show you my faith by what I do" (James 2:18). As some governments have begun to seek ways to restrict religious practice to a narrow understanding of worship, the public side of faith is being challenged. Today, you can often hear politicians and others talk about freedom of worship rather than freedom of religion. By this, they mean that people of faith are free to have their unique beliefs and to

---

[22] This isn't a requirement only for the church. In the Hebrew Scripture, the Jewish people were similarly expected to engage in acts of public service as expressions of their faith. Proverbs 19:17 declares, "Whoever is generous to the poor lends to the Lord, and he will repay him for his deed." Isaiah 58:6–7 describes the act of meeting the needs of others—such as helping people escape sinful behavior; freeing the oppressed; and providing food, shelter, and clothing to those in need—as the evidence of true spiritual dedication. Helping those in need is a common element of the world's religions. Islam has a requirement to help others known as *Zakat*. Hinduism, Buddhism, and Sikhism refer to the practice of generosity toward others in need as *Dāna*.

worship within their buildings but are not free to live their lives in society in a way that runs contrary to established public policy. They believe that once a person enters public space, he is bound to obey the law just like anyone else.

There is a kernel of truth to this. Christians, for example, are bound by Scripture to obey the civil authorities (Rom. 13:1–6). On the other hand, this directive has limitations. The requirement for faithful Christians to submit to civil authority is limited by the higher calling to obey God in all things. The most famous biblical example of this limitation occurs in the book of Acts. In this instance, the disciples had been preaching the gospel of faith in Jesus for the forgiveness of sin. The Jewish leaders hauled them in for preaching views contrary to Jewish teaching and ordered them to desist. The apostles rightly responded, "We must obey God rather than men" (Acts 5:29).

The takeaway for people of faith is that obedience to the civil authority ends when that authority requires them to disobey the express commands of God. The early church did not believe government had the authority to make them abandon their core values in order to function in society. The authority of human government is not absolute. The authority of the human government is to bow to God's authority and not interfere with people of faith as they live out the requirements of their faith in the public square.[23]

The Southern Baptist Convention's statement of faith, *The Baptist Faith & Message*, explains this aspect of religious freedom with succinct clarity. The final sentence in its paragraph on religious liberty states, "A free church in a free state is the Christian ideal, and this implies the right of free and unhindered access to God on the part of all men, and the right to form and propagate opinions in the sphere of religion without interference by the civil power."[24]

Religious freedom is God's gift to humanity, not the benevolent kindness of government. When government recognizes the right of people to worship, or not worship, to practice the requirements of their faith, or to not, according

---

[23] Paul Marshall ("Human Rights," in *Toward an Evangelical Public Policy*, ed. Ronald Sider and Diane Knippers [Grand Rapids, MI: Baker Books, 2005], 315) concludes, "Each of us has a right to be a servant of God, to fulfill our particular office and calling for God's glory." The purpose of the political order is to enable people to "express themselves as God's imagers." Typically, people of faith are insistent about this requirement when it involves requisite activities of their faith. Some are less inclined to support this freedom for people of other faiths within their communities. But it is only religious freedom when all people are free to live out the public requirements of their faith, within appropriate boundaries of respect for others, of course.

[24] Southern Baptist Convention, *The Baptist Faith & Message, 2000*, Article XVII, "Religious Liberty," http://www.sbc.net/bfm2000/bfm2000.asp.

to the dictates of their conscience, it is not bestowing a freedom on its citizens; it is acknowledging a right that exists outside of and beyond its authority. The purpose of government is to assist people to fulfill God's design for them—not its own design for them. To the extent that it gets that right, it is acting in a legitimate way, according to God's design for government. As it deviates from God's intention and usurps authority not given to it by God, it becomes illegitimate. Nicholas Wolterstorff puts it succinctly: "The state is but one authority structure among many."[25]

Conclusion

This brief chapter has argued that the Bible supports the universality of religious freedom in the individual, the ecclesial, and the civil spheres. It might be claimed that I am making arguments from silence about the universal nature of religious freedom in these spheres. I have acknowledged that my arguments must be inferred from the various texts I've examined and that some claims of universality must be extrapolated from the available evidence. Nevertheless, there appears to be adequate evidence to support this view.

The universal nature of religious freedom in the individual sphere seems indisputable. In the garden, when God was the only available external authority who could have interfered with the choices Adam and Eve were making, he didn't. The same can possibly be said for the conflict between Cain and Abel. These individuals were free to make their choices.

I believe the Apostle Paul adds to our understanding of the universal nature of the individual sphere of religious freedom. When he stood before the Areopagus in Athens, Paul claimed that God "intended" that every person "seek him and perhaps reach out for him and find him" (Acts 17:27). What makes this statement especially relevant for the current argument is that Paul made this claim within the context of God's establishment of the nations (see Acts 17:26). It seems that a primary purpose of the state is to ensure the freedom of every person to seek God and to find him. It is not the state's job to guide people in their search or to correct them when they are in error in that search. This chapter has demonstrated that, within appropriate moral boundaries, that part of the journey is between each person and God. We are all free to seek God, to find God, and to follow God according to the dictates of our conscience. We are even free to get it wrong.

---

[25] Nicholas Wolterstorff, "Theological Foundations for an Evangelical Political Philosophy," in *Toward an Evangelical Public Policy*, 159.

Arguing for universal religious freedom in the ecclesial, or faith community, sphere is more difficult. The Bible does not address directly some of the specifics we would like to see to argue for a universal right to religious freedom in all faith communities. Nevertheless, I believe it is appropriate to claim that what is good for the goose is good for the gander. If God permits those who have come to him through his son Jesus to freely choose the extent to which they will live faithfully before him within the church, it is reasonable to assume that he permits all people to have a similar level of freedom in their various religious communities, even those in grave error. People may find themselves excluded from their community because of their choices, but they are still free to make those choices. At the very least, I have provided some guidance for those in the church as they try to understand their responsibility for their brothers and sisters in Christ.

A final observation about religious life in the ecclesial sphere is also necessary. While the individual sphere appears to be the primary of the three spheres, the spheres do not exist independently of each other. I've demonstrated from Bible passages that the individual is free to make personal choices and decisions within the ecclesial sphere, even errant choices. Within that sphere, however, the individual is called on to curb the exercise of his or her individual freedom, at times, for the sake of others within that community.

The same interconnectedness occurs within the civil sphere. Both Paul and Peter directed the church to obey the civil authorities. Paul said the civil authority is God's minister for good (Rom. 13:1–7), and Peter repeated this guidance (1 Pet. 2:13–17). Again, however, the civil sphere doesn't subsume the other spheres. Its authority has limitations, and the realm of religion is one of those areas of limitation. For example, the early disciples insisted on the priority of the ecclesial sphere over the state in fulfilling God's calling to it. Also, I have noted that Paul wanted the church to settle its disputes without involving the civil authority. Additionally, the first disciples declared, "We must obey God rather than men" (Acts 5:29).

This declaration isn't only applicable for adherents to the Christian faith. I noted earlier that Paul described God's desire that all men seek him and find him within the context of the establishment of the nations (Acts 17:26–27). The civil sphere protects the right of people to seek God. Period. For God to desire that all men would seek him and find him and then to empower a civil authority to hinder that search is the equivalent of creating people to need water to live and then denying them access to water. The realm of faith does not belong to the civil authority. The civil authority comes closest to its divine design when it protects the freedom of all people to exercise faith or to hold to no faith, according to the dictates of their individual conscience within God-ordained civil protections.

Finally, just because people make choices under God's watchful eye that are contrary to God's revealed will and of great spiritual consequence doesn't mean that God prefers those choices. Nevertheless, he clearly allows people to make those choices. Eventually, God will hold all people to account. Until then, though, it appears that people are free to make their own decisions in matters of religion, as individuals, in community, and within the state. God will sort it out in the end. Nothing less than eternity is at stake, however. May each person find God as he has revealed himself in and through Jesus, and may we all do our part to respect one another in that pursuit.

Chapter 4

Freedom to Flourish: The New Testament, Conscience, and Religious Freedom

Hugh C. Whelchel
Executive Director, IFWE

On May 6, 1776, thirty-two "sons of Virginia" representing every county of the state met at Williamsburg to pass a resolution calling for the Virginia delegates at the Continental Congress to move for independence from Britain.[1] This Virginia Convention was also tasked with drafting a bill of rights and a constitution for the now independent state of Virginia.

At the age of fifty-one, elder statesman George Mason of Gunston Hall emerged from retirement to represent Fairfax County and agreed to write the first draft of both the Virginia Declaration of Rights and the Virginia Constitution. After a few changes and additions, the Declaration of Rights was read to the entire convention on May 27, 1776. In section 16 on religion, Mason, following the thinking of the era, wrote that government must uphold "toleration in the exercise of religion." Religious tolerance was understood as permission given by the state to individuals and groups to practice religion. Mason's language echoed John Locke's writings and the movement toward religious tolerance in England.

However, a young James Madison (then twenty-five years old) objected to Mason's toleration clause and successfully led an effort to modify Mason's original language. Madison argued that religious liberty was a natural and inalienable right. It was possessed equally by all citizens and had to be beyond the reach of civil magistrates. The problem with religious tolerance, he argued, was that what the state gave, it could also take back. Madison changed Mason's

---

[1] The Second Continental Congress was convened on May 10, 1775, at Philadelphia's State House, to consider if the colonies should declare independence. By May of 1776 they were close to passing the resolution, which necessitated the Virginia Convention actions. Less than two months after the Virginia Convention's vote, the Second Continental Congress, on July 2, 1776, released the Declaration of Independence written by another Virginian, Thomas Jefferson.

"toleration in the exercise of religion" to "free exercise of religion." The revised Declaration of Rights was passed unanimously on June 11, 1776.

With this small but significant change in the Declaration's language, Virginia moved from toleration to full religious freedom—a precedent that would help shape not only the new nation's commitment to free exercise of religion but also its very political theology.[2] Government would no longer have the power to decide which groups to "tolerate" and what conditions to place on the practice of their religion. This revolutionary idea was designed to protect and promote a vital role for religion in public life.

The other twelve states adopted this idea of "religious liberty" and had it written into their constitutions. Eventually, it was Madison who codified it in the First Amendment of the U.S. Constitution as one of the cornerstones of the U.S. Bill of Rights. For the first time, religious freedom and the liberty of conscience it sustains became an inalienable right.[3] Madison would later write, "The Religion then of every man, must be left to the conviction and conscience of every man to exercise it as these may dictate."[4]

Madison's idea of religious liberty emerged as one of the unique contributions of the American experiment,[5] but where did it originate? As this chapter will demonstrate, it was not an idea that originated with the Enlightenment, as some claim; rather, it emerged from the rich teaching of the holy Scripture as understood throughout the history of the church. The seeds of religious freedom were found in the Scriptures, sown by the early church fathers, and grown in the rich soil plowed by the Reformers. It began to bear fruit with the founding fathers and a nation birthed, in part, by a desire for religious freedom. This chapter will examine the Christian church's theological development of religious freedom, which was based on the New Testament, and the impact it had on the founding fathers.

---

[2] Political theology is the study of the intersection of theology, politics, society, and economics. While historically affiliated with Christianity, it is currently discussed with relation to all religions.

[3] This did not happen for everyone right away; the issue of slavery would take another hundred years and a civil war to resolve.

[4] George Madison makes this comment in a track he wrote in 1785 titled *Memorial and Remonstrance against Religious Assessments*. The track was anonymously published to oppose a proposed tax that would fund preachers in the state of Virginia and to support Thomas Jefferson's Bill for Establishing Religious Freedom in Virginia.

[5] Daniel Dreisbach, lecture at Reformed Theological Seminary in Washington, DC, February 2008.

Where Did the Idea of Religious Freedom Originate?

There is a conventional narrative taught in the majority of today's colleges that is generally accepted as historical fact by most academics. It attributes modern western political thought, including the rise of religious tolerance, to a process of secularization that occurred in Europe during the seventeenth century called the Great Separation. Mark Lilla describes this event in his book *The Stillborn God*:

> Something happened—or rather, many things happened—and their combined force would eventually bring the reign of political theology to an end in Europe. Not just Christian political theology, but the underlying assumptions upon which all political theology had rested. Christianity as a religious faith survived, as did its churches. The Christian tradition of thinking about politics that depended on a particular conception of the divine . . . did not. It was replaced by a new approach to politics focused exclusively on human nature and human needs. A Great Separation took place, severing Western political philosophy from cosmology and theology. It remains the most distinctive feature of the modern West to this day.[6]

This story of the Great Separation begins in medieval and Renaissance Europe where political theology was informed by Christian thought and seen in the context of the Scripture's call to live our lives based on God's design and desire. As the story goes, by the end of the sixteenth century, this worldview, with its biblically informed "political theology," began to erode, and by the seventeenth century, it had totally collapsed. This tectonic shift was supposedly driven by many events across multiple disciplines. Distressed by the horrors of the Wars of Religion, philosophers rejected the claims of biblical authority and saw religion as inherently dangerous to civil peace. This intellectual upheaval was fueled by new scientific discoveries coupled with the strident philosophical skepticism of men like Montaigne and Charron. As Harvard professor Eric Nelson writes:

> It is this separation, we are told, that is responsible for producing the distinctive features of modern European political thought, including (but by no means limited to) its particular notion of individual rights, its account of the state, and its embrace of religious toleration. These

---

[6] Mark Lilla, *The Stillborn God* (New York: Random House, 2007), 57.

innovations could not appear on the scene until religion had effectively been sequestered from political science. It is, then, the peculiar achievement of the seventeenth century to have bequeathed us a tradition of political thought that has been purged of political theology.[7]

This idea that individual rights, freedom of conscience, religious toleration, and limited, constitutional government were all fruits of banishing religion from the public sphere is not new. It was widely taught in this country by the 1970s, and, by some accounts, modernity itself emerged from this great separation.[8] Today, these ideas are so widely accepted that, for many, it is difficult to imagine any other way of seeing the world. But is this narrative true?

This chapter will examine the truth about the rise of two of these liberal ideas: freedom of conscience and religious toleration. It will look at how their development can be found in another story that begins fifteen hundred years before the Enlightenment, in the birth of the early Christian church, and how believers over the centuries have understood and applied the teaching of the Old and New Testaments to their everyday lives.

Is the Idea of Religious Freedom Biblical?

"Thou shalt not encroach upon the religious liberty of your fellow citizens" is not something you will find in the Bible. Yet, even H. L. Mencken, normally a strong critic of religion, wrote the following in a 1926 essay titled *Equality before the Law*:

> The debt of democracy to Christianity has always been underestimated. . . . Long centuries before Rousseau was ever heard of, or Locke or Hobbs (sic), the fundamental principles of democracy were plainly stated in the New Testament, and elaborately expounded by the early fathers, including St. Augustine.[9]

The Bible teaches that God the Creator, who is the supreme authority over his entire creation, appoints lesser authorities, to whom we are to submit, to rule in certain areas (Rom. 13:1–7). As the Apostle Paul explains, government is one example where God appoints authorities for the support of public order and the common good. He makes it clear that government's responsibilities

---

[7] Eric Nelson, *The Hebrew Republic* (Cambridge: Harvard University Press, 2011), 1.

[8] Lilla, 55–101.

[9] H. L. Mencken, "Equality before the Law," *Chicago Tribune*, (February 28, 1926), 73.

include upholding the rule of law and encouraging good behavior. Scripture also teaches, however, that the rule of civil magistrates over us is not absolute. Only God's moral law binds our consciences. We are to obey God, even if it means disobeying lesser rulers in certain situations.

It is the tension between these two principles—established government and personal responsibility before God—that we see acted out in the New Testament. In the book of Acts, we read of government officials telling Peter and John not to talk about Jesus:

> Then they called them in again and commanded them not to speak or teach at all in the name of Jesus. But Peter and John replied, "Judge for yourselves whether it is right in God's sight to obey you rather than God. For we cannot help speaking about what we have seen and heard." (Acts 4:18–20)

The apostles were echoing the spirit of religious protest sounded some five hundred years before by Daniel's three friends. Faced with the threat of death, they flatly refused to worship before the religious and civil statue of Babylon's king:

> Shadrach, Meshach, and Abednego replied to him, "King Nebuchadnezzar, we do not need to defend ourselves before you in this matter. If we are thrown into the blazing furnace, the God we serve is able to deliver us from it, and he will deliver us from Your Majesty's hand. But even if he does not, we want you to know, Your Majesty, that we will not serve your gods or worship the image of gold you have set up." (Dan. 3:16–18)

As the early Christian church was persecuted, they struggled to apply these two biblical principles. Out of this struggle was born the important idea of an "unconstrained conscience," which, at its very core, requires immunity from religious coercion and contains the seeds of religious liberty.[10] These early believers understood from Scripture that no one should be compelled to violate his conscience by being forced to embrace another religion against his will. Nor should someone be kept from expressing freely and publicly deeply held religious convictions by being forbidden to worship God according to the dictates of his or her conscience. For these early believers, this was not just an intellectual exercise; many were martyred because they would not betray the dictates of conscience.

---

[10] J. M. Roberts, *The Penguin History of Europe* (London: Penguin Books, 1996), 94.

Commenting on this very idea, the early church father Tertullian, in 197 AD, in a letter to the magistrates of Rome, writes that he and other Christians cannot be coerced into sacrificing to pagan gods because "we stand immovable in loyalty to our conscience."[11] In the same treatise, he effectively invents (or discovers) the principle of religious freedom and, in fact, becomes the first person in history to use the phrase "religious liberty."[12] Fifteen years later, he writes to a Roman proconsul:

> It is a fundamental human right, a privilege of nature, that every man should worship according to his own convictions. One man's religion neither harms nor helps another man. It is assuredly no part of religion to compel religion, to which free will and not force should lead us.[13]

Tertullian was not a lone voice on this subject in the early church but was joined by others, including Lactantius.[14] The influence of these early church fathers on the emperor Constantine can be seen clearly in his so-called Edict of Milan in January 313, which was signed by both Roman emperors, Constantine, who ruled in the West, and Licinius in the East. This agreement establishes religious freedom throughout the entire Roman Empire. As the church historian Eusebius commented at the time:

> . . . every man, according to his own inclination and wish, should be given permission to practice his religion as he chooses. . . . Christians and non-Christians alike should be allowed to keep the faith of their own religious beliefs and worship. . . . This we have done to make it plain that we are not belittling any rite or form of worship.[15]

Using Scripture as their source, these early church fathers centered the argument for religious freedom around two ideas: "religion as an inner conviction that cannot be coerced and the freedom and dignity of human beings made in the image of God."[16] These two ideas would lay the groundwork for the later,

---

[11] Tertullian, *Apologeticus*.

[12] Timothy Shah, "The Roots of Religious Freedom in Early Christian Thought," in *Christianity and Freedom: Volume 1 Historical Perspectives*, ed. Timothy Samuel Shah and Allen D. Hertzke (New York: Cambridge University Press, 2016), 55.

[13] Tertullian, *Ad Scapulam*.

[14] Robert Lewis Wilkin, "The Christian Roots of Religious Freedom," in *Christianity and Freedom: Volume 1 Historical Perspectives*, 62–89.

[15] Eusebius, *The History of the Church*, bk. 10, para. 5.

[16] Robert Louis Wilken, *The Christian Roots of Religious Freedom* (Milwaukee, WI: Marquette University Press, 2014), 69.

fuller doctrine of natural rights and a more robust vision of religious freedom. We will concentrate our discussion around the biblical idea of freedom of conscience; for a more in-depth analysis of human dignity and the image of God, see Chapter Two by John Redd.

In 380 AD, with the Edict of Thessalonica, Christianity became the *ex facto* state church of the Roman Empire, and persecution diminished along with the need for religious freedom.[17] Over the next thousand years in the Western church, Tertullian's ideas of religious freedom would be replaced by the concept of religious tolerance, while two other significant ideas would be more fully developed: conscience and separation of church and state.

Religious Liberty, Conscience, and the New Testament

In 2009, speaking on religious liberty, Princeton professor Robert George, the late Charles Colson, and Baptist theologian Timothy George, stated the following in the Manhattan Declaration:

> Immunity from religious coercion is the cornerstone of an unconstrained conscience. No one should be compelled to embrace any religion against his will, nor should persons of faith be forbidden to worship God according to the dictates of conscience or to express freely and publicly their deeply held religious convictions. What is true for individuals applies to religious communities as well.

Where do we find this in Scripture? While the Bible may not comment specifically on religious liberty, it does have something to say about conscience and, as we see in the statement above, the connection between religious liberty and conscience is strong.

The Greek word *suneidēsis* (συνείδησις), which is translated as *conscience* in the New Testament, never occurs in the four Gospels. It is used thirty times in the rest of the New Testament,[18] twenty of those by the Apostle Paul in his letters.[19] While *suneidēsis* is used almost exclusively by Paul (eleven times in 1 and 2 Corinthians alone), five references are found in the book of Hebrews and one in 1 Peter. Interestingly, the Hebrew Old Testament has no word for

---

[17] Sidney Ehler and John Morrall, ed. *Church and State through the Centuries* (New York: Burns & Oates, 1954), 6.

[18] The Greek word *suneidēsis* is used thirty-one times in the New Testament if you include the possible usage in a variant in John 8:9.

[19] Paul A. Hartog, "Conscience," in *The Lexham Bible Dictionary*, ed. J. D. Barry et al. (Bellingham, WA: Lexham Press, 2016).

conscience, although the idea is often expressed in the word *heart* (1 Sam. 24:5). While the idea of the Christian conscience is complex, a thematic review of the occurrences of *suneidēsis* in the New Testament reveals three major ideas.[20]

First, one of the functions of conscience is as a "witness" to an internal value system, based upon the knowledge that one accepts to be true (Rom. 9:1; 2 Cor 1:12, 4:2, 5:11). Conscience does not represent an independent authority but facilitates making moral judgments regarding right and wrong based on what the person believes. A close examination of 1 Corinthians 8 and 10 illustrates this principle. In Paul's rebuke of the Corinthian church, we see an example of a weak conscience that is without adequate knowledge regarding idols and meat and suffers feelings of guilt as a result. By contrast, the strong have a proper understanding of the issue in question and are therefore free of guilt.[21]

Second, God has given humanity conscience as a means to exercise self-critique, to judge one's self whether something is rightfully or wrongly done after the fact. Paul's concept of clear conscience is illustrated in both 1 Corinthians 4:4 and Acts 24:16. In 1 Corinthians 4:4, when reflecting on his ministry and motives, Paul claims he "knows nothing against himself" (*sunoida*; translated "my conscience is clear" by the NIV) but confirms he is still subject to critique by God.[22] Paul clearly understands his conscience does not have the final say but is subject to God's judgment.

The third idea relates to our discussion regarding religious liberty. Paul does not shame the weak believers in chapter 8 of 1 Corinthians because of their incorrect views but instead warns the stronger believer not to coerce them into going against their values—not to bind their conscience. In Romans 14:17 and Colossians 2:16–17, Paul makes it clear that our Christian liberty cannot be bound by personal conviction of extra-biblical nonessentials. Only

---

[20] G. Kittel, G. Friedrich, and G. W. Bromiley, *Theological Dictionary of the New Testament: Abridged in One Volume* (MI: Eerdmans, 1985), 1122.

[21] "Knowledge" is used almost as a substitute for conscience in Paul's discussion, both here and in the Roman 14 discussion.

[22] The discussion in Romans 2:14–15 further illustrates this point. Paul is claiming that the Gentiles are, in one sense, superior to the Jews. The Gentiles' "self-critique mechanism," or conscience, based on their own law or values makes them more consistent than the Jews are to the true law. The Jews resist, while the Gentiles' conscience works, even though it is based on inferior values. Paul uses the illustration to shame the Jews in their position of greater privilege. The point of Romans 2:14–15 is to illustrate how the concept of conscience functions.

the word of God can bind the Christian's conscience. As theologian A. A. Hodge writes:

> God alone is the Lord of human conscience, which is responsible only to his authority. God has authoritatively addressed the human conscience only in his law, the only perfect revelation of which in this world is the inspired Scriptures. Hence God himself has set the human conscience free from all obligation to believe or obey any such doctrines or commandments of men as are either contrary to or aside from the teachings of that Word. Hence, to believe such doctrines, or to obey such commandments as a matter of conscience, is to be guilty of the sin of betraying the liberty of conscience and its loyalty to its only Lord; and to require such obedience of others is to be guilty of the sin of usurping the prerogative of God and attempting to destroy the most precious liberties of men.[23]

"Liberty of conscience," then, is defined by the New Testament as freedom from the doctrines and commandments of men that are contrary to God's word.[24] Therefore, no one, including the civil magistrate, can bind the conscience of a believer with laws or commands outside the bounds of Scripture, unless it is with their willful consent. The problem, as we will see, is how Paul's teaching on binding the conscience is ignored and often abused in the period between the Reformation and the late eighteenth century.

The Reformation and Further Development of Religious Liberty

It is Martin Luther who helps return to the biblical concept of conscience in the Protestant Reformation. On October 31, 1517, Luther posts his Ninety-Five Theses on the church door in Wittenberg, launching the Reformation in earnest. The Reformation produced a new focus on freedom of conscience, with dramatic social and political consequences. It created modern notions of religious liberty as well as new frameworks for civic life. At the same time, the Reformers, building upon centuries of religious thought on conscience, dignity, and freedom, found additional support from new resources.

Luther and the other Reformers more fully develop this idea of conscience in their struggle with the Roman church. Luther's famous "Here I Stand" speech

---

[23] A. A. Hodge, *The Confession of Faith* (Carlisle, PA: Banner of Truth, 2004), 265.
[24] As Paul tells the Corinthians, "For why is my freedom being judged by another's conscience?" (1 Cor. 10:29); also see *WCF* 20.2.

at the Diet of Worms is a classic example of how the early Reformers saw the rights of a free conscience being bound by Scripture:

> Unless I am convicted by Scripture and plain reason—I do not accept the authority of popes and councils, for they have contradicted each other—my conscience is captive to the Word of God. I cannot recant, and I will not recant anything, for to go against conscience is neither right nor safe. Here I stand, I can do no other. God help me. Amen.[25]

For Luther, it was the Bible that informed his conscience. J. I. Packer writes, "The Christian's conscience . . . as Luther memorably declared at Worms in 1521, is and must be subject to the Word of God—which means the teaching of Holy Scripture."[26] Luther's stance against the Roman church was not just due to his autonomous conscience telling him they were wrong; instead, it was because the church's teaching was in clear violation of Scripture. To act contrary to the urging of one's conscience is wrong, for actions that go against the conscience cannot arise out of faith[27] (1 Cor. 8:7–13, 10:23–30).

John Calvin, like Luther, also supported liberty of conscience informed by God's Word. For example, Calvin writes in his *Institutes of the Christian Religion*: "The restraint thus laid on the conscience is unlawful. Our consciences have not to do with men but with God only."[28] Yet, Luther and Calvin's most significant contributions to religious liberty were in principle, not practice.[29]

Further development of the foundational principles of conscience and religious liberty would await the work of later Reformers like John Knox, Theodore Beza, Johannes Althusius, and John Milton. These Reformers, and those who

---

[25] Martin Luther, quoted by Roland Bainton in *Here I Stand* (Nashville: Abingdon Press, 1990), 144.

[26] J. I. Packer, *A Quest for Godliness* (Wheaton, IL: Crossway, 1990), 107.

[27] R. F. Youngblood, F. F. Bruce, and R. K. Harrison, *New Illustrated Bible Dictionary* (Nashville: Thomas Nelson, 1995).

[28] John Calvin, *Institutes of the Christian Religion*, Bk. IV, chap. 10, sect. 5.

[29] Luther, speaking in the context of the state not having the right to compel an individual toward a particular religion, writes, "Furthermore, every man is responsible for his own faith, and he must see to it for himself that he believes rightly. . . . Since, then, belief or unbelief is a matter of every one's conscience, and since this is no lessening of the secular power, the latter should be content and attend to its own affairs and permit men to believe one thing or another, as they are able and willing, and constrain no one by force." ("Secular Authority: To What Extent It Should Be Obeyed," in *Martin Luther: Selections from His Writings*, ed. John Dillenberger (New York: Doubleday, 1961), 385. This statement is typical of the early Reformers' use of "liberty of conscience" merely as the idea that no authority can compel a person to believe the truth.

would follow them, applied Calvin's insights to the nature of corporate rule and created "a robust constitutional theory of the state that rested on the pillars of the rule of law, democratic process and individual liberty."[30]

> In the Calvinist Tradition, religious rights were first, for they were the easiest for persecuted Calvinists to conceive; other rights developed gradually and sporadically over the next centuries, and with varying intellectual foundation and institutional force. From the start, religious rights were the cornerstones of Calvinist rights theories—freedom of conscience, freedom of exercise, and freedom of the church.[31]

The efforts of these later Reformers would be significantly enhanced by two unlikely sources, the Torah and a full array of ancient rabbinic sources.

The Reformed commitment to "*Sola Scriptura*" triggered a revival of interest in original (Hebrew) Old Testament texts beginning in the sixteenth century, and it would continue for the next two hundred years. As Eric Nelson writes in his book *The Hebrew Republic,* the study of the Bible as a Christian duty "led Protestants back to the original texts of the Hebrew Bible and the New Testament to an unprecedented degree."[32] As Hebrew texts and grammars became more widely available in Christian Europe, scholars also turned to the "full array of rabbinic sources" that had also become available, including the Talmud, the Midrash, Targums, and medieval law codes. It is in these sources that scholars began to uncover the argument that in the first five books of the Bible, God reveals to man the ideal form of government: the republic. Nelson goes on to convincingly argue that the ideas of religious tolerance, rough material equality, and republican government entered Western political thought not because of the Great Separation, but because they were discovered in the Hebrew Bible. Therefore, in the seventeenth century, we see Reformation political theology reentering mainstream European intellectual life. Os Guinness echoes this idea in his book *Last Call for Liberty,* writing:

> The precedent and pattern of the Sinai covenant was rediscovered and developed by the Reformation. Along with the truths of calling and

---

[30] John White Jr., "Calvinist Contributions to Freedom in Early Modern Europe," in *Christianity and Freedom: Volume 1 Historical Perspectives,* ed. Timothy Samuel Shah and Allen D. Hertzke (New York: Cambridge University Press, 2016), 217.

[31] White, "Calvinist Contributions to Freedom in Early Modern Europe," 229.

[32] Nelson, *Hebrew Republic,* 13.

conscience, it became one of the three most decisive gifts of the Reformation that shaped the rise of the modern world.[33]

These discoveries significantly enhanced and reinforced two essential ideas that were, as mentioned earlier, beginning to be more fully developed at the onset of the Reformation: religious toleration and separation of church and state. As Nelson argues,

> The pursuit of toleration was primarily nurtured by deeply felt religious convictions, not by their absence; and it emerged to a very great extent out of the Erastian effort to unify Church and State, not out of the desire to keep them separate. Once again, I argue that the Hebrew revival played a crucial role in forging this nexus between a pious Erastianism and toleration. It was a particular understanding of what the Jewish historian Josephus had meant by the term "theocracy," mediated through a series of rabbinic sources, which convinced a wide range of seventeenth-century authors that God's own thoroughly Erastian republic had embraced toleration.[34]

Unfortunately, because of the Reformers' distorted understanding of the Bible's teaching on conscience, it would take more than two centuries for these truths to be fully embraced by the heirs of the Reformation—America's founding fathers.

By the second half of the sixteenth century, many Reformed Confessions stated, "Godly magistrates, like the good kings of Judah, were to overthrow idolatry and punish crimes against the first table of the law."[35] The Second Helvetic Confession was typical of this era, clearly authorizing the magistrate to draw their swords against blasphemers and heretics.[36] These new Protestant governments continued, as the Roman church had done, to see the state as the instrument of the church. Not only were heretics put to death whenever the Protestants seized power, but they also suppressed the worship of other faiths, including the Catholic Mass. John Marshall writes, "To every one of the leading magisterial Reformation thinkers of the sixteenth century, toleration was simply a diabolical doctrine."[37] While this may be a little over the top, most of the

---

[33] Os Guinness, *Last Call for Liberty* (Downers Grove, IL: IVP, 2018), 23.

[34] Nelson, *Hebrew Republic*, 4.

[35] John Coffey, "John Owen and the Puritan Toleration Controversy, 1646–59," in *The Ashgate Research Companion to John Owen's Theology*, ed. Kelly Kapic and Mark Jones (Farnham: Ashgate, 2012), 227–48.

[36] Alexander Jaffray, *The Diary of Alexander Jaffray Profost of Aberdeen*, ed. John Barclay (London: Darton and Harvey, 1834), 38–39.

[37] John Marshall, *John Locke, Toleration and Early Enlightenment Culture* (Cambridge:

Reformers of this period were in agreement that "liberty of conscience," as supported by the few dissenters like Sebastian Castellio, the Socinians, and the Anabaptists, was a misnomer. Only the true believers were the ones who had a right to "freedom of conscience." Those in error had no rights.

By the mid-seventeenth century, England had become ground zero for the fierce assault against religious coercion. Published in 1647, the Westminster Confession of Faith continued to teach that the civil magistrate had a duty to preserve the unity of the church and the purity of its doctrine and to suppress "all blasphemies and heresies."[38] The next year, the Presbyterian-dominated English Parliament passed a blasphemy ordinance that prescribed the death penalty for those who publicly denied the authority of the Scriptures and the Trinity, and imprisonment for promoting Arminianism and other lesser heterodoxies.[39] Numbers of other statements and treatises were written against religious toleration, defending the traditional Reformed view of the magistrate's power in matters of religion.[40] All this was done in an attempt to quell the rising tide of individuals and groups advocating for religious toleration, or what they called "liberty of conscience." The movement was led by men like Roger Williams, the founder of Rhode Island; writer John Milton; Sir Henry Vane, former governor of Massachusetts; and, one of the most influential members of the English Parliament of the time, Enlightenment thinker John Locke.[41] Even the Puritan John Owen, whose view on the subject significantly changed over his

---

Cambridge University Press, 2007), 325. Marshall's monograph thoroughly documents Protestant support for religious coercion in the sixteenth and seventeenth centuries.

[38] "Westminster Confession of Faith," in *Creeds of the Evangelical Protestant Churches*, ed. Philip Schaff, vol. 3 Creeds of the Evangelical Protestant Churches (New York: Harper and Brothers, 1877), 653.

[39] C. H. Firth and R. S. Rait, ed. *Acts and Ordinances of the Interregnum*, 3 vols. (London: Wyman and Sons, 1911), 1:1133.

[40] See John Coffey, "The Toleration Controversy," in *Religion in Revolutionary England*, ed. Christopher Durston and Judith Maltby (Manchester: MUP, 2006), 42–68. For other concise surveys of the mid-seventeenth-century English debate, see Andrew Murphy, *Conscience and Community: Revisiting Toleration and Religious Dissent in Early Modern England and America* (University Park, PA: Penn State University Press, 2001), chap. 3; Perez Zagorin, *How the Idea of Religious Toleration Came to the West* (Princeton: Princeton University Press, 2003), chap. 6.

[41] In his Bible-based writings on religious tolerance, Locke, like Williams and Penn, influenced the views of many in both England and colonial America. In 1669, Locke helped write the constitution for the colony of Carolina in America, which notably allowed for freedom of belief despite the state having an official state church. Carolina's state church was more tolerant than those in other colonies like Massachusetts, Connecticut, and Virginia. See David Armitage, "John Locke, Carolina, and the 'Two Treatises of Government'," *Political Theory* 32, no. 5 (2004): 602–27, http://www.jstor.org/stable/4148117.

lifetime, wrote, "But these things stand not in the relation imagined. Liberty of conscience is of natural right, Christian liberty is a gospel privilege, though both may be pleaded in unwarrantable impositions on conscience."[42] These advocates for religious tolerance argued that "true religion" would eventually overwhelm "false religion" without using force. They also argued that the doctrine of religious coercion was unbiblical based on Paul's teaching on conscience, causing more harm than good by relentlessly suppressing godly reformers as evil heretics.[43]

During this same period, views both for and against religious toleration and freedom of conscience found their way across the Atlantic to America with the Puritans and the English Separatists who found themselves persecuted for what they believed in the changing European religious landscape. It is this contingent that leaves Europe and heads to a new world seeking a place where they can live their lives free from religious persecution. J. I. Packer points out that the Puritans viewed conscience as "the mental organ in men through which God brought his word to bear on them."[44] As we will see, it is this definition that will continue to cause great hardship for many in the founding of what would become America. In the first two hundred years of American colonization, persecution of minority protestant groups, Catholics, and Jews was almost as widespread as it was in Europe.

Religious Freedom, America, and the Founding Fathers

The seventeenth-century American colonists crossed the Atlantic with a robust notion of personal freedom. As William Penn writes, "Every Free-born subject of England is heir by Birth-right unto that unparalleled privilege of Liberty and Property, beyond all the Nations in the world beside."[45] And as Os Guinness writes, they brought with them two centuries of developed political theology:

> [T]he rule of law, the consent of the governed, the responsibility of rights, the separation of powers, the notion of prophetic critique and social criticism, transformative servant leadership, the ethics of responsibility, the primacy of the personal over the political—all of these ideals and more are the legacy of Exodus, and their effect was to provide a

---

[42] John Owen, *Works of John Owen, vol. 21*, ed. Thomas Russell (London: 1827), 295.

[43] John Coffey, "Puritanism and Liberty Revisited: The Case for Toleration in the English Revolution," *Historical Journal* 41 (1998): 461–85.

[44] Packer, *Quest for Godliness*, 107.

[45] William Penn, quoted in Daniel Hannan, *Inventing Freedom: How the English-Speaking Peoples Made the Modern World* (New York: HarperCollins, 2013), 127.

massive boost for the ancient liberties of the English. Most importantly, the Sinai covenant at the heart of the Exodus story came to America with the English and put its stamp on American history through its decisive contribution to the U.S. Constitution and the notion of constitutionalism.[46]

The majority of European settlers coming to the new colonies during the seventeenth century came from countries with established national churches, and for them, a society without an established church was unimaginable. What they did not realize was that the deep-seated conflict between their view of freedom of conscience, religious tolerance, and the state-established church would soon be apparent.

Liberty of conscience, from the perspective of the Reformation, does not give us the freedom to do anything we want; it instead binds our conscience to the will of God. Also, our consciences should not be bound by false religion or extra-biblical scruples and traditions, because we are ultimately answerable only to God. The problem in the new American colonies was that once the early settlers became the ruling authority, they strictly applied these principles to everyone and began to persecute all those who disagreed with their specific interpretation of Scripture. They reasoned that the concept of liberty of conscience did not allow men or women to believe in false religion or give them the freedom to hold to unbiblical positions on moral issues.

Puritan minister Roger Williams provides an excellent example of this. The Puritans in Massachusetts felt called by God to establish a holy commonwealth, a new Israel, based on a covenant between themselves and God. Williams challenged the Puritan vision and argued God had a very different plan for human society. He claimed that the civil authorities of Massachusetts had no authority in matters of faith. According to Williams, the true church was a voluntary association of God's elect. "Soul liberty," as Williams called it, was understood as the freedom to follow an individual's heart in matters of faith, without outside coercion by the government. Williams's argument for separating church and state was centered on his conviction that every individual's conscience must remain free to accept or reject the word of God. In 1635, after being banished from Massachusetts, Williams founded what became the state of Rhode Island. Williams's colony did not have an established church, making it the first society in America to grant liberty of conscience to everyone.

---

[46] Guinness, *Last Call for Liberty*, 23.

In 1670, Quaker William Penn wrote a comprehensive statement on religious toleration, which serves as a theoretical foundation for his experiment in the practice of religious liberty in Pennsylvania. Penn makes an inherently religious argument for religious toleration, resting his appeal on divine authority. Penn claimed that intolerance violates liberty of conscience and is not only an offense against others but also, ultimately, an offense against God.[47]

What we see in this period, from the early founding of the first colonies to 1750, is a gradual extension of a new vision of religious tolerance that broadens the Christian view of liberty of conscience. The idea that religious liberty can also include others, even those with whom "we" disagree, slowly becomes a central American conviction. This vision coalesces around a view of liberty of conscience from the Scriptures that endorses religious tolerance. It is this principle that provided the promise of full freedom for people of all faiths and that laid the groundwork for the establishment of true religious freedom by the founding fathers.

With a keen historical awareness of the inherent dangers of wedding the political powers of the government with the church, the founding fathers looked to balance religious obligations with Madison's rediscovered religious freedom. Gregory Wallace notes the following:

> For Madison and others, religious obligations were paramount. Defining the proper relation between religion and civil government meant drawing a jurisdictional boundary between two potentially competing authorities, one spiritual and the other political. That line was drawn with the understanding that duty to God, as perceived within the individual conscience, is superior to political, legal, or social obligations. Religion thus posited an ultimate limit on the power of the state. In this sense, the First Amendment was intended to function as a sort of religious "supremacy clause" which presumes that God exists and makes claims on human beings and that those claims are first in both time and importance to the claims of the state.[48]

Thomas Jefferson, in his *Notes on the State of Virginia* in 1782, wrote what many believe is the quintessential liberal formation of an individual's right to religious freedom:

---

[47] William Penn, *Selected Works of William Penn in Five Volumes*, 3rd ed. (London: James Phillips, 1782), 3:12–13.

[48] E. Gregory Wallace, "Justifying Religious Freedom: The Western Tradition," *Penn State Law Review*, 114, no. 2 (2009): 490.

Our rulers can have authority over such natural rights only as we have submitted to them. The rights of conscience we never submitted, we would not submit. We are answerable for them to our God. The legitimate power of government extends to such acts only as are injurious to others. But it does me no injury for my neighbor to say there are twenty gods or no god. It neither picks my pocket nor breaks my leg.[49]

In the margin on the original copy of *Notes,* across from the passage above, Jefferson wrote, in his own hand, a quote in Latin from Tertullian's *Ad Scapulam.*[50] As noted earlier, the quote from Tertullian contains the first articulation of religious freedom as a universal human right ever written. As you can see, the two passages are strangely similar. It has been suggested that Jefferson somehow found out about the passage after he wrote *Notes.* Timothy Shah makes the following remarks about Jefferson's journey to understanding the idea of religious freedom:

> One can imagine Thomas Jefferson, trudging up the religious freedom mountain, step by arduous step. And when he reached the top of the conceptual mountain, argument by argument, and reached his radical conclusions about religious freedom—not mere toleration—as a universal natural right, for all people, regardless of creed, one can imagine his surprise: When he finally got to the top, he discovered that a North African Church Father was already sitting there—and had been for some sixteen hundred years.[51]

The founders believed virtue derived from religion was indispensable to limited government. Therefore, Madison's Constitution guaranteed religious free exercise while prohibiting the establishment of a national religion: "This constitutional order produced a constructive relationship between religion and state that balances citizens' dual allegiances to God and earthly authorities without forcing believers to abandon (or moderate) their primary loyalty to God."[52]

---

[49] Thomas Jefferson, *Notes on the State of Virginia* (query VII).

[50] See full quote on page 7.

[51] Shah, "Roots of Religious Freedom in Early Christian Thought," 58.

[52] Jennifer Marshall, "Why Does Religious Freedom Matter?" The Heritage Foundation, accessed March 8, 2019, https://www.heritage.org/religious-liberty/report/why-does-religious-freedom-matter.

Madison and the other founding fathers' brilliant model of religious liberty is at the center of the success of the American experiment. Freedom of conscience wasn't just about Christianity or even religion for Madison and the other founding fathers. Instead, they wanted the country to accommodate all citizens—religious or not; therefore, they needed to establish freedom for religion. This meant an openness to political and societal tolerance for the religious choices of others—Muslims, Buddhists, humanists, and, yes, Christians.

Madison and the founding fathers crafted a unique political theology, in part, by doing two things that had never been done. First, they built upon the Reformers' biblical view of liberty of conscience, incorporating the ideas of tolerance that had been expressed since the beginning of the Reformation. Incorporating the work of men like Williams, Locke, and Penn, the founding fathers then broadened the Reformers' view of liberty of conscience, letting it apply to all members of the community. The second thing they did was to put this new tolerant view of liberty of conscience beyond the reach of the civil magistrates, creating, for the first time in history, true religious freedom.

For the founding fathers, the term "liberty of conscience" had three aspects. First was the notion that everyone had freedom of belief. All individuals in a society were at liberty to choose the religious creed they wanted to embrace or to choose to embrace none. Second, was the idea of freedom of observance. Individuals were at liberty to practice their religion lawfully without outside interference. Third, all members of society were to have equal status under the law. In other words, all religions and their believers, as well as nonpractitioners of religion, would receive equal treatment under the law by the civil magistrate.

Conclusion: Practical Considerations for Christians Today

Historically, we see the best examples of human flourishing where people enjoy freedom—religious, economic, and political. Of course, the three freedoms are interrelated, but the foundational freedom is religious freedom, because without freedom to be guided by faith-based morals, economic freedom and political freedom are at greater risk of corruption.[53] As America's founders correctly

---

[53] See Section Three of this volume.

observed, "freedom requires virtue, virtue requires faith, and faith requires freedom."[54]

Unfortunately, our exercise of the inalienable right of religious freedom, as defined by James Madison and America's founders, is threatened today. The current momentum in our country is toward replacing religious freedom with religious tolerance, or more extreme yet—allowing anti-discrimination laws to trump religious freedom completely. One example of this subtle but dangerous shift is the 2009 U.S. immigration exam that says that the First Amendment protects "freedom of worship" rather than the "free exercise of religion."[55]

Other challenges to the constitutional definition of religious freedom abound and are playing out in state judiciaries and the U.S. Supreme Court (see Section Four). A circuit court case in 2012 revealed a very troubling argument made by the Department of Justice in *Newland v. Sebelius*. In this case, the Catholic owners of Hercules Industries challenged the government mandate to provide free contraception and sterilization surgeries to employees. This was the government's argument in defense of the mandate:

- Seeking profit is a wholly secularist pursuit.
- Once people go into business, they lose their religious freedoms in the context of those activities.
- Everyone who engages in secular undertakings must acquiesce to the principles of secular ideology.
- The government establishes this ideology through the passage of laws and the promulgation of regulations.

It is hard to believe that a government based on a constitution that so clearly defines religious freedom as untouchable by the state, a definition that has been so carefully debated and articulated, could make such an argument. It is an argument aiming to redefine religious freedom out of existence, or at least back two hundred fifty years, to the concept of religious tolerance. The *Newland v. Sebelius* case helps us not only see how religious freedom is essential to the ability to freely exercise our beliefs and follow our consciences in all spheres of life (including work and what we do in the public square) but also how religious freedom in our country is in jeopardy.

---

[54] Os Guinness, *A Free People's Suicide: Sustainable Freedom and the American Future* (Downers Grove, IL: IVP, 2012), 93–129.
[55] Ryan T. Anderson, *Truth Overruled: The Future of Marriage and Religious Freedom* (Washington, DC: Regnery Publishing, 2015), 198.

Christians have argued that for followers of Jesus Christ, nothing is secular; everything we do is spiritual. Our work, which occupies two-thirds of our time, is a ready example of this. As the Apostle Paul reminds the Corinthians:

> So whether you eat or drink or whatever you do, do it all for the glory of God. (1 Cor. 10:31)

And again, he tells the Colossians:

> Whatever you do, work at it with all your heart, as working for the Lord, not for human masters, since you know that you will receive an inheritance from the Lord as a reward. It is the Lord Christ you are serving. (Col. 3:23–24)

Therefore, whatever we do in our work, even in the work we do in the public square, is done to glorify God, serve the common good, and further God's kingdom. This is our high calling, and it is *all* spiritual activity.

Thankfully, in *Newland v. Sebelius,* the judge did not rule for the government;[56] however, over the last six years, there have been numerous examples of men, women, and children whose First Amendment rights have been violated by those trying to redefine religious freedom and force faith out of the public square. Some politicians and members of the media belittle individuals' claims of religious conscience, treating religious freedom as an obstacle to be overcome rather than as an important value to protect. As Os Guinness observes,

> America is now experiencing an open assault on freedom of religion and conscience. What was the founders' "first liberty" and the freedom that (Lord Acton wrote) "secures the rest" is in danger of being dislodged from its central and time-honored place in American life.[57]

Religious freedom is not just important for U.S. Christians because it's in the Constitution. Religious freedom is important because the principles that support it flow from God's Word and are designed to bless all people. True religious liberty provides the freedom to live and work within a Christian worldview seven days a week, fulfilling God's call in our families, churches, communities, and vocations. We must always remember that, in Christianity,

---

[56] Timothy Jost, "*Newland v. Sebelius*: The General Welfare, Religious Liberty, and Contraception Coverage under the ACA," *Health Affairs* (blog), July 30, 2012, accessed March 8, 2019, https://www.healthaffairs.org/do/10.1377/hblog20120730.021584/full.
[57] Guinness, *Last Call for Liberty*, 144.

human liberty is both a theological and political telos.[58] As Lord Acton once said, "liberty is not a means to a higher political end, it is itself the highest political end."[59]

Leading historians are rediscovering the unappreciated role that Christianity has played in the development of fundamental human rights and freedoms, from the times of the early church fathers through today. This role includes contributing to "radical notions of dignity and equality, religious freedom, liberty of conscience, limited government, consent of the governed, economic liberty, autonomous civil society, and church-state separation, as well as . . . democracy, human rights, and human development."[60] While there certainly is not a straight line from the early church fathers through the Reformation to the founding fathers, scholars are documenting how the seeds of freedom sown by men like Tertullian produced fruit in Madison's republic.[61]

James Madison and the other founding fathers called religious freedom our first freedom and believed it was the foundation of all others.[62] In a December 1790 speech to the Congress, Madison declared ". . . above all, it is the particular glory of this country, to have secured the rights of conscience which in other nations are least understood or most strangely violated."[63] Madison strongly believed religious freedom was the prerequisite to fulfilling our obligation to God. Placing that freedom outside the reach of the coercive powers of the state was the only way to preserve its important purpose: "The Duty which we owe our Creator, and the manner of our discharging it, can be governed only by Reason and Conviction, not by Compulsion or Violence; and therefore all men

---

[58] Remi Brague, "God and Freedom, Biblical Roots of the Western Idea of Liberty," in *Christianity and Freedom: Volume 1 Historical Perspectives*, ed. Timothy Samuel Shah and Allen D. Hertzke (New York: Cambridge University Press, 2016), 391–402.

[59] Lord Acton, "An Address Delivered to the Members of the Bridgnorth Institute February 26, 1877," accessed November 9, 2018, https://acton.org/research/history-freedom-antiquity.

[60] Timothy Shah, "Introduction" in *Christianity and Freedom: Volume 1 Historical Perspectives*, ed. Timothy Samuel Shah and Allen D. Hertzke (New York: Cambridge University Press, 2016), 5.

[61] An example is a collection of essays in Timothy Samuel Shah and Allen D. Hertzke, ed. *Christianity and Freedom: Volume 1 Historical Perspectives* (New York: Cambridge University Press, 2016).

[62] Michael Novak, "The First of All Freedoms Is Liberty of Conscience," in *Religious Liberty: Essays on First Amendment Law*, ed. Daniel N. Robinson and Richard N. Williams (Cambridge: Cambridge University Press, 2016), 175–86.

[63] James Madison, *James Madison's "Advice to My Country,"* ed. David B. Mattern (Charlottesville, VA: University of Virginia Press, 1997), 25.

are equally entitled to the full and free exercise of it according to the dictates of conscience, unpunished and unrestrained by the Magistrate."[64]

As the historical record clearly shows, religious freedom did not *originate* with the Enlightenment. Instead it arose from the teaching of the Bible as understood by God's people for over almost two millennia. And, although the journey was fraught with difficulties, Madison and the other founders returned to the biblical understanding of religious freedom voiced by the early church fathers.

Today, America is at a crossroads. What we do in the next twenty years will have significant impact on the direction our country takes, both now and through the end of this century. Religious freedom, one of the core ideals of our republic, is facing challenges not only because of the rise of populism on the right and democratic socialism on the left, but also because of an ever-growing government that seeks to have more control over its citizens and to turn religious freedom back to religious tolerance. Religious freedom, an important part of our Christian heritage and a key component in America's flourishing, needs to be restored in our current age; it must be retaught and sustained so that future generations of all faiths might live free.

---

[64] Thomas F. Farr, *World of Faith and Freedom: Why International Religious Liberty Is Vital to American National Security* (New York: Oxford Press, 2008), 87.

The History of Religious Freedom

Chapter 5

The Religious Origins of Religious Freedom in Western Thought

E. Gregory Wallace

Professor of Law, Campbell University School of Law

Early Christian Views on Church and State

Tension between church and state was inevitable from the very beginning of the Christian religion.[1] Unlike the Hebrew theocracy, in which the civil and ecclesiastical were merged into a single institution and God was the constitutional source of all authority, over things both secular and religious, early Christianity taught that civil governments, while established by and subject to God, have no jurisdiction over spiritual matters. From the outset, there was always the possibility that Christian believers would be faced with conflicting obligations as they lived under two sovereigns.

The Teachings of Jesus and the Apostles

Early Christian teaching distinguished between the claims of God and the claims of the state. Jesus taught his followers to "give back to Caesar what is Caesar's, and to God what is God's."[2] Christian believers thus were to fulfill their obligations, to the fullest extent possible, to both God and the state. But Jesus also indicated that there are limits to the jurisdiction of earthly rulers. Caesar's image is on those things necessary for the proper functioning of civil society; therefore, civil government legitimately exerts power over this realm. But the state has no right to regulate what God has put his image on—those things that belong to God as creator, redeemer, and sovereign. And since human beings bear the *imago Dei*, their allegiance to God takes precedence over their allegiance to the state. Jesus further emphasized the deliberate nature of

---

[1] This chapter is adapted from E. Gregory Wallace, "Justifying Religious Freedom: The Western Tradition," *Penn State Law Review* 114, no. 2 (2009): 485–570.

[2] Luke 20:25.

genuine faith. He taught that the "first and greatest commandment" is to "[l]ove the Lord your God with all your heart and with all your soul and with all your mind" (Matt. 22:37–38). Implicit in this command is the idea that not only must devotion to God come before all other commitments but also that such devotion must be voluntary, and not coerced. Love for God is not genuine unless it comes willingly and fully from the inner person; forced love is a contradiction.

The Apostle Paul taught that civil authorities must be obeyed because they are established by God (Rom. 13:1–7). Submission is necessary not just because of the threat of punishment but also because of conscience (Rom. 13:5). While civil authorities are agents of God, they cannot lay claim to the absolute authority that belongs to God. Their power is limited, and there are matters beyond their jurisdiction and control (Rom. 13:7). Similarly, the Apostle Peter taught that Christians are to "fear God" and "honor the King" (1 Pet. 2:17 NASB). They are to do both, whenever possible. Yet Peter also recognized that civil authorities cannot exercise ultimate power over spiritual matters. When faced with conflicting commands from God and earthly leaders, Peter declared, "We must obey God rather than men!" (Acts 4:18–20, 5:29 NASB).

Early Christian teaching thus drew a rudimentary distinction between religion and the state that is essentially jurisdictional. The starting point is that there are two sovereigns with distinct spheres of authority. Because God is sovereign over all, the believer owes God his ultimate allegiance. The civil magistrate's jurisdiction has been established by God and is limited to matters properly delegated to the realm of human government. Believers are to obey both God and civil authorities; when that is not possible, the commands of God take precedence over the commands of the state. The jurisdictional boundaries delineated by Jesus and the apostles were given to help individual believers understand what to do when faced with conflicting commands from God and the state. They were not part of a political model of church-state relations; nor were they given primarily to instruct civil rulers about the limits of their authority over religious believers. They nevertheless provide the basis for future understandings about the proper relationship between religious and civil authority.

Early Christian teaching also emphasized the voluntariness of genuine religious devotion. There was no sanction in early Christian doctrine or examples for forced imposition of religious orthodoxy. Christ came to establish a new kingdom—one not spread through force or violence, but through persuasion and example (Matt. 28:19–20; 2 Tim. 2:24–25 NASB). He urged his followers to love their enemies, turn the other cheek, and do to others as they would have others do to them (Matt. 5–7 NASB). As political philosopher John Locke later observed, "the Gospel frequently declares that the true disciples of Christ must suffer persecution; but that the church of Christ should persecute others, and force others by fire and sword, to embrace her faith and doctrine, I could never yet find in any of the books of the New Testament."[3] Although doctrinal unity is prized,[4] the New Testament never authorizes civil coercion of those who embrace heresies or cause divisions.[5] The remedy for heresy and schism is first to admonish the offender and then, if that is unsuccessful, to reject and avoid him, which typically means expulsion from the Christian church and community.[6]

These teachings provided the elements that might be constructed into a theology of religious freedom. The idea that temporal rulers do not have jurisdiction over spiritual matters was radical. The English historian Lord Acton wrote that "the vice of the classic State was that it was both Church and State in one. Morality was undistinguished from religion and politics from morals; and in religion, morality, and politics there was only one legislator and one authority."[7] Brian Tierney, a leading historian of religious freedom, observes that the most common form of human government has been some form of theocratic absolutism: "The order of society was seen as a part of the divine order of the cosmos; the ruler provided a necessary link between heaven and earth."[8] He adds that "[t]ypically, in such societies, religious liberty was neither conceived of nor desired."[9] By contrast, as law professor and judge John Noonan explains, early Christian teaching contained the fundamental concepts of religious freedom:

> By the first century AD there is in the Mediterranean world a religion, which will spread widely in the West, that carries the concepts of a God, living, distinct from and superior to any human being, society, or state; of obligations to that God, distinct from and superior to any society or

---

[3] John Locke, *A Letter Concerning Toleration* (1689; repr., Amherst: Prometheus Books, 1990), 25.

[4] See, for example, Rom. 16:17 NASB and 1 Cor. 1:10 NASB.

[5] For an extended discussion of this point, see Perez Zagorin, *How the Idea of Religious Toleration Came to the West* (Princeton: Princeton University Press, 2003), 17–21.

[6] See, for example, Titus 3:10 NIV: "Warn a divisive person once, and then warn him a second time. After that, have nothing to do with him."

[7] John Emerich Edward Dalberg-Acton, "An Address to the Members of the Bridgnorth Institution at Agricultural Hall on the History of Freedom in Antiquity (Feb. 26, 1877)," in *The History of Freedom and Other Essays*, ed. John Neville Figgis and Reginald Vere Laurence (London: MacMillan, 1907), 1, 16–17.

[8] Brian Tierney, "Religious Rights: A Historical Perspective," in *Religious Liberty in Western Thought*, ed. Noel B. Reynolds and W. Cole Durham Jr. (Grand Rapids, MI: Eerdmans, 1996), 34.

[9] Tierney, "Religious Rights," 34.

state; of authorized teachers who can voice these obligations and judge any society or state; of an inner voice of reason that is one way God speaks as well as by His authorized teachers. According to these concepts as taught by this religion, each person, individually . . . will have to account to God as Judge for every thought and deed. Collectively, these concepts are at the core of liberty of conscience and liberty of religion.[10]

That God exists is a necessary premise to the argument for religious freedom. Without God, there is no higher sovereign, no superior duty, and no individual accountability.

Persecution in the Early Roman Empire

The principles taught by Jesus and the apostles provided clarity for early Christians, who, at times, found themselves persecuted by the Roman state for refusing to engage in state-mandated emperor worship. Such persecution was sporadic in the beginning, became more systematic with the edict of Decius in AD 250, and reached its peak during the reign of Diocletian in 284–305. Christians suffered confiscation of property, imprisonment, torture, and even execution. Their immediate concern was dealing with persecution, not constructing a theory of church-state relations. That question does not assume practical importance until the fourth century.[11]

Although Roman persecution of Christianity was infrequent in the first two centuries, it was not because official policy required religious toleration. The word for "toleration" comes from the Latin verb *tolerare*, which means "to bear or endure" and indicates a "grudging and temporary acceptance of an unpleasant necessity."[12] Peter Garnsey, a leading historian of classical antiquity, explains that toleration is "disapproval or disagreement coupled with an unwillingness to take action against those who are viewed with disfavor in the interest of some moral or political principle."[13] Rome often appeared tolerant

---

[10] John T. Noonan Jr., *The Lustre of Our Country: The American Experience of Religious Freedom* (Berkeley: University of California Press, 1998), 44–45.

[11] For a helpful discussion of persecution and toleration in the first four centuries, see W. H. C. Frend, *Martyrdom and Persecution in the Early Church: A Study of Conflict from the Maccabees to Donatus* (Oxford: Basil Blackwell, 1965).

[12] Randolph C. Head, "Introduction: The Transformations of the Long Sixteenth Century," in *Beyond the Persecuting Society: Religious Toleration before the Enlightenment,* ed. John Christian Laursen and Cary J. Nederman (Philadelphia: University of Pennsylvania Press, 1998), 97.

[13] Peter Garnsey, "Religious Toleration in Classical Antiquity," in *Persecution and Toleration*, ed. W. J. Shiels (Hoboken: Blackwell, 1984), 1.

either because its polytheism absorbed other religions or because it lacked the will or resources to engage in systematic persecution.[14] Historian Perez Zagorin explains that "the Romans were willing to accept foreign cults and practices; this de facto religious pluralism is entirely attributable to the polytheistic character of Roman religion and had nothing to do with principles or values sanctioning religious toleration, a concept unknown to Roman society or law and never debated by Roman philosophers or political writers."[15]

Rome's religious pluralism no longer extended to Christianity after the second century. The turning point was Caracalla's edict issued in 212, which granted Roman citizenship to the empire's free inhabitants and required them, as part of their obligations of citizenship, to pay homage to Roman deities.[16] Caracalla's edict had profound consequences for Christians. Loyalty to the Roman state was demonstrated not merely by denying the Christian faith but also by participating in the Roman imperial cult.[17] Christians were considered treasonous because, following the teachings of Jesus, their first allegiance was to God, not Caesar. Christians suffered because they refused to recognize the supremacy of the state over their religious practices.

The appeal to Rome for toleration originated not with secular philosophers but with Christian thinkers. No arguments for religious toleration appear in the pagan literature of the first three centuries.[18] Near the end of the second century, Christian advocates first urged that state-enforced religion was incompatible with basic assumptions about God and religious faith. Justin Martyr, for example, wrote that "nothing is more contrary to religion than constraint"[19] and "compulsion is not an attribute of God."[20] The task of giving these ideas their theoretical underpinnings was taken up by Tertullian and Lactantius.

---

[14] Elizabeth DePalma Digeser, *The Making of a Christian Empire: Lactantius and Rome* (Ithaca: Cornell University Press, 2000), 119.

[15] Zagorin, *Religious Toleration*, 4. On the absence of a principled concept of toleration in Roman society, see Garnsey, "Religious Toleration in Classical Antiquity," 9–12.

[16] Digeser, *Lactantius and Rome*, 50–51.

[17] J. B. Rives, *Religion and Authority in Roman Carthage: From Augustus to Constantine* (New York: Clarendon Press, 1995), 252.

[18] Garnsey, "Religious Toleration in Classical Antiquity," 9–12.

[19] Justin Martyr, quoted in M. Searle Bates, *Religious Liberty: An Inquiry* (New York: Harper and Bros., 1945), 137.

[20] Justin Martyr, "Letter to Diognetus 7," in *From Irenaeus to Grotius: A Sourcebook in Christian Political Thought*, ed. Oliver O'Donovan and Joan Lockwood O'Donovan (Grand Rapids, MI: Eerdmans, 1999), 14.

Tertullian's Call for Religious Freedom

Tertullian, a rhetorician, lawyer, and leading Christian theologian of the late second and third centuries, broke new ground in the struggle against Roman persecution. He asserted that it is a "fundamental human right, a privilege of nature, that every man should worship according to his own convictions."[21] He was the first to argue for religious toleration as a general principle and, in so doing, coined the phrase "freedom of religion" (*libertas religionis*).[22]

Tertullian offered a theological rationale for religious freedom when he wrote that the basis for religious freedom is found in God's own disposition toward the devotion he seeks:

> Look to it, whether this may also form part of the accusation of irreligion—to do away with one's freedom of religion [*libertas religionis*], to forbid a man choice of deity . . . so that I may not worship whom I would, but am forced to worship whom I would not. No one, not even a man, will wish to receive reluctant worship.[23]
>
> It is assuredly no part of religion to compel religion—to which free-will and not force should lead us. . . . You will render no real service to your gods by compelling us to sacrifice. For they can have no desire of offerings from the unwilling, unless they are animated by a spirit of contention, which is a thing altogether undivine.[24]

Tertullian went on to explain that genuine faith is freely held, not coerced. To be authentic, one's devotion and duty to God must be voluntary: "[T]he injustice of forcing men of free will to offer sacrifice against their will is readily apparent, for . . . a willing mind is required for discharging one's religious obligations. It certainly would be considered absurd were one man compelled by another to honor gods whom he ought to honor of his own accord and for his own sake."[25] Tertullian thus opposed state coercion of religious faith not because it is ineffective but because it is contrary to the

---

[21] Tertullian, "Ad Scapulam," in *The Ante-Nicene Fathers*, ed. A. Roberts and J. Donaldson (New York: C. Scribner's Sons, 1885), 105.

[22] Garnsey, "Religious Toleration in Classical Antiquity," 16.

[23] Tertullian, "Apology 24," translated in Garnsey, "Religious Toleration in Classical Antiquity," 14. For an alternate translation, see http://www.ccel.org/ccel/schaff/anf03.iv.iii.xxiv.html.

[24] Tertullian, "Apology 24."

[25] Tertullian, "Apology 28," in *The Fathers of the Church: Tertullian, Apologetical Works*, trans. Rudolph Arbesmann, Emily Joseph Daly, and Edwin A. Quain (Washington, DC: Catholic University of America Press, 1950), 83. For an alternate translation, see http://www.ccel.org/ccel/schaff/anf03.iv.iii.xxviii.html.

ways of God and the character of true religion. The state should not coerce because God does not coerce—it is not in God's nature or will to force humans to believe in him.

There are two striking features about Tertullian's argument for religious freedom. First, while Tertullian's understanding of God obviously was shaped by Christian theism, his argument had a much broader appeal: the desire for voluntary worship is a characteristic basic to any deity. The rationale is religious, but not specifically Christian. Tertullian's justifications for tolerance were accessible to anyone who has even a rudimentary conception of deity. Second, although not explicit, the juxtaposition of Tertullian's claim to worship the one true God with his insistence on religious freedom as a fundamental human right suggests that religious faith can be exclusive and yet tolerant of those who disagree. One can believe that his or her religion is true, but still understand that true religion is not served by forcing others to accept it. For Tertullian, these were not incompatible views.

While Tertullian was the first to articulate a general principle of religious freedom, his arguments were not well developed and had a limited effect. His writings, however, were the most important Christian source for Lactantius, who "draws on Tertullian for his idea that religion requires liberty" and provides Constantine with the basis for a remarkably progressive policy of religious freedom.[26]

Lactantius and Religious Freedom under Constantine

The church-state question was profoundly complicated by the conversion of Emperor Constantine in the fourth century and the subsequent adoption of Christianity as the official religion of the Roman empire. The alliance of Christianity with the state and its coercive power posed new questions: Does this alliance somehow relegitimize the claim of the emperor to supremacy in all things, including matters of religion? To what extent, if any, should the state's coercive power be applied to convert unbelievers and to correct heretics? These questions would vex the church for the next millennium.

Once Constantine took the throne, he realized that it was neither possible nor desirable to eliminate Christianity, so he sought a solution that would reconcile the empire's need for religious validation with the Christians' refusal to worship any other deity. The Constantinian solution was to secure Christian

---

[26] Digeser, *Lactantius and Rome*, 112.

support of the empire by creating a polity in which Christians and pagans could participate on equal terms under an umbrella of general monotheism.[27]

The centerpiece of Constantine's religious policy was the Edict of Milan, issued with his co-emperor Licinius in 313, which proclaimed religious freedom in the Roman Empire. The edict was remarkable in that it recognized that religious devotion should not be coerced. The emperors granted "to the Christians and others full authority to observe that religion which each prefer[s]," because no one should be denied "the opportunity to give his heart to the observance of the Christian religion, [or to] that religion which he should think best for himself."[28] Religious observance may occur "freely and openly, without molestation"[29] so that "each one may have the free opportunity to worship as he pleases."[30] Historian H. A. Drake explains that these features made the edict more radical and far-reaching than a simple grant of toleration to Christians:

> The Edict of Milan embodied a far more creative and daring solution, defining state security in terms of a general monotheism, thereby opening an umbrella that would cover virtually any form of worship—a policy with no losers, only winners. The edict constitutes a landmark in the evolution of Western thought—not because it gives legal standing to Christianity, which it does, but because it is the first official government document in the Western world to recognize the principle of freedom of belief.[31]

Robert Wilken, a leading historian of Christian thought, echoes this point when he writes that "[b]y mentioning not only Christianity (the immediate

---

[27] H. A. Drake, *Constantine and the Bishops: The Politics of Intolerance* (Baltimore: Johns Hopkins University Press, 2000), 191. Drake provides a fascinating and extensively documented account of the origins, implications, and consequences of Constantine's religious policy and Christian coercion in the fourth century.

[28] Lactantius, "Edict of Milan," in *De Mortibus Persecutorum*, chap. 48; "Galerius and Constantine: Edicts of Toleration 311/313," Internet Medieval Sourcebook, accessed July 14, 2019, http://www.fordham.edu/halsall/source/edict-milan.html/.

[29] Lactantius, "Edict of Milan," in *De Mortibus Persecutorum*.

[30] Lactantius, "Edict of Milan," in *De Mortibus Persecutorum*.

[31] Drake, *Constantine and the Bishops*, 194. Sanford Cobb describes the Edict of Milan as the "ordination of the fullest religious liberty the world has known until the foundation of the American republic." Sanford Cobb, *The Rise of Religious Liberty in America* (New York: Macmillan, 1905; photo. repr. 1968), 26.

occasion for the decree) but other forms of worship, the decree sets forth a policy of religious freedom, not simply the toleration of a troublesome sect."[32]

Constantine's grant of religious freedom in the Edict of Milan reflected the influence of Lactantius, a Christian scholar and rhetorician who had fled to the West during the persecution ordered by Diocletian in 303. He subsequently joined the court of Constantine and became tutor to his eldest son, Crispus. Between 305 and 310, Lactantius wrote the *Divine Institutes* to counter the arguments of Porphyry, a Greek philosopher in the court of Diocletian who had provided a philosophical justification for the persecution of Christians. By arguing for why religion of any sort cannot be coerced, the *Divine Institutes* provided the underpinnings of Constantine's religious policy.[33] Michel Perrin calls book five of the *Divine Institutes* a "manifesto for the liberty of religion."[34]

Few in history have voiced the argument for religious freedom more eloquently than Lactantius. He is the first Western thinker to present a comprehensive argument for religious freedom that is rooted not in secular notions of toleration but in the nature of God and authentic religious belief.[35] The object of true religion is a loving God, he argued, and thus, by its very nature, religion is not something that can be coerced.[36] "For nothing is so much a matter of free-will as religion," he wrote, "in which, if the mind of the worshipper is disinclined to it, religion is at once taken away, and ceases to exist."[37] Those who use force, Lactantius wrote, "neither know themselves nor their gods."[38] True deities do not seek compelled devotion:

> For unless it is offered spontaneously, and from the soul, it is a curse; [this is the case] when men sacrifice, compelled by proscription, by injuries, by prison, by tortures. If they are gods who are worshipped in

---

[32] Robert Louis Wilken, "In Defense of Constantine," review of *Constantine and the Bishops: The Politics of Intolerance,* by H. A. Drake; Elizabeth De Palma Digeser, "The Making of a Christian Empire: Lactantius and Rome," *First Things,* no. 112 (April 2001): 38, https://www.firstthings.com/article/2001/04/in-defense-of-constantine.

[33] See, generally, Drake, *Constantine and the Bishops*; Digeser, *Lactantius and Rome.* Digeser provides the most useful insight into the theological and philosophical aspects of Lactantius's thinking and its influence on Constantine's policy.

[34] Michel Perrin, *"La 'Révolution Constantinienne' vue a Travers L'oeuvre de Lactance,"* in *L'Idée de Révolution* 88 (1991), trans. in Digeser, *Lactantius and Rome,* 133.

[35] Wilken, "In Defense of Constantine," 38.

[36] Lactantius, *Divine Institutes,* 5:20, in *The Ante-Nicene Fathers,* 7:157. http://www.ccel.org/ccel/schaff/anf07.iii.ii.v.xx.html.

[37] Lactantius, *Divine Institutes,* 5:20.

[38] Lactantius, *Divine Institutes,* 5:20.

this manner, if for this reason only, they ought not to be worshipped, because they wish to be worshipped in this manner: they are doubtless worthy of the detestation of men.[39]

Lactantius insisted that genuine religious devotion must be voluntary. "There is no need of force and injury," he wrote, "because religion cannot be forced. It is a matter that must be managed by words rather than blows, so that it may be voluntary."[40] Force and violence only defile religion and produce hypocrisy:

> For they are aware that there is nothing among men more excellent than religion, and that this ought to be defended with the whole of our power; but as they are deceived in the matter of religion itself, so also are they in the manner of its defence. For religion is to be defended, not by putting to death, but by dying; not by cruelty, but by patient endurance; not by guilt, but by good faith. . . . For if you wish to defend religion by bloodshed, and by tortures, and by guilt, it will no longer be defended, but will be polluted and profaned.[41]

His arguments showed Roman persecutors that Christianity—not pagan religion—was committed to rational dialogue, which had been the hallmark of classical thought. "Let them imitate us in setting forth the system of the whole matter," Lactantius wrote, "for we do not entice, as they say; but we teach, we prove, we show."[42]

Lactantius's argument for religious freedom is strikingly similar to that made by Tertullian, but more thoughtful, far-reaching, and accessible. He maintained that religious freedom is fundamental to all other freedoms, and that authentic religion, by its very nature, is not something that can be forced. Lactantius's views presuppose that God exists but do not require a rejection of religious exclusivism. Wilken observes that "[h]is argument is not that Christianity should be tolerated because there are many ways to God and no one can know which way is correct (a conventional defense of religious toleration). Rather, Lactantius claims that coercion is inimical to the nature of religion. This is the first theological rationale for religious freedom, because it is the first rationale to be rooted in the nature of God and of devotion to God."[43] This

---

[39] Lactantius, *Divine Institutes*, 5:21, in *The Ante-Nicene Fathers*, 7:158.

[40] Lactantius, *Divine Institutes*, 5:20, in *The Fathers of the Church*, 378; for an alternate translation, see *Ante-Nicene Fathers*, 3:156.

[41] Lactantius, *Divine Institutes*, 5:20, in *The Ante-Nicene Fathers*, 7:157.

[42] Lactantius, *Divine Institutes*, 5:20, in *The Ante-Nicene Fathers*, 7:156.

[43] Wilken, "In Defense of Constantine," 38.

rationale, Wilken contends, "lays bare the spiritual roots of Western notions of religious liberty. For he saw that religious freedom rests on a quite different philosophical foundation than toleration of religion."[44]

Although in many ways a minor historical character, Lactantius was the first to conceive of a comprehensive and principled theological argument for religious freedom. The immediate influence of his thinking on Constantine's religious policy resulted in a remarkably novel commitment by the state to religious freedom, something heretofore unrealized in his day. We should not be surprised to learn, therefore, that prominent sixteenth- and seventeenth-century advocates for religious freedom frequently turned to Lactantius as a source for their ideas.[45]

The Rise of Intolerance in Early and Medieval Christendom

Constantine's policy of toleration gave way to imperial preference for Christianity by the end of the fourth century. The emperors who came to power after Constantine's death in 337 were increasingly willing to use the coercive powers of the state to punish Christian dissidents and suppress pagan religions. Constantine's successors convened and dissolved church councils, interjected themselves into theological controversies, enforced uniformity of religious belief and practice by civil punishments, and gave aid to the organized church.[46] Laws against heresy became increasingly severe beginning in the latter half of the fourth century. Heretics suffered confiscation of their churches and other property, were forbidden from assembling in public or private for religious purposes, and were denied the right to devise or inherit property.[47]

While the emperors considered Christianity a means to unifying a vast and complex empire and consolidating their power over it, their repressive measures were not solely affairs of state. Church leaders sought full partnership with civil authorities in the fight against heresy. For example, Nestorius proposed in his sermon to emperor Theodosius, "Give me, my Prince, the earth purged of heretics, and I will give you heaven as a recompense. Assist me in destroying heretics, and I

---

[44] Wilken, "In Defense of Constantine," 38.

[45] For a helpful discussion of Lactantius's influence on the development of Christian ideas about religious freedom and comparing Lactantius's religious understanding of religious freedom with James Madison's, see Wilken, "In Defense of Constantine," 38.

[46] Bates, *Religious Liberty: An Inquiry*, 134. For a fuller discussion of the policies of Constantine's successors toward both heretics and pagans, see Joseph Lecler, *Toleration and the Reformation*, trans. T. L. Westow (New York: Association Press, 1960), 1:39–46.

[47] See Bates, *Religious Liberty: An Inquiry*, 135; Lecler, *Toleration and the Reformation*, 1:46; Zagorin, *Religious Toleration*, 23.

will assist you in vanquishing the Persians."[48] If it were not for the views advocated by Tertullian and Lactantius in the earlier period, this later-adopted coercive strategy might be understood as the inevitable product of Christian exclusivism.

Augustine, a philosopher-turned-Christian who wrote at the beginning of the fifth century, gave the church a powerful and coherent justification for state coercion of religious dissidents. For him, the aim of such coercion was not to punish, but to win back, the dissident to the true faith and thereby ensure the dissident's salvation. He defended religious persecution, so long as its ends were redemptive. Such compulsion was beneficial and remedial, like the forceful restraint of someone about to throw himself over a cliff. His most famous rationale for civil coercion is his exegesis of the parable Jesus told about a rich master who prepared a great banquet. When the master's invited guests did not show up, he told his servants, "Go out into the highways and along hedges, and compel them to come in" (Luke 14:23 NASB). Those found in the highways and hedges, according to Augustine, are those in "heresies and schisms."[49] For Augustine, the key words were the last ones: "compel them to come in." Such constraint, he maintained, was to be exercised by the civil authority—the church acting "through the faith of kings."[50]

For the next millennium, the church pursued a policy of suppressing religious dissent, made respectable by Augustine's theory of "just persecution," which sought to effect a change of heart through the use of force and fear of suffering. The religious justifications for religious toleration and freedom, so eloquently stated by early Christian advocates such as Tertullian and Lactantius, were lost to church and society at large. It was not until their arguments came to prevail again in the sixteenth century that modern religious freedom emerged.

Advocates for Religious Freedom in the Sixteenth Century

The sixteenth-century Reformation did little to end the intolerance and persecution of the Middle Ages.[51] Persecution by Catholic regimes intensified because of the new and more powerful threat to the unity of Christendom.[52]

---

[48] Quoted in Socrates Scholasticus, *Ecclesiastical History* 7:29, in *Nicene and Post-Nicene Fathers of the Christian Church,* ed. Philip Schaff and Henry Wace (series II, 1886), 2:169. http://www.ccel.org/ccel/schaff/npnf202. ii.x.xxix.html.

[49] Augustine, "Epistle to Boniface" 185:6.24, in *Nicene and Post-Nicene Fathers,* 4:642 (series I). This letter is otherwise known as *A Treatise Concerning the Correction of the Donatists.*

[50] Augustine, "Epistle to Boniface."

[51] John Coffey, *Persecution and Toleration in Protestant England, 1558–1689* (Abington: Routledge, 2000), 23. The best and most complete modern work on the Reformation and the problem of toleration is Lecler, *Toleration and the Reformation.*

[52] Coffey, *Persecution and Toleration,* 23.

Despite their rejection of Catholic hegemony, the major Protestant Reformers often were zealous advocates of persecution.[53] They embraced Augustine's vision of the coercive Christian state.[54] While Luther wrote strongly in favor of toleration in the early 1520s, he later reverted to the view that the Christian magistrate could punish heretics.[55] John Calvin, perhaps the most influential Reformer, established in Geneva a legalistic regime that did not easily tolerate heresy.[56] In 1553 Genevan authorities executed the anti-Trinitarian heretic Michael Servetus with Calvin's support, something that earned Calvin the approval of other Reformers.[57] Calvin's special reputation for intolerance prompted historian Roland Bainton to write, "If Calvin ever wrote anything in favour of religious liberty, it was a typographical error."[58] Historian John Coffey similarly affirms, "If Protestantism was all about religious freedom, no one told the Reformers."[59]

Yet the contribution of Protestantism to the demise of the confessional state should not be overlooked. As law and religion scholar John Witte points out, the Reformation was "at its core, a fight for religious liberty—liberty of the individual conscience from intrusive canon laws and clerical controls, liberty of political officials from ecclesiastical power and privilege, liberty of the local clergy from central papal rule and oppressive princely controls."[60] Protestantism brought revolt against the authority of a unified Christendom, spawned multiple new religious groups, and helped recover what it meant to be a true Christian by shifting attention away from liturgies and doctrinal uniformity in nonessential matters back to fundamental Christian virtues such as faith, humility, love, and forbearance.

---

[53] See Lord Acton, "The Protestant Theory of Persecution," in *The History of Freedom and Other Essays* (London: Macmillan, 1907), 150–87.

[54] Coffey, *Persecution and Toleration*, 23.

[55] Coffey, *Persecution and Toleration*, 23.

[56] Coffey, *Persecution and Toleration*, 24.

[57] Coffey, *Persecution and Toleration*, 24.

[58] Roland H. Bainton, introduction to *Concerning Heretics: Whether They Are to Be Persecuted and How They Are to Be Treated: A Collection of the Opinions of Learned Men, Both Ancient and Modern* (preface by Sebastian Castellio), trans. Roland H. Bainton (1554; repr. New York: Columbia University Press, 1935), 74.

[59] Coffey, *Persecution and Toleration*, 24.

[60] John Witte Jr. "Moderate Religious Liberty in the Theology of John Calvin," in *Religious Liberty in Western Thought*, ed. Noel B. Reynolds and W. Cole Durham Jr. (Grand Rapids, MI: Eerdmans, 1996), 119.

There were numerous advocates for toleration in the sixteenth century, especially among radical Protestants in Europe. The Anabaptists, one of the most savagely persecuted Christian minorities of the century, repudiated all religious violence. They were among the first in the sixteenth century to develop a systematic theory of religious freedom based upon their understanding of the nature of faith, the gospel, and the church.[61] Most influential of all were mainstream Reformed intellectuals like Sebastian Castellio and Dirk Coornhert. Castellio's writings were familiar to seventeenth-century English writers, and Coornhert was highly influential with Remonstrant theologians who later established the Arminian tolerationist tradition.[62] Dutch Arminians like Philip van Limborch and Jean LeClerc were close friends with John Locke.[63] As seen in the short descriptions that follow, religious justifications for toleration were prominent among leading sixteenth-century Christian thinkers.

Martin Luther (1483–1546)

Luther's most significant contribution to the development of religious freedom is found in his famous doctrine of two kingdoms (one spiritual and one temporal) and two governments (church and state). Building on the two-kingdoms theology of Augustinian thought,[64] Luther explained these doctrines in his *On Temporal Authority: To What Extent It Should Be Obeyed*, in which he sharply distinguished the secular and spiritual domains.[65]

> God has ordained two governments: the spiritual, by which the Holy Spirit produces Christians and righteous people under Christ; and the temporal, which restrains the un-Christian and wicked. . . . [O]ne must carefully distinguish between these two governments. Both must be permitted to remain; the one to produce righteousness, the other to bring about external peace and prevent evil deeds. Neither one is sufficient in the world without the other.[66]

---

[61] William R. Estep, *Revolution within the Revolution: The First Amendment in Historical Context 1612–1789* (Grand Rapids, MI: Eerdmans, 1990), 28.

[62] Coffey, *Persecution and Toleration*, 52.

[63] Coffey, *Persecution and Toleration*, 53.

[64] See Augustine, *The City of God*, trans. Marcus Dods (New York: Modern Library, 1950), 376–77.

[65] Martin Luther, "On Temporal Authority," in *Luther's Works*, Vol. 45 ed. Jaroslav Pelikan and Helmut T. Lehmann (St. Louis: Concordia, 1955), 81–129.

[66] Luther, "On Temporal Authority," 45:92.

While affirming both the right and necessity of the secular power to use force to maintain civil order, Luther was concerned that "it extend too far and encroach upon God's kingdom and government."[67]

Luther asserted that the state has no right to intervene in matters of faith because God has confined it to a strictly temporal sphere. Human authorities have power only over bodies, properties, outward things; they legitimately may tax subjects for public services, maintain moral standards, and restrain by threat and force those who injure others.[68] But only God has authority over the spiritual realm:

> The temporal government has laws which extend no further than to life and property and external affairs on earth, for God cannot and will not permit anyone but himself to rule over the soul. Therefore, where the temporal authority presumes to prescribe laws for the soul, it encroaches upon God's government and only misleads souls and destroys them. . . . [T]he soul is not under the authority of Caesar; he can neither teach it nor guide it, neither kill it nor give it life, neither bind it nor loose it, neither judge it nor condemn it, neither hold it fast nor release it. . . . Over what is on earth and belongs to the temporal, earthly kingdom, man has authority from God; but whatever belongs to heaven and to the eternal kingdom is exclusively under the Lord of heaven.[69]

For Luther, the distinction between the two kingdoms of church and state had its most significant application in bringing to an end the state's jurisdiction over spiritual matters. Government must no longer be seen as omnicompetent—it has neither the ability nor prerogative to manage those matters that belong exclusively to the province of the spiritual sovereign. Although Luther ultimately did not act consistently with his two-kingdoms theology, the doctrine later was elaborated and refined within both Lutheran and Calvinist traditions[70] and eventually had a profound influence on the development of religious freedom in America.[71]

---

[67] Luther, "On Temporal Authority," 45:104.

[68] Luther, "On Temporal Authority," 45:110–12.

[69] Luther, "On Temporal Authority," 45:105, 111.

[70] See, for example, John Calvin, *Institutes of the Christian Religion*, vol. 2, ed. John McNeill, trans. Ford L. Battle (Philadelphia: Westminster Press, 1975), 184.

[71] See, generally, Arlin M. Adams and Charles J. Emmerich, *A Nation Dedicated to Religious Liberty: The Constitutional Heritage of the Religion Clauses* (Philadelphia: University of Pennsylvania Press, 1990), 3, 56–57; Estep, *Revolution within the Revolution*; Michael W. McConnell, "The Problem of Singling Out Religion," *DePaul Law Review* 50 (2000): 1, 16–19.

The Anabaptists

The Anabaptists were one of the fringe groups of early Protestantism that were part of the Radical Reformation. They were mostly a grassroots movement of disaffected commoners who preferred a simple, personal religious faith, free from the control of political or religious hierarchies. They rejected the leadership of prominent Reformers such as Luther or Calvin and instead formed numerous loosely-related Christian sects in Switzerland, Germany, and the Netherlands beginning in the 1520s.[72] They also, as church historian William Estep observes, "were the first in the sixteenth century to develop a thorough-going position on religious liberty based upon their understanding of the nature of faith, the gospel, and the church."[73]

Anabaptists were persecuted by both Catholics and Protestants alike for their views on church and state. Their rejection of church-state establishments resulted in them being branded as extremists and anarchists.[74] Balthasar Hubmaier (1481–1528) stated most clearly the Anabaptist position on religious freedom in a 1524 tract titled *Concerning Heretics and Those Who Burn Them*.[75] Estep writes that Hubmaier's tract "was a closely reasoned treatise arguing not merely for toleration but for complete religious freedom as a universal principle."[76] Hubmaier set forth arguments for religious freedom that were based on the will of God, the nature of authentic faith, and the essential differences between church and state. Estep suggests that "[t]hese are possibly the most revolutionary set of ideas about the subject that the sixteenth century produced."[77]

Dirk Philips (1504–1568), an Anabaptist leader in Danzig, published a tract titled *The Church of God* around 1560, which sets forth a fairly typical Anabaptist argument against religious persecution.[78] Philips gave four reasons why those who persecute others cannot call themselves true Christians: first, Jesus is the final "judge of the souls and consciences of men";[79] second, the task of the Holy Spirit is to convict the world of sin and unbelief, and such reproof is not

---

[72] See Zagorin, *Religious Toleration*, 83.

[73] Estep, *Revolution within the Revolution*, 28.

[74] Estep, *Revolution within the Revolution*, 28.

[75] Balthasar Hubmaier, "Concerning Heretics and Those Who Burn Them," in *Religious Pluralism in the West: An Anthology*, ed. David G. Mullen (Hoboken: Wiley-Blackwell, 1998), 94–98.

[76] Estep, *Revolution within the Revolution*, 30.

[77] Estep, *Revolution within the Revolution*, 30.

[78] Dirk Philips, "The Church of God," in *Religious Pluralism in the West: An Anthology*, ed. David G. Mullen (Hoboken: Wiley-Blackwell, 1998), 98–100.

[79] Philips, "The Church of God," 99 (citing John 5:22).

done with violence "but by God's word and power";[80] third, the only remedy authorized by Christ for known heretics is excommunication;[81] and fourth, the parable of the tares[82] shows that Christ does not want heretics systematically rooted out and punished until the final judgment.[83] To the argument that the state should wield the sword to purify the church, Philips responded: "The higher power has received the sword from God, not that it shall judge therewith in spiritual matters (for these things must be judged by the spiritual, and only spiritually . . .), but to maintain the subjects in good government and peace, to protect the pious and punish the evil."[84]

Menno Simons (1496–1561), the most effective protagonist of moderate Dutch Anabaptism, whose followers later adopted the name Mennonites, also wrote extensively on religious toleration. Simons declared that faith cannot be coerced and that the civil magistrate has no authority to force men to believe: "Faith is a gift of God; therefore it cannot be imposed by any temporal authority nor by the sword; it can only be obtained from the Holy Spirit, as a gift of grace, through the means of the pure doctrine of the sacred Word and a fervent and humble prayer."[85] Spiritual matters "are not subject to human authority, but are the exclusive concern of God Almighty."[86] Simons urged civil authorities not to invade Christ's jurisdiction over those matters which he has reserved for himself: "With your earthly and temporal power do not try to make laws for things that belong to the jurisdiction and kingdom of Christ . . . [and] do not judge and strike with your sword of iron what is reserved to the judgment of the Most High, that is, faith and what belongs to faith."[87] Joseph Lecler explains the significance of moderate Anabaptist teachings:

> What stands out among the moderate Anabaptists—and this particularity is most important for the future—is their doctrine on the nature of the Church and on the relations between Church and State. When the humanists protested against the violent persecution of heretics, they did not dream of depriving the princes of their religious privileges.

---

80 Philips, "The Church of God," 99 (citing John 16:8).
81 Philips, "The Church of God," 99 (citing Rom. 16:17; 1 Cor. 5:10; 1 Thess. 5:14; Titus 3:10).
82 See Matt. 13:24–43.
83 Philips, "The Church of God," 99 (citing Matt. 13:29).
84 Philips, "The Church of God," 99.
85 Menno Simons, *Opera Omnia Theologica, of, Alle de Godtgeleerde Wercken van Menno Symons*, ed. Johannes van Veen (Amsterdam:1681): 149, trans. and quoted in Lecler, 214.
86 Simons, *Opera Omnia Theologica*, 334, trans. and quoted in Lecler, 214.
87 Simons, *Opera Omnia Theologica*, 499, trans. and quoted in Lecler, 215.

Their irenic inclination was not based on a radical distinction between the spiritual and the temporal. It was different with the Mennonites. . . . They built their community on the model of a sect and so were led to affirm, for all practical purposes, the separation of church and state; they rejected the state in this sinful world, from which they had separated themselves voluntarily, and consequently denied it any jurisdiction in the spiritual order. In such a system, freedom of conscience is secured by the very fact of this separation.[88]

Half a century after Simons' death in 1561, his writings commanded a following among English refugees in the Netherlands, among whom were John Smyth and Thomas Helwys, influential leaders of English Baptists who advocated for religious freedom.[89]

Sebastian Castellio (1515–1563)

While leading Reformers like John Calvin supported persecution of heretics, there were calls for toleration within mainstream Reformed churches from Christian intellectuals such as Sebastian Castellio in Switzerland and Dirk Coornhert in the Netherlands. Castellio, a Frenchman who was a professor of Greek and linguistics in Basle, strongly criticized the religious intolerance of Calvin, his former mentor, for having agreed to the execution of heretic Michael Servetus.[90] He stressed that the issue was not Servetus's heresy but the fact of his execution:[91] "[T]o kill a man is not to defend a doctrine, it is to kill a man," Castellio wrote, "[r]eligious doctrine is not the affair of the magistrate, but of the doctor. What has the sword to do with doctrine?"[92] While modern scholars often overlook Castellio and his influence on the development of religious freedom, Mario Turchetti describes Castellio as "the lone voice proclaiming the true open-minded and definitive tolerance, which both the Catholics and the

---

[88] Lecler, *Toleration and Reformation*, 215–16.

[89] On the link between continental Anabaptists and the English Baptist movement, see Estep, *Revolution within the Revolution*, 33–54.

[90] The best sources on Castellio are Hans R. Guggisberg, *Sebastian Castellio, 1515–1563: Humanist and Defender of Religious Toleration in a Confessional Age*, ed. and trans. Bruce Gordon (Abington: Routledge, 2003); Zagorin, *Religious Toleration*, 93–144; and Roland H. Bainton, "Sebastian Castellio, Champion of Religious Liberty" in *Studies on the Reformation* (Boston: Beacon Press, 1963), 139–81.

[91] Steven E. Ozment, *Mysticism and Dissent: Religious Ideology and Social Protest in the Sixteenth Century* (New Haven: Yale University Press, 1973), 173.

[92] Sebastian Castellio, *Against Calvin's Book*, quoted in Zagorin, *Religious Toleration*, 119.

Protestants detested."[93] Perez Zagorin calls Castellio "the first champion of religious toleration."[94]

Castellio's work represents the beginnings of a systematic conceptualization of the case for religious freedom. His most effective writing, *Concerning Heretics and Whether They Should Be Persecuted, and How They Should Be Treated*, was first published anonymously in 1554, the year after Servetus's death.[95] The book is an anthology of texts from early Christian writers and from contemporary works of the first half of the sixteenth century. Among the early Christians quoted are Lactantius, Hilary, Chrysostom, and Jerome. Sixteenth-century sources appear, in part, under pseudonyms (including some of Castellio's own writing) and, in part, with the full names of the authors, which include Martin Luther, Sebastian Franck, and Erasmus. Leonard Levy calls *Concerning Heretics* "the sixteenth century's first book on religious liberty,"[96] while Brian Tierney says that the tract "provided the first full-scale argument for freedom of conscience."[97]

Castellio deployed two major arguments against religious persecution in *Concerning Heretics*. The first was that religious persecution is contrary to the nature and will of God. Castellio's desire for toleration was sustained by the deeply held belief that persecution is cruel and inhumane and therefore contrary to Christ's character and teachings. There is nothing in Scripture, he argued, that sanctions the use of civil punishment or violence to protect the church from heresy. Such persecution is attributable to evil, not to God. Castillo's second argument was that the civil magistrate is neither authorized nor competent to judge or punish religion. Spiritual offenses can be judged only by the word of God and are punishable, at most, by excommunication.

Concerning Heretics was the opening salvo in a long-running battle between Castellio and Calvin over the ideas that led to Servetus's death.[98] In 1554,

---

[93] Mario Turchetti, "Religious Concord and Political Tolerance in Sixteenth- and Seventeenth-Century France," *Sixteenth Century Journal*, 22, no. 1 (Spring 1991): 15, 19.

[94] Zagorin, *Religious Toleration*, 93.

[95] Sebastian Castellio, *Concerning Heretics: Whether They Are to be Persecuted and How They Are to be Treated: A Collection of the Opinions of Learned Men, Both Ancient and Modern*, trans. Roland H. Bainton (1554; New York: Columbia University Press, 1935). In the discussion that follows, I use Bainton's English translation. The book's contents are discussed in Lecler, *Toleration and Reformation*, 1:336–47; Guggisberg, *Sebastian Castellio, 1515–1563*, 81–86; and Zagorin, *Religious Toleration*, 102–14.

[96] Leonard Levy, *Blasphemy: Verbal Offense against the Sacred, from Moses to Salman Rushdie* (New York: Knopf, 1993), 226.

[97] Tierney, "Religious Rights," 47.

[98] Zagorin, *Religious Toleration*, 114.

Castellio wrote *Against Calvin's Book,* as an answer to Calvin's *Defense of the Orthodox Faith*, which had set forth a justification for persecution of heretics.[99] A main theme in Castellio's criticism was his questioning of Calvin's claim that civil rulers and magistrates have a duty to defend true doctrine with force. Here, Calvin was relying on Augustine's older argument that civil penalties are aimed at making heretics reflect on their error and restraining them from continuing to do what is evil. Castellio found Augustine's logic to be unpersuasive. Constraint in religion is contrary to Scripture, Castellio argued, and "forces people to pretend to believe."[100] We must, he said, "obey God rather than Saint Augustine."[101]

Castellio's arguments for religious freedom are themselves grounded in his theology. As Zagorin observes, since Castillo's works were "very largely a Christian indictment of the persecuting spirit, it is easy to understand why . . . he quoted only the Bible, upon whose authority he relied exclusively."[102] His opposition to state persecution of religious dissenters was dictated not by religious skepticism or political expediency but by an abiding concern for the welfare of authentic Christianity. Castillo's ideas influenced important seventeenth-century tolerationists, most notably William Walwyn, Jeremy Taylor, Roger Williams, and John Locke.[103]

Summing Up: Christian Thought and Religious Freedom

The justifications for religious freedom, first proposed by early Christian thinkers such as Tertullian and Lactantius and then rediscovered by sixteenth-century tolerationists, are almost wholly religious in nature: God is sovereign over all things spiritual and temporal; duty to God is superior to civil obligations; the state has neither the jurisdiction nor competence to judge spiritual matters; authentic faith must be voluntary, not coerced; and the true Christian displays love, humility, and forbearance toward those with differing views. While these were not the only arguments for religious freedom during these periods, they were at the forefront of opposition to the persecuting state. These

---

[99] For a helpful and extended discussion of Castellio's arguments in *Against Calvin's Book,* see Zagorin, *Religious Toleration*, 114–22.
[100] Quoted in Zagorin, *Religious Toleration*, 129.
[101] Quoted in Zagorin, *Religious Toleration*, 129.
[102] Zagorin, *Religious Toleration*, 112.
[103] Guggisberg, *Sebastian Castellio, 1515–1563*, 247–49; Tierney, "Religious Rights," 49.

arguments highlight certain misconceptions that can distort our modern discussion about religious freedom.

One misconception is that religious freedom came about primarily through the efforts of skeptical rationalists who sought to avoid civil conflict over religious matters. According to this view, the emergence of religious freedom began sometime in the seventeenth century and reached its pinnacle in the Jeffersonian rationalism of the late eighteenth century, which produced our constitutional commitment to religious freedom. The impetus purportedly behind this movement was twofold: first, a growing skepticism toward the truth claims of religion; and second, a desire to put an end to civil strife and persecution brought about by religious conflict. Secular Enlightenment rationalists, the argument goes, were skeptical of religious claims and horrified by religious conflict, so they sought to dislodge religious authority from its close connection with the state.[104]

This view overlooks the fact that the ideas and practices of religious freedom were available and in use long before the Enlightenment. They originated with people who were deeply religious and thus had a significant stake in the outcome. The most prominent advocates were not skeptical rationalists; rather, they were thoughtful Christians who were concerned with both the purity of the church and the freedom of religious conscience. From Tertullian and Lactantius of late antiquity, to Sebastian Castellio and the radical Protestants of sixteenth century, to seventeenth-century tolerationists in England and Europe such as William Walwyn and John Locke, to early American advocates such as Roger Williams, William Penn, Elisha Williams, Isaac Backus, John Leland, Thomas Jefferson, and James Madison, the justifications advanced for religious freedom were predominantly, if not exclusively, based on religious principles. To understand why religious freedom became such an important value—important enough to be enshrined in the First Amendment to the Constitution—we cannot be satisfied with any inquiry that neglects the deeply religious nature of its preconstitutional rationales. Religious freedom has not and cannot be grounded reliably in radical skepticism about religion.

A second misconception involves the modern idea of separation of church and state: there are those who argue that the essential consequence of this

---

[104] Alan Levine, "Introduction: The Prehistory of Toleration and Varieties of Skepticism," in *Early Modern Skepticism and the Origins of Toleration,* ed. Alan Levine (Lanham: Lexington Books, 1999), 9.

separation is that government and politics must be thoroughly secular.[105] But this view largely misapprehends the historic aims for severing the connections between church and state. As we have seen, the most compelling arguments for religious freedom drew a jurisdictional boundary between spiritual and civil authority. The state in classic antiquity laid claim to complete control over the order and structure of human society. Religious and civil authority were unified—pagan gods and political rulers were one, church and state were indistinguishable, and the individual's religious allegiance was bound up with his political allegiance. Political rulers asserted authority over the spiritual decisions of their subjects, frequently applying the coercive power of civil government to ensure orthodox belief and practice. Religious toleration, if it existed at all, was a matter of expediency rather than principle.

The coming of Christianity and the fundamental distinction it drew between spiritual and civil power brought recognition of a separate spiritual authority that sought to check the unrestrained power of the state. Christianity severs the individual's religious obligation from his political obligation, as expressed in Jesus's injunction to "give back to Caesar what is Caesar's, and give to God what is God's" (Luke 20:25). It proclaims that a person's supreme duty is to God, who transcends all temporal and political orders, thereby placing spiritual matters fundamentally outside the sphere of civil command. As such, government is neither authorized nor competent to enforce religious truth.

To be sure, the implications of this dualism were slow to be recognized, and the jurisdictional lines again blurred. For over a millennium, often with the Christian church's complicity, the state reasserted its power over spiritual matters, maintaining religious unity by force and, in the latter centuries, executing heretics and dissenters when necessary. But the horrors of religious persecution provoked Christian thinkers once again to challenge the assumption that there is an essential identity between civil and spiritual authority.

The reason for disconnecting civil and spiritual was not so much to confine the church and state to separate spheres of authority institutionally—as modern separationism emphasizes—but to end the state's jurisdiction over spiritual matters. While the church's exercise of institutional authority over political matters was sometimes controversial, the predominant concern voiced by advocates of religious toleration and freedom was over the state's use of its coercive power to enforce religious uniformity. Separating the civil from the

---

[105] See, for example, Isaac Kramnick and R. Laurence Moore, *The Godless Constitution: A Moral Defense of the Secular State* (New York: W. W. Norton, 2005).

spiritual meant limiting the state's power to define or control a person's relationship to God. This was done to protect religion, not the state.

Comprehending the nature (and limits) of the civil-spiritual disconnection is vital to understanding what our constitutional commitment to religious freedom means. While modern views of church-state separation emphasize keeping church and state apart, with some urging that religion be excluded altogether from the civil-political sphere, the historical disconnection of civil from spiritual meant something more limited—the state was disempowered from defining, controlling, or enforcing religion. The fuller implications of this disconnection remain a matter for consideration, but at the very least, it suggests that our church-state debate should carry a different emphasis.

Chapter 6

The Pursuit of Religious Liberty in the American Constitutional Tradition

Daniel L. Dreisbach
Professor of Legal Studies, American University

Since the first permanent settlements were established in British North America, religion has been integral to the identity and mission of the American people and their political pursuits.[1] The First Charter of Virginia in 1606 commended the colonists' "humble and well intended desires" to further, "by the providence of Almighty God," a noble work "in propagating [the] Christian religion to such people, as yet live in darkness and miserable ignorance of the true knowledge and worship of God."[2] The signatories to the Mayflower Compact in 1620 undertook their voyage "for the Glory of God, and Advancement of the Christian Faith, and the Honour of our King and Country."[3] An invocation of divine blessing and acknowledgment of a sacred mission to spread the Gospel were recurring themes in the colonial charters and in other expressions of the colonists' political pursuits.

The New England Puritans, especially, believed they were called by God, in the words of Matt. 5:14, to build a "city set upon a hill." These pious settlers committed themselves to establishing Bible commonwealths and remaking the world in conformity with God's laws, as they understood them. Christianity and its sacred text, especially the laws of Moses, informed early colonial charters and codes. This was true not only in New England but also in Virginia. The "Articles, Lawes, and Orders, Divine, Politique, and Martiall for the Colony in

---

[1] Portions of this chapter are adapted from the introduction and notes in *The Sacred Rights of Conscience: Selected Readings on Religious Liberty and Church-State Relations in the American Founding*, ed. Daniel L. Dreisbach and Mark David Hall (Indianapolis, IN: Liberty Fund, 2009) [hereinafter *Sacred Rights of Conscience*].

[2] "The First Charter of Virginia" (1606), in *The Statutes at Large; Being a Collection of all the Laws of Virginia, from the First Session of the Legislature, in the Year 1619*, ed. William Waller Hening (Richmond, VA: J & G Cochran, 1821), 1:58.

[3] "The Mayflower Compact" (1620), in *Sacred Rights of Conscience*, 86.

Virginea," written in 1610 and enlarged in 1611, was designed to restore discipline in the colony. These rules and regulations have been described as "the earliest extant English-language body of laws in the western hemisphere."[4] Like the legal codes subsequently framed in Puritan commonwealths to the north, it bore the unmistakable influence of the Ten Commandments (Exod. 20:1–17), as interpreted through the lens of their religious tradition. It prohibited and punished harshly speaking "impiously or maliciously against the holy and blessed Trinitie, . . . [or] the Christian faith"; blaspheming God's "holy name"; subjecting God's "holy word" to derision; Sabbath-breaking; murdering; swearing false oaths; bearing false witness; and committing adultery, fornication, sodomy, and other sexual offenses.[5]

Early expressions of law in colonial New England were often based explicitly on the Bible. The colonists, to be sure, did not adopt all aspects of biblical law, and the Bible was not the sole source of their laws. Nonetheless, the Bible was a vital, authoritative source of law in their new political communities. For example, the "Fundamental Orders of Connecticut" (1639), arguably the first written constitution in North America, declared that a governor and his council "shall have power to administer justice according to the Lawes here established, and for want thereof according to the rule of the word of God."[6] The "Massachusetts Body of Liberties" (1641), sometimes described as the first bill of rights in North America, stated that "No custome or prescription shall ever prevaile amongst us in any morall cause, our meaneing is maintaine anythinge that can be proved to bee morallie sinfull by the word of god."[7] The "Body of Liberties" borrowed from Mosaic law, as interpreted within the colonists' theological tradition, mandating the death penalty for "worship[ping] any other god, but the lord god"; "Blasphem[ing] the name of God, the father, Sonne, or Holie ghost"; witchcraft; murder; man-stealing (kidnapping); perjury with intent to secure the death of another; bestiality; homosexuality; and adultery.[8] Lest there be doubt about the source of these laws, New England codes often gave specific biblical authority for provisions.

---

[4] Brent Tarter, "Lawes Divine, Morall and Martiall," *Encyclopedia Virginia,* Virginia Foundation for the Humanities online, January 20, 2012, accessed February 15, 2019.

[5] "Articles, Lawes, and Orders, Divine, Politique, and Martiall for the Colony in Virginea" (1610, 1611), in *Sacred Rights of Conscience,* 84–86.

[6] "Fundamental Orders of Connecticut" (1639), in *Sacred Rights of Conscience,* 89.

[7] "Massachusetts Body of Liberties" (1641), in *Colonial Origins of the American Constitution: A Documentary History,* ed. Donald S. Lutz (Indianapolis, IN: Liberty Fund, 1998), 79.

[8] "Massachusetts Body of Liberties" (1641), in Lutz, *Colonial Origins,* 83–84.

Religious Diversity and the Pursuit of Religious Liberty

Most of the colonies eventually established state churches, following a model they had known in Europe. Congregationalism enjoyed legal favor in much of New England, and the Church of England was established in the southern colonies. Religious dissenters were afforded a measure of toleration in most colonies, although they were often burdened in the exercise of their religion and denied certain civic prerogatives.

As settlements grew in number and size throughout the colonies, the diversity of religious sects also increased. Many European immigrants from diverse religious traditions, burdened in the practice of their faith in their homelands, were drawn to the New World by the promise of the right to practice their religion without fear or persecution. The resulting extraordinary religious diversity in the colonies was a potential source of rivalry and conflict among denominations competing for adherents and public recognition (and, sometimes, the legal and financial favor of the civil state). Some minority sects, unfortunately, suffered persecution in Britain's North American colonies. In mid-seventeenth-century Massachusetts, in an especially dark episode in colonial history, members of the Society of Friends (Quakers) experienced persecution, including public execution by hanging, for their religious beliefs. For understandable reasons, the dramatic sectarian clashes capture much attention; however, the story of religions in America is most remarkable for the amity and general respect that was demonstrated among the diverse sects that were planted and flourished side by side in the American soil.

In communities where the governors and the governed are *all* of one faith, there is little demand for a policy of religious liberty. But where both civil authorities and ordinary citizens come from many denominations, and where multiple sects compete for followers and public favor, peaceful coexistence requires a workable policy of toleration. Therefore, religious diversity in the colonies required Americans to develop policies of, initially, religious toleration and, eventually, religious liberty. Early in the colonial experience, Americans began to wrestle with these contentious issues, a process that culminated in the bold policies of religious liberty enshrined in the Virginia Declaration of Rights (1776), the Virginia Statute for Establishing Religious Freedom (1786), and the First Amendment to the U.S. Constitution (1791).

By the time the national constitution was crafted in the late 1780s, a declining number of Americans supported an exclusive ecclesiastical establishment in their respective states, and few advocated for a national establishment. The religious diversity in the new nation meant that the establishment of a national church was practically untenable. No denomination was sufficiently dominant to claim the legal favor of the federal regime, and there was little likelihood that a political consensus would emerge as to which sect or combination of sects should constitute a "Church of the United States." Nonetheless, many influential citizens, despite some Enlightenment influences, continued to believe that religion must play a public role in the polity.

Few Americans of the seventeenth and eighteenth centuries, even among those who supported disestablishment, doubted the value and utility of a vibrant religious, specifically Christian, culture. There was a consensus that religion fosters the civic virtues and social discipline that give citizens the capacity to govern themselves. Authoritarian rulers use the whip and rod to compel social order, but this is unacceptable for a free, self-governing people. Religion, alternatively, develops an internal moral compass that prompts citizens to behave in a responsible, orderly manner. A moral people respect social order, legitimate authority, oaths and contracts, private property, and the like; and such civic virtue, many eighteenth-century Americans believed, was nurtured by the Bible and the Christian religion. For this reason, John Adams, among other founders, described the Bible as "the most republican book in the world," because he believed that "without national morality a republican government cannot be maintained" and that "[t]he Bible contains the most profound philosophy, the most perfect morality, and the most refined policy, that ever was conceived upon earth."[9] For this reason, many Americans of the age viewed Christianity and its sacred text as vital to their experiment in republican self-government. Accordingly, they thought about how best to nurture popular religion and extend its influence in society.

By the mid-eighteenth century, two distinct, conflicting schools of thought had emerged regarding how best to promote a vibrant religious culture. Dr. Benjamin Rush of Philadelphia, a respected signer of the Declaration of

---

[9] "John Adams to Benjamin Rush," February 2, 1807, in *The Spur of Fame: Dialogues of John Adams and Benjamin Rush, 1805–1813*, ed. John A. Schutz and Douglass Adair (San Marino, CA: The Huntington Library, 1966), 75–76. Recognizing Christianity's vital contributions to social virtues, John Dickinson similarly wrote, "The Bible is the most republican Book that ever was written." (John Dickinson, notes [n.d.]. R. R. Logan Collection, Historical Society of Pennsylvania, copy provided courtesy of The John Dickinson Writings Project, University of Kentucky.) Elsewhere, he mused that "[t]he Bible is the most republican Book in the World—and therefore forbidden to be read in so many parts of Christendom at Large." (John Dickinson, notes [n.d.]. Copy provided courtesy of The John Dickinson Writings Project, University of Kentucky.)

Independence, said "[t]here are but two ways of preserving visible religion in any country. The first is by establishments. The second is by the competition of different religious societies."[10]

The first way, which was the practice in Europe and most of the colonies, was to maintain a legally established church. A dominant view in the early colonial period was that, because religion was indispensable to social order and political happiness, the civil state must officially and legally maintain a particular church or denomination, which citizens had a duty to support. These establishmentarians feared that a failure to establish a church with the civil state's sustaining aid would impair religion's ability to extend its influence into civil society.

In the second half of the eighteenth century, an unlikely coalition of religious dissenters, nonconformists, and moderate Enlightenment rationalists advanced a second way to nurture a vibrant religious culture. They advocated for dismantling the old arrangement of one state, one church—that is, terminating legal privileges for one particular sect or combination of sects over all others—and replacing it with a disestablished regime in which all sects were on an equal footing before the law and could compete for adherents and their support in an open marketplace of ideas. They believed the multiplicity of religious sects that would flourish in this disestablished regime would foster religious liberty and harmony, as multiple sects would check any one sect from working in concert with the civil state to oppress and persecute other sects.[11] This approach was in the ascendancy by the end of the eighteenth century. As jurisdictions abandoned ecclesiastical establishments toward the end of the eighteenth century and the start of the nineteenth century, matters regarding

---

[10] "Benjamin Rush to Granville Sharp," April 27, 1784, in *Letters of Benjamin Rush*, 2 vols., ed. L. H. Butterfield (Princeton, NJ: Princeton University Press, 1951), 1: 330–31.

[11] See James Madison, "Speech in the Virginia Convention," June 12, 1788, in *The Papers of James Madison*, ed. Robert A. Rutland et al. (Charlottesville: University Press of Virginia, 1977), 11:130–31: "This freedom [of religion enjoyed by the states] arises from that multiplicity of sects, which pervades America, and which is the best and only security for religious liberty in any society. For where there is such a variety of sects, there cannot be a majority of any one sect to oppress and persecute the rest. . . . [T]he United States abound in such a variety of sects, that it is a strong security against religious persecution, and is sufficient to authorise a conclusion, that no one sect will ever be able to out-number or depress the rest." See also Publius (James Madison), *The Federalist* no. 51, in *The Papers of James Madison*, ed. Robert A. Rutland et al. (Chicago: University of Chicago Press, 1977), 10:478–79: "In a free government, the security for civil rights must be the same as that for religious rights. It consists in the one case in the multiplicity of interests, and in the other, in the multiplicity of sects." See also Thomas Jefferson, *Notes on the State of Virginia*, query XVII, in *Sacred Rights of Conscience*, 292: "Difference of opinion is advantageous in religion. The several sects perform the office of a Censor morum over each other."

religious belief or disbelief and association with and support of a particular minister or religious society were left to the voluntary choice of individual citizens; and, increasingly, the civil rights and prerogatives of citizens were no longer conditioned on their religious beliefs. Each sect or church, an increasing number of Americans came to believe, should be free to compete in an open marketplace of ideas where, as Thomas Jefferson confidently predicted, "truth is great and will prevail if left to herself . . . unless by human interposition disarmed of her natural weapons, free argument and debate."[12]

These opponents of state churches argued that disestablishment and competition among religious sects, in the words of James Madison, resulted "in the greater purity & industry of the pastors & in the greater devotion of their flocks."[13] Disestablishment required sects to compete to survive. Churches and their clergy had to be exemplary and industrious, demonstrating to the world the purity and efficacy of their faith. Churches were forced to rely on the voluntary support of adherents rather than on the benevolence of the civil state. In short, there was a growing belief in the late-eighteenth century that state churches (state ecclesiastical monopolies) tended to become complacent, corrupt, and intolerant.[14] Disestablishment, by contrast, facilitated a vibrant

---

[12] "A Bill for Establishing Religious Freedom, Virginia," in *Sacred Rights of Conscience*, 251. See also Jefferson, *Notes on the State of Virginia* (1782), query XVII, in *Sacred Rights of Conscience*, 292: "It is error alone which needs the support of government. Truth can stand by itself" and John Locke, "A Letter Concerning Toleration," in *The Second Treatise of Government (An Essay Concerning the True Original, Extent and End of Civil Government) and a Letter Concerning Toleration*, edited with an introduction by J. W. Gough (New York: Macmillan, 1956), 153: "For the truth certainly would do well enough if she were once left to shift for herself."

[13] "James Madison to Jasper Adams," September 1833, in *Sacred Rights of Conscience*, 613. See also "James Madison to Robert Walsh," March 2, 1819, in *Sacred Rights of Conscience*, 594–95: "On a general comparison of the present & former times, the balance is certainly & vastly on the side of the present, as to the number of religious teachers the zeal which actuates them, the purity of their lives, and the attendance of the people on their instructions. It was the Universal opinion of the Century preceding the last, that Civil Govt. could not stand without the prop of a Religious establishment, & that the Xn. religion itself, would perish if not supported by a legal provision for its Clergy. The experience of Virginia conspicuously corroborates the disproof of both opinions. The Civil Govt. tho' bereft of everything like an associated hierarchy possesses the requisite stability and performs its functions with complete success; Whilst the number, the industry, and the morality of the Priesthood, & the devotion of the people have been manifestly increased by the total separation of the Church from the State." Adam Smith, *The Wealth of Nations* (1776), in *Sacred Rights of Conscience*, 76: the exertion, zeal, and industry of religious teachers who rely "upon the voluntary contributions of their hearers" is "likely to be much greater" than that of the religious teachers who derive funds from legal establishments.

[14] See Madison, "A Memorial and Remonstrance against Religious Assessments" (1785), in *Sacred Rights of Conscience*, 311–12: "What have been its fruits [fruits of ecclesiastical

religious culture in which the best and purest religion would dominate. Disestablishmentarians argued with growing confidence that the combination of competition among sects, disestablishment, and religious liberty created an environment in which a vital, robust religious culture would emerge and beneficently influence public culture. This, they contended, was good for the church, good for society, and good for the civil state.

After the separation from England, the former colonies began to revise their laws to bring them into conformity with republican principles. They gave particular attention to the model of ecclesiastical establishment inherited from England. Nowhere was this process more dramatic and, in the end, more influential than in Virginia. The Virginia Convention that assembled in Williamsburg in May 1776 instructed its delegates at the Continental Congress to press for independence. This bold initiative raised difficult questions about the nature of civil authority in the Commonwealth. Believing, perhaps, that they had reverted to a state of nature, the delegates thought it necessary to frame a new social compact, beginning with a declaration of man's natural rights, followed by a new plan of civil government. The convention appointed a committee to prepare a state declaration of rights and constitution. George Mason and the young delegate from Orange County, James Madison Jr., were among those appointed to the committee.

Mason framed initial drafts of both a declaration of rights and a constitution. Although Madison was certainly interested in all portions of the declaration, only the last article, "providing for religious toleration, stirred him to action." In "his first important public act" in a long and distinguished career in public service,[15] Madison objected to Mason's use of the word "toleration" because it dangerously implied that religious exercise was a mere privilege that could be granted or revoked at the pleasure of the civil state and was not assumed to be a natural, indefeasible right.[16] Mason's draft reflected the most

---

establishments]? More or less in all places, pride and indolence in the Clergy, ignorance and servility in the laity, in both, superstition, bigotry and persecution."

[15] "Editorial Note," in *The Papers of James Madison*, ed. William T. Hutchinson and William M. E. Rachal (Chicago: University of Chicago Press, 1962), 1:171.

[16] In his so-called autobiography, Madison wrote: "Being young & in the midst of distinguished and experienced members of the Convention he [Madison referring to himself in the third person] did not enter into its debates; tho' he occasionally suggested amendments; the most material of which was a change of the terms in which the freedom of Conscience was expressed in the proposed Declaration of Rights. This important and meritorious instrument was drawn by Geo. Mason, who had inadvertently adopted the word *toleration* in the article on that subject. The change suggested and accepted, substituted a phraseology which—declared the freedom of

enlightened, liberal policies of the age and went further than any previous declaration in force in Virginia, but it did not go far enough to satisfy Madison. He wanted to replace "toleration" with the concept of absolute equality in religious belief and exercise.

As early as 1774, Madison had come to think of religious toleration, the ultimate objective of most reformers of his day, as an inadequate goal because, as Thomas Paine declaimed in 1791, "Toleration is not the *opposite* of Intolerance, but is the *counterfeit* of it. Both are despotisms. The one assumes to itself the right of withholding Liberty of Conscience, and the other of granting it. The one is the Pope armed with fire and faggot, and the other is the Pope selling or granting indulgences."[17] What is the difference between religious *toleration* and religious *liberty*, as Madison, Paine, and others saw it? The former often assumes an established church and is always a revocable grant of the civil state rather than a natural, inalienable right. In Madison's mind, the right of religious exercise was too important to be cast in the form of a mere privilege allowed by civil authorities and enjoyed as a grant of governmental benevolence. Instead, he viewed religious liberty as a fundamental, natural, and irrevocable right, possessed equally by all citizens, located beyond the reach of civil magistrates and subject only to the dictates of a free conscience. He concluded, in short, that religious toleration, whether granted by the civil state or by a religious establishment, was inconsistent with freedom of conscience.[18]

Madison proposed revisions to Mason's draft article on religion that punctuated his aversion to the concept of toleration. He proposed replacing Mason's

---

conscience to be a *natural and absolute* right." Douglass Adair, ed., "James Madison's Autobiography," *William and Mary Quarterly* 2 (3rd Series, 1945): 199; emphasis in the original.

[17] Thomas Paine, *Rights of Man* (1791), in *The Writings of Thomas Paine*, 4 vols., ed. Moncure Daniel Conway (New York: G. P. Putnam's Sons, 1894), 2:325.

[18] For other expressions of this idea, see John Leland, *The Virginia Chronicle* (Fredericksburg, VA, 1790), 40: "The liberty I contend for, is more than toleration. The very idea of toleration is despicable, it supposes that some have a pre-eminence above the rest, to grant indulgence; whereas all should be equally free, Jews, Turks, Pagans and Christians." Tench Coxe, *A View of United States of America* (Philadelphia, 1794), 103–04: "Mere toleration is a doctrine exploded by our general constitution; instead of which have been substituted an unqualified admission, and assertion, that their own modes of worship and of faith equally belong to all the worshippers of God, of whatever church, sect, or denomination." Charles Fenton James, *Documentary History of the Struggle for Religious Liberty in Virginia* (Lynchburg, VA: J. P. Bell, 1900), 201: "By religious liberty is meant the right of every one to worship God, or not, according to the dictates of his own conscience, and to be held accountable to none but God for his belief and practice. It differs from religious toleration . . . in that toleration implies the right to withhold, or to refuse license, whereas religious liberty means that the civil power has nothing to do with a man's religion except to protect him in the enjoyment of his rights."

statement, "all Men shou'd enjoy the fullest Toleration in the Exercise of Religion, according to the Dictates of Conscience," with the phrase, "all men are equally entitled to the full and free exercise of [religion] accord[in]g to the dictates of Conscience." He recognized that religious duties are prior to civil obligations. The logic of Mason's phrasing stemmed from the idea that because religion "can be governed only by Reason and Conviction, not by Force or Violence," for practical reasons "all Men shou'd enjoy the fullest Toleration."[19] By contrast, the practical difficulty of governing religious opinion, whether by coercion or persuasion, concerned Madison less; rather, he sought to remove religion—and matters of conscience—from the cognizance of the civil state. Key to Madison's restatement was the word "equally," which the Virginia Convention retained in subsequent drafts. This language underscored that the unlearned Separate Baptists of the central Piedmont had religious rights equal to those of the well-heeled Anglican aristocrats of the Tidewater. All citizens enjoyed absolute equality in religious belief. In the end, Madison's view prevailed and was enshrined in the fundamental law of Virginia. Article XVI of the Virginia Declaration of Rights, adopted on June 12, 1776, declared the following:

> That religion, or the duty which we owe to our CREATOR, and the manner of discharging it, can be directed only by reason and conviction, not by force or violence; and therefore all men are equally entitled to the free exercise of religion, according to the dictates of conscience; and that it is the mutual duty of all to practise Christian forbearance, love, and charity, towards each other.[20]

Instituting religious liberty in the place of toleration is one of America's great contributions to, and innovations of, political society. This great achievement of the American experiment was reaffirmed in the Virginia Statute for Establishing Religious Freedom and the First Amendment to the U.S. Constitution. George Washington also recognized it in an eloquent 1790 address to the Hebrew Congregation in Newport, Rhode Island:

> The Citizens of the United States of America have a right to applaud themselves for having given to mankind examples of an enlarged and

---

[19] "Declaration of Rights and Form of Government in Virginia," May 16–June 29, 1776, in *The Papers of James Madison*, ed. William T. Hutchinson and William M. E. Rachal (Chicago: University of Chicago Press, 1962), 1:172–75. See, generally, Daniel L. Dreisbach, "George Mason's Pursuit of Religious Liberty in Revolutionary Virginia," *Virginia Magazine of History and Biography* 108, no. 1 (2000): 5–44.

[20] "Virginia Declaration of Rights, art. XVI" (1776), in *Sacred Rights of Conscience*, 241.

liberal policy: a policy worthy of imitation. All possess alike liberty of conscience and immunities of citizenship. It is now no more that toleration is spoken of, as if it was by the indulgence of one class of people, that another enjoyed the exercise of their inherent natural rights. For happily the Government of the United States, which gives to bigotry no sanction, to persecution no assistance requires only that they who live under its protection should demean themselves as good citizens, in giving it on all occasions their effectual support.[21]

There were differences of opinion in the founding era regarding the precise meaning of religious liberty in the American context. Among the issues debated were the extent to which the civil state, consistent with the principles of religious liberty, could identify with religion or cooperate with and aid religious institutions. Some Americans maintained that religious liberty did not preclude official recognition and even promotion of religion in general, while others argued that religious liberty necessitated a separation between the institutions of the church and the civil state.[22] (Interestingly, religious liberty guarantees coexisted with various manifestations of religious establishment in many late eighteenth- and early nineteenth-century state constitutions.) The content, scope, and application of religious liberty were debated in the early republic, and they continue to agitate the public mind today.

Virginia was not alone among the former colonies in reconsidering the prudential and constitutional place and role of religion in civic life in their post-independence constitutions and laws. The Massachusetts Constitution of 1780, for example, was attentive to religion's place in the polity, adopting a church-state model that differed in key respects from Virginia's. It acknowledged "the duty of all men in society, publicly, and at stated seasons, to worship the SUPREME BEING." It also affirmed the citizen's right to worship "GOD in the manner and season most agreeable to the dictates of his own conscience," without being "hurt, molested, or restrained," so long as one does

---

[21] "George Washington to the Hebrew Congregation in Newport, Rhode Island," August 18, 1790, in *The Papers of George Washington*, Presidential Series, ed. Dorothy Twohig et al. (Charlottesville: University Press of Virginia, 1996), 6:285.

[22] For further discussion on the historical origins and purposes of the guarantee of free exercise of religion, see, generally, Philip A. Hamburger, "A Constitutional Right of Religious Exemption: An Historical Perspective," *George Washington Law Review* 60 (1992): 915–48; Michael W. McConnell, "The Origins and Historical Understanding of Free Exercise of Religion," *Harvard Law Review* 103 (1990): 1409–517; Ellis M. West, "The Right to Religion-Based Exemptions in Early America: The Case of Conscientious Objectors to Conscription," *Journal of Law and Religion* 10 (1993–94): 367–401.

"not disturb the public peace, or obstruct others in their religious worship." It further stated that "the happiness of a people, and the good order and preservation of civil government, essentially depend upon piety, religion, and morality; and . . . these cannot be generally diffused through a community but by the institution of the public worship of GOD, and of public instructions in piety, religion, and morality." Therefore, the constitution authorized the legislature to mandate political bodies or religious societies to provide for religious worship and instruction, require attendance at public worship, and compel a tithe for the support of public worship and ministers.[23] Proponents believed this arrangement appropriately balanced the establishment of one public religion with the maintenance of a protected space for various private religions in which they could worship and enjoy the support of adherents. Every polity, they thought, must maintain by law some expression of public religion responsible for disseminating the values and civic virtues that promote social order and give citizens the capacity for self-government. A stable civil state and political prosperity could not long endure if it remained neutral or indifferent toward religion.

Religion and the American Constitution

Against this backdrop of state constitutions, national leaders turned their attention to creating a plan of government conducive to the safety and happiness of the former colonies and the American people. The national constitution framed in Philadelphia in mid-1787, together with the First Amendment to it, defined a place and role for religion in public life. The constitutional bases for this distinctively American approach to church-state relations are Article VI, Clause 3, and the First Amendment. The first declares that "no religious Test shall ever be required as a Qualification to any Office or public Trust under the United States," and the second provides that "Congress shall make no law respecting an establishment of religion, or prohibiting the free exercise thereof." The former is binding only on federal officeholders. It did not invalidate religious tests that existed under state laws. Similarly, the latter provision did not initially alter church-state arrangements and practices at the state and local levels.

The Article VI religious test-ban in the original, unamended constitution followed language instructing all national and state officeholders to take an oath or affirmation to support the constitution. Charles Pinckney of South

---

[23] "Massachusetts Constitution" (1780), in *Sacred Rights of Conscience*, 246.

Carolina, who thought the national legislature should "pass no Law on the subject of Religion,"[24] was the chief proponent of a test-ban. He purportedly told delegates at the Constitutional Convention in May 1787 that "the prevention of Religious Tests, as qualifications to Offices of Trust or Emolument . . . [, is] a provision the world will expect from you, in the establishment of a System founded on Republican Principles, and in an age so liberal and enlightened as the present."[25] Three months later, Pinckney raised the subject again, this time proposing that "No religious test or qualification shall ever be annexed to any oath of office under the authority of the United States."[26] At the end of August, during debate on qualifications for federal office and employment, Pinckney urged the convention to adopt the religious test-ban. Following a brief debate, the delegates approved Pinckney's amendment and forwarded it to the Committee on Style, which shaped the final language incorporated into Article VI.[27]

The provision generated lively debate in the state ratifying conventions. A recurring theme emphasized the role of morality, fostered by the Christian religion, in promoting the civic virtues and social order essential to a system of self-government. The ban on religious tests, critics said, suggested inattentiveness to the vital task of selecting rulers committed to protecting and nurturing religion and morality. Once it is conceded that not all religions are conducive to good civil government and political order, then there are plausible grounds for excluding adherents of some religions from public office. Accordingly, in the words of Luther Martin of Maryland, "it would be *at least decent* to hold out some distinction between the professors of Christianity and downright infidelity or paganism."[28] Proponents of a federal test-ban framed the debate in terms of religious liberty. Oliver Ellsworth of Connecticut defended the ban, arguing that "the sole purpose and effect of it is to exclude persecution and to secure to you the important right of religious liberty. . . . [A] good and peaceable citizen," he continued, should receive "no penalties or incapacities on account of his religious sentiments."[29]

The inclusion of religious tests in the laws of many states of the era indicates some measure of support for them. Moreover, religious tests coexisted

---

[24] Max Farrand, ed., *The Records of the Federal Convention of 1787* (New Haven, CT: Yale University Press, 1911), 3:599 (hereinafter *Records*).

[25] Farrand's *Records*, 3:122.

[26] Farrand's *Records*, 2:335, 342.

[27] Farrand's *Records*, 2:461, 468.

[28] Luther Martin, *The Genuine Information* (1788), in *Sacred Rights of Conscience*, 382.

[29] A Landholder (Oliver Ellsworth), No. 7 (December 17, 1787), in *Sacred Rights of Conscience*, 377.

with free exercise and nonestablishment provisions in some state constitutions. The founding generation apparently did not consider these concepts necessarily incompatible. Interestingly, some delegates at the Constitutional Convention who endorsed the federal ban had previously participated in crafting religious tests for their respective state laws. Can these positions be reconciled? The Constitution of 1787, as a matter of federalism, denied the national government all jurisdiction over religion, including the authority to administer religious tests. There was a consensus that religion was a matter best left to individual citizens and to their respective state governments. Many in the founding generation, it would seem, supported a federal test-ban because they valued religious tests required under state laws and did not want the federal regime to mandate a test that would displace existing state test oaths and religious establishments.[30]

A number of states conditioned their support for the proposed constitution on the adoption of amendments—including an amendment protecting religious liberty. Early in the first Congress under the Constitution, Representative James Madison proposed the following amendment: "The civil rights of none shall be abridged on account of religious belief or worship, nor shall any national religion be established, nor shall the full and equal rights of conscience be in any manner, or on any pretext, infringed."[31] The House gave this proposal little attention before debating the topic on August 15, 1789. Five days later, the House revisited the measure, eventually adopting this language: "Congress shall make no law establishing religion, or to prevent the free exercise thereof, or to infringe the rights of conscience."[32] The measure was then forwarded to the Senate, which, after consideration of several proposals, approved this text: "Congress shall make no law establishing articles of faith or a mode of worship, or prohibiting the free exercise of religion."[33] The House declined to accept the Senate version; thus, the matter was sent to a conference committee that drafted the final language adopted by the House on September 24 and by the Senate the following day. This text was ratified by the requisite number of states and added to the constitution in December 1791.

Although diverse interpretations can be drawn from this text and its legislative history, there is broad agreement on several modest conclusions. First, the

---

[30] See, generally, Daniel L. Dreisbach, "The Constitution's Forgotten Religion Clause: Reflections on the Article VI Religious Test Ban," *Journal of Church and State* 38 (1996): 261–95.

[31] Madison, "Speech in Congress," June 8, 1789, in *Sacred Rights of Conscience*, 420.

[32] House debate, August 20, 1789, in *Sacred Rights of Conscience*, 430.

[33] Senate debate, September 9, 1789, in *Sacred Rights of Conscience*, 432.

framers proscribed the creation of a national church like the established church in England. Congress was prohibited from conferring legal preferences or special favors on one church and denying them to others. The nonestablishment provision was not meant to silence religion or require civil government to hold all religions in utter indifference. Second, the amendment implicitly affirmed that the states retained authority to define church-state relationships within their respective jurisdictions. Moreover, Congress was not only prohibited from establishing a national church but also denied authority to interfere with existing state religious establishments. (This purpose was turned on its head by the incorporation of the First Amendment into the Fourteenth Amendment.)[34] Third, the amendment protected citizens from actions by the federal regime that inhibited the free exercise of religion. The free-exercise guarantee, at the very least, prevented Congress from compelling or prohibiting religious worship. It affirmed a right to worship God, or not, according to the dictates of conscience, free from coercion, interference, discrimination, or punishment by the national government.

While the legislative history reveals aspects of the First Amendment's original understanding and purposes, many questions about its application remain unanswered. For example, what role, if any, does the Constitution permit religion to play in the formulation of public policy? Or to what extent is the federal government authorized to assist or encourage religion generally? Or does the free exercise provision relieve a believer of an obligation to comply with a valid, facially neutral law of general applicability on the ground that the law inhibits the adherent's religious exercise? These questions plague modern church-state relations.

Ratification of the First Amendment changed little, at least initially, in church-state policies and practices in the new nation. It merely made explicit that which was already implicit in the constitutional arrangement—that is, authority in matters pertaining to religion was denied to the national government and retained by the individual, by religious societies, and by the respective states. At least half of the states in 1791, the year the First Amendment was ratified, retained some form of religious establishment, and a handful of states—including Connecticut, New Hampshire, and Massachusetts—

---

[34] In the mid-twentieth century, the U.S. Supreme Court incorporated the First Amendment religion provisions into the "liberties" protected by the Fourteenth Amendment's due process of law clause, thereby making them applicable to state and local authorities. This constitutional development prohibited state laws and practices "respecting an establishment of religion" or prohibiting religious exercise. The free exercise and nonestablishment of religion provisions were incorporated into the Fourteenth Amendment in *Cantwell v. Connecticut*, 310 U.S. 296, 303 (1940) and *Everson v. Board of Education*, 330 U.S. 1, 15 (1947), respectively.

continued to maintain religious establishments well into the nineteenth century. Ratification of the First Amendment, which explicitly restricted the U.S. Congress only, left these church-state arrangements unchanged at the state level. Moreover, the new national legislature continued to appoint and pay for legislative chaplains, as had been the practice in the Continental Congress. Presidents George Washington and John Adams followed the tradition set by state chief executives and the Continental Congress in setting aside days in the public calendar for prayer and thanksgiving. These and other arguably religious practices continued under the First Amendment with relatively little controversy.

The election of 1800 provided an early test for religion's place in national politics. Opponents of candidate Thomas Jefferson contended that his heterodoxy raised doubts about his fitness for high office. In an influential pamphlet published in 1800, the Presbyterian minister John Mitchell Mason declaimed that it would be "a crime never to be forgiven" for the American people to confer the office of chief magistrate "upon an open enemy to their religion, their Redeemer, and their hope, [and it] would be mischief to themselves and sin against God." Mason alleged that Jefferson's "favorite wish [is] to see a government administered without any religious principle among either rulers or ruled." He repudiated the notion gaining currency among Jeffersonians that *"Religion has nothing to do with politics."*[35]

Jefferson's supporters denied that their candidate was an atheist or an infidel and, in response, advanced a separationist policy that would eventually exert much influence on American politics. "Religion and government are equally necessary," intoned Tunis Wortman, "but their interests should be kept separate and distinct. No legitimate connection can ever subsist between them. Upon no plan, no system, can they become united, without endangering the purity and usefulness of both—The church will corrupt the state, and the state pollute the church."[36]

The incumbent, John Adams, similarly contended with political smears on account of religion. When President Adams recommended a national "day of solemn humiliation, fasting, and prayer," adversaries depicted him as a tool of establishmentarians intent on legally uniting the Presbyterian church with the

---

[35] [John Mitchell Mason], *The Voice of Warning to Christians, on the Ensuing Election of a President of the United States* (New York: G. F. Hopkins, 1800), 6, 20, 25; emphasis in original.

[36] Timoleon [Tunis Wortman], *A Solemn Address, to Christians & Patriots, upon the Approaching Election of a President of the United States: In Answer to a Pamphlet, Entitled, "Serious Considerations,"* &c. (New York: David Denniston, 1800), 7.

new federal government.[37] This allegation alarmed religious dissenters, such as the Baptists, who feared persecution by a legally established church. Disclaiming any involvement in such a scheme, Adams reported that he "was represented as . . . at the head of this political and ecclesiastical project."[38] He thought the allegation, which drove dissenters into Jefferson's camp, cost him the election.

Once elected, President Jefferson provoked controversy by refusing to issue religious proclamations, departing from the precedent of his presidential predecessors. To his detractors, this was proof that he was an infidel, if not an atheist. On New Year's Day, 1802, the president penned a missive to a Baptist Association in Danbury, Connecticut. The New England Baptists, who had supported Jefferson in the election, were a beleaguered religious and political minority in a region where a Congregationalist-Federalist alliance dominated public life. In his letter, the president endorsed the persecuted Baptists' aspirations for religious liberty. Affirming his belief that "religion is a matter which lies solely between Man & his God" and is not among the legitimate concerns of civil government, Jefferson famously asserted that the First Amendment had built "a wall of separation between Church & State."[39] According to his own account, Jefferson wanted this letter, with its figurative barrier, to explain why he, as president, had refrained from issuing executive proclamations setting aside days for public prayer and thanksgiving. Because the national government could exercise only those powers expressly granted to it by the Constitution and because no power to issue religious proclamations had been so granted, Jefferson maintained that the national government could not issue such proclamations. Insofar as Jefferson's wall was a metaphor for the First Amendment, it imposed restrictions on the national government only. As a matter of federalism, his wall had less to do with the separation between church and state than with the separation between state governments and the national government on matters pertaining to religion, such as religious proclamations. Regardless of Jefferson's understanding of the metaphor, courts and commentators have embraced the "wall of separation" as a "proof-text" for a strict separationist construction of the First Amendment and the organizing theme of church-state jurisprudence.

---

[37] "Proclamation for a National Fast," March 6, 1799, in *Sacred Rights of Conscience*, 457.

[38] "John Adams to Benjamin Rush," June 12, 1812, in *Sacred Rights of Conscience*, 519.

[39] "Thomas Jefferson to Messrs. Nehemiah Dodge, Ephraim Robbins, and Stephen S. Nelson, a Committee of the Danbury Baptist Association in the State of Connecticut," January 1, 1802, in Daniel L. Dreisbach, *Thomas Jefferson and the Wall of Separation between Church and State* (New York: New York University Press, 2002), 48.

From the founding era to the present day, Americans have debated the prudential and constitutional relationships between church and state and between religion and politics. Few controversies today involving religion and public life raise wholly novel issues; indeed, many contemporary conflicts are variations on disputes that have engaged prior generations of Americans. Much church-state debate turns on the interpretation of the First Amendment provisions respecting the nonestablishment and free exercise of religion. Significantly, the U.S. Supreme Court has counseled that this amendment should be construed "in the light of its history and the evils it was designed forever to suppress," and many of its church-state rulings have relied on the court's interpretation of history.[40] Accordingly, reflection on the relations between religion and American public life in the last four centuries casts light not only on the past but also on the future of relations between the civil polity and religion.

---

[40] *Everson*, 330 U.S. at 14–15.

The Relationship between Religious, Economic, and Political Freedom

Chapter 7

Foundations of Freedom

Art Lindsley
Vice President of Theological Initiatives, IFWE

Freedom should not be taken for granted. In the United States, in particular, we fought the Revolution for our freedom, and it has been a U.S. cornerstone ever since. The Declaration of Independence notes that certain "inalienable rights" include "life, liberty and the pursuit of happiness." Patrick Henry famously said, "Give me liberty or give me death." And the First Amendment states, "Congress shall make no law respecting an establishment of religion, or prohibiting the *free* exercise thereof" (emphasis added). Freedom of speech, freedom of the press, and freedom of assembly are all guaranteed. These freedoms are still upheld, but without vigilance, there is always the prospect of lawmakers, executive orders, and the courts taking away some of those freedoms we have assumed will always be there.

Outer, political threats are not the only ones with the potential to erode our freedom. There are philosophical and moral threats as well. As relativism increasingly encroaches on our society, the notion of objective truth has been discarded by many. Reality is what you want it to be. Instead of conforming their desires to the truth, many would rather conform "truth" to their desires. With nothing any longer inalienable (or objective), what will become of life and liberty?

We, as believers, need to go back to the source—the Bible—and look anew at the biblical view of freedom. In this chapter, we will explore the biblical view of freedom, with a special focus on the contrast between "freedom from" (virtue and faith) and "freedom to" (live in a way that is ordered by faith-based moral values). In the final section, we will explore the three-legged stool—the necessary relationship between political, economic, and religious freedom. I will show that a nation cannot be stable or flourish without political, economic, and religious freedom, with religious freedom being a prerequisite. Politics and economics need to be grounded in a faith-based moral foundation.

Defining Freedom

Throughout human history, people of all cultures have sought freedom. Some have emphasized inner spiritual or emotional freedom, and others, freedom from external restraints (such as slavery)—otherwise known as political freedom. Hindus seek an experience of oneness with the universe that frees them from the illusion of this world of distinction. Buddhists seek enlightenment that involves a detachment from desiring anything in this world. Atheists want to be free from the constraints of any objective moral rules.

In the political arena, there are a variety of liberation theologies.[1] Gustavo Gutiérrez wrote his *Theology of Liberation* with a focus on the political and economic situation in Latin America. James Cone wrote *A Black Theology of Liberation* to develop a black theology that identified with the oppressed. Others have developed feminist liberation theology that focuses on cultural problems that have limited women's freedom. Most of the above perspectives involve a freedom from constraints but are not as clear about what the liberated situation would look like. This "freedom from (constraints)" perspective is at the heart of our secular culture. In this chapter, we will discuss the biblical view of freedom, first contrasting it with other views so we can see its significance more clearly.

Many people in our culture believe freedom to be a lack of norms, rules, or laws restraining us from doing what we want to do or be. You often hear the refrain, "Whatever is true for you is true for you, and whatever is true for me is true for me. Nobody can tell me what to do." People who hold to this view believe in "freedom from" any external values. This freedom is limited if God exists. In his film *Crimes and Misdemeanors*, Woody Allen portrays God as a cosmic eye who is always watching us. You can't escape his gaze and his judgment of your life. Jean Paul Sartre, the atheist existentialist, went so far as to argue that if God exists, we couldn't be free. God would be like a cosmic voyeur, always looking through the keyhole, watching every little thing in our lives.

This kind of "freedom from" something is not the biblical view of freedom. Biblical freedom, in contrast to other views, does not mean doing whatever you feel like doing. It means being free to serve Christ and others. Freedom

---

[1] Liberation theology is not easily defined. There are many types and varieties that come from different concerns about problems in society. Gutiérrez spawned a whole variety of responses that fall under the general category of Latin American liberation theology, but because they are so diverse, it's hard to find one common denominator that fits them all. The same thing could be said for black liberation theology because there were many books written in response to and inspired by Cone's foundational work.

paradoxically involves throwing off the bondage of sin and becoming a servant of Christ. It is only in this state that we can know the freedom and flourishing that we were created to experience.

First, we will examine how the concept of freedom developed both historically and biblically. We will look at inner and outer freedom and how the biblical view of freedom lends itself to the outer freedoms of religious, economic, and political freedom. Lastly, we will look at how all the "outer" freedoms are interdependent and, all together, are essential for societies to grow and flourish.

Historical and Biblical Ideas about Freedom

Freedom in Greek philosophy. There have been different perspectives on freedom throughout history. The Greek view is perhaps the most directly influential in our culture.

In Greek philosophy, freedom, *eleutheros*, was primarily used in a political sense. First, someone who was free was a full citizen of the city-state, or *polis*, in contrast to a slave who did not have the rights of a citizen. To be free meant to have freedom to speak openly and decide what you want to do. But, in order to preserve freedom, there needed to be political order governed by law that was enforced. Note the following:

> Freedom, for Plato and Aristotle, is essential to a state. The best constitution guarantees the greatest freedom (Thucydides). This freedom is freedom within the law which establishes and secures it. . . . Law protects freedom against the caprice of the tyrant or the mass. . . . Democracy achieves this best by allowing the same rights to all citizens (cf. Plato, Aristotle, Herodotus). [However, if] the law of self replaces the law of the *politeía* . . . it leads to the rise of demagogues and opens the door to tyranny.[2]

In Stoic philosophy, freedom was inwardly directed. Since people could not always control external events, emphasis was placed on an internal detachment from this world and anything that would bind you to it, such as anger, anxiety, pity, and the fear of death. Individual reason was to be brought into harmony with the cosmic reason. There was a constant struggle to maintain this detachment (*atarchia*). Freedom was inner freedom for the Stoics and primarily outer freedom for Plato and Aristotle.

---

[2] G. Kittel, G. Friedrich, and G. W. Bromiley, ed. *Theological Dictionary of the New Testament: Abridged in One Volume* (Grand Rapids, MI: Eerdmans, 1985), 224.

Freedom in the Old Testament. In the Old Testament, freedom was primarily a freedom from slavery. There was provision in the law for the freedom of Israelite slaves (probably like indentured servants) every seven years in the sabbatical year (Exod. 21:2ff.). The previous "owner" was to be generous in giving gifts that would enable these freed ones to set up a new life (Deut. 15:12ff.).

In a larger sense, freedom was precarious for the Israelites. God, by his grace, delivered them from slavery in Egypt (Exod. 20:2; Deut. 7:8). They repeatedly needed to be delivered from foreign oppression by the Judges. Time and again, a generation came along that didn't know and follow the Lord, and a foreign conqueror would make their lives difficult until the Lord raised up a deliverer. When God's people were disobedient, they often lost their freedom. The Assyrian conquest of the kingdom (2 Kings 17:7–23) and the Babylonian captivity of the southern kingdom (2 Kings 21:10–15, 22:19f, 23:25ff) are illustrations of this pattern. In later Judaism, freedom movements arose to gain political freedom in order to allow religious freedom (among other things). The Maccabeans and the Zealots are only a couple illustrations of such movements.

This freedom was often referenced in the prophets. Jesus's inaugural sermon echoed this theme (Luke 4:18–19). Isaiah 61:1 says,

> The Spirit of the Lord God is upon me,
> Because the Lord has anointed me
> To bring good news to the afflicted;
> He has sent me to bind up the brokenhearted,
> To proclaim liberty to the captives,
> and freedom to the prisoners.

This proclamation of "liberty" and "freedom" was a mark of the Messiah's message.

In addition to political, or outer, freedom, there is a consistent thread through the Old Testament pointing to the need for inner and spiritual renewal. Ezekiel 36:26–30 says,

> Moreover, I will give you a heart of flesh. And I will put my Spirit within you and cause you to walk in my statutes, and you will be careful to observe my ordinances and you will live in the land that I gave your forefathers . . . and I will call for the grain and multiply it, and I will not bring famine on you. And I will multiply the fruit of the tree and the produce of the field.

Notice here that the inner rebirth leads to outer flourishing and safety:

Similarly, the classic passage in 2 Chronicles 7:14 says, "If . . . my people who are called by my name humble themselves and pray and seek my face and turn from their wicked ways, then I will hear from heaven, will forgive their sin, and will heal their land." Again, the inner change leads to outer or external consequences that extend not only to forgiveness but to healing in the land. Both inner and outer freedom are valued.

Freedom in the New Testament. The predominant note of the New Testament is not political freedom but freedom in Christ from bondage to sin, the law, Satan, the old man, and death. It is not that political freedom or freedom from slavery was unimportant but that there was an even deeper bondage that had to be overcome first. The Greeks had a somewhat simple view of the problem; they saw it as being in the mind. In the New Testament, the problem was the bondage of the will. Even if you were politically free, you could still be in bondage.

This is still true today. Human will is not, at present, neutral but is captivated by sin. Humans, by nature, "love the darkness" and "hate the light" (John 3:19–20). Jesus speaks about this freedom in the classic verses in John 8:31–32: "Jesus therefore was saying to those Jews who had believed in Him, 'If you abide in my words, then you are truly disciples of mine, and you shall know the truth, and the truth shall make you free.'"

The scribes and Pharisees immediately respond to this statement, arguing that they are Abraham's offspring and have never been slaves and wondering how can Jesus say, "You shall become free." Jesus responds that anyone who sins becomes a slave of sin, but "if therefore the Son shall make you free, you shall be free indeed" (John 8:36). Graciously applied to our lives, Jesus's death and resurrection liberates us from bondage to sin so that we can live a redirected life. Calvin points out that although we have freedom, it may not be perfect. "Freedom has its degrees according to the measure of their faith; and, therefore, Paul, though clearly made free, still groans and longs after perfect freedom (Rom. 7:24)."[3]

In the New Testament, we learn it is the truth that will make us free. We are, in our natural sinful state, captive to lies. We don't see reality as it is. We deny what we know deep down is true (Rom. 1:20–25), "exchanging the truth of God for a lie" (Rom. 1:25). We live in a state of unreality. If truth is that which corresponds to reality, then throwing off lies and deception frees us to see reality for what it is. We see our own slavery to sin and can receive forgiveness and

---

[3] John Calvin, *Commentary on the Gospel of John* (Grand Rapids, MI: Baker Book House, 1989), 1:342.

new power to live in accordance with reality. We can be what we were created to be. Truth leads to freedom.

We are historical beings that have a past, present, and future. We don't reinvent ourselves at each moment but are influenced by past patterns and choices. We are, according to the old self (sinful nature), directed away from God, saying, in effect, "My will be done." In Christ, we are freed from this bondage in order to say, "Thy will be done." We were headed down a road away from God and have been turned around 180 degrees by God's grace, so that we are now pursuing our Lord rather than running away from him. We were serving sin, but now we are serving Christ.

But how can service or being a servant be freedom? Because we are made in a particular way, for a specific purpose, and to function in a designated fashion. One analogy sometimes used is a train. If a train stays on the tracks, it can function well in transporting people and goods from one place to another. If the train goes off the tracks, it leads to pain (and death) for people and a destruction of its cargo. The train needs the tracks to function as it is designed to. There are limits to where that train can go and the path it needs to follow.

Just as with the train, there are certain laws, rules, and norms that need to be followed in order to flourish as a human being. We need to follow the creator's instructions for recommended use as given in the Bible. God's laws or Jesus's commands are not arbitrary but show us the way to joy. This way to joy must involve saying no to certain actions or patterns of life that will get us off-track. God's character, his revelation in the Bible, and our own nature correspond to each other. We are to be holy because God is holy (1 Pet. 1:16). To act in an unholy fashion is to violate God our Creator, his Word, and our own being. There are direct consequences for violating God's specifications for how to live. We need an intimate relationship with God, closeness to other people, clear vocational direction, proper sexual conduct, sleep, exercise, and nutrition. If we habitually fall short in any of these areas it can lead to dissatisfaction, lack of purpose, a feeling of inadequacy, or even a crisis of meaning or purpose in our life.

There is a structure to reality rooted in God's nature, his creation, and our own being. We can choose to live autonomously, attempting to be "free from" any restriction, but we will never experience true freedom by following that path. True freedom is living the way we were created to live. Another way of describing this life after the Fall is that we serve Christ our Redeemer. We are created in, through, by, and for him (Col. 1:16). This service, not surprisingly, leads to flourishing. This truth will make us free (John 8:32).

The Apostle Paul expounds on the implications of this freedom more fully. Romans 6:18ff. says we are "freed from sin" so that we can be "slaves to righteousness" (Rom. 6:18). Later, he writes that we are "freed from sin" to be "enslaved to God" (Rom. 6:22). Being "enslaved to God" leads to "eternal life" (vv. 22 and 23) and a fullness of life in the present time.

In addition to being freed from sin through coming to faith in Jesus Christ, we are also freed from death. Paul says that the outcome of our sin is death (Rom. 6:21) and that the "wages of sin is death" (Rom. 6:23). But Christ has now freed us from the power of death. Note, "Death is swallowed up in victory. O death, where is your sting? . . . but thanks be to God, who gives us the victory through our Lord Jesus Christ" (1 Cor. 15:54–57). We may fear dying, but we need not fear death itself.

We are also freed from the law (Rom. 7:3–6). We are freed from the obligation of earning our salvation, from seeing duty as a wearisome practice, from suffering the condemnation in our own natures, from disobeying the law. We are not "under the law but under grace" in that sense (Rom. 6:14). Jesus does not contradict the message of grace, or freedom from the law, when he says, "If you love me, you will obey my commandments." We are now freed from the condemnation and external adherence to the law in order to now serve out of hearts full of grace, out of desire (not merely duty), and out of joyous obedience.

The New Testament, in effect, calls us to freedom. Paul writes in Galatians, "It was for freedom that Christ set us free" (Gal. 5:1) and "You were called to freedom" (Gal. 5:13). We now experience the glorious liberty of being children of God (Rom. 8:21). We have the Spirit, and "where the Spirit of the Lord is there is liberty" (2 Cor. 3:17).

We are free but, nevertheless, subject to the "law of liberty" (James 1:25, 2:12). Peter Davids says of James's phrase, "He feels perfectly comfortable with enjoying grace within the structure of ethical rules."[4] Similarly, Alec Motyer maintains, "When we come into bondage to the Word of God we come into freedom, because the Word liberates us from the lustful pull of our own nature, and brings us on via the pathway of hard obedience, into new realms of living for God. It is the Law of Liberty."[5]

Law and liberty are not contradictory. Just as a train needs tracks in order to experience "trainness," so humans need to follow the creator's manual of guidelines to experience "humanness" and the freedom to be all God created us to be.

---

[4] Peter Davids, *New International Biblical Commentary: James* (Peabody, MA: Hendrickson, 1989), 74.
[5] J. A. Motyer, *The Tests of Faith* (London: IVP, 1972), 36.

The Fruits of Inner Freedom

The inner freedom emphasized in the New Testament is not explicitly political, economic, or religious freedom. However, there is a sense in which we can say, as we saw in the Old Testament, that new inner freedom eventually leads to consequences in the outer world.

Jesus did not fight, as some expected the Messiah to do, for a violent revolutionary overthrow of the Romans. But there are passages that point toward the importance of personal and political freedom. In 1 Corinthians 7, Paul emphasizes that the believer should stay in the condition in which they were called (vv. 20, 24). However, if the slave had an opportunity to be free, he or she should take it. "Were you called while a slave? Do not worry about it; but if you are able also to become free, rather do that" (1 Cor. 7:21). In Paul's letter to Philemon, the apostle asks him to receive back Onesimus, who is "no longer a slave but more than a slave, a beloved brother" (Philem. 16).

The inner freedom Christ came to bring has often been the garden out of which other freedoms grow. The themes of Exodus ("Let my people go") and of Jesus's sermon at his home synagogue in Luke 4 (freedom to the captive) have often been preached. Like Jesus, we "proclaim justice" (Matt. 12:18–21) with mercy and compassion. The Holy Spirit is sent to convict us concerning sin, righteousness, and judgment (John 16:7f). It seems that this applies not only in personal life but in public life as well. We are to be prophetic—proclaiming his excellencies in a world of darkness (1 Pet. 2:9–10). While we can have inner freedom without outer freedom, it is better to have both. The inner freedom gives birth to freedom in public life.

Redemption, above all, applies to all of life. Not only are we redeemed from our sin (personal); we are also brought into a new community—the body of Christ (1 Cor. 12:13) (corporate). Our redemption, though, extends beyond the personal and corporate to the whole cosmos. Acts 3:21 says that God's ultimate goal is the "restoration of all things." The whole "creation itself will also be set free from its slavery to corruption into the freedom of the glory of the children of God" (Rom. 8:21). We will ultimately live on a new earth. There are two Greek words for "new"—*neos*, meaning "totally new," and *kainos*, meaning "renewed." Almost every time the Bible uses the word "new," *kainos* (renewed) is meant. God's redemption will extend to all of life.

Freedom cannot be limited to inner transformation but must, of necessity, extend to all of life. Jesus not only preached and taught but also healed people's bodies. People were freed inwardly and outwardly. It should not be surprising that where Christ's inner freedom is experienced, the natural outworking is toward justice and political, economic, and religious freedom. There are many biblical passages and themes that demonstrate the holistic freedom and redemption that Jesus came to inaugurate.

It is no wonder, then, that Christians have been on the forefront of freedom movements for the abolition of slavery both past (i.e., William Wilberforce) and present (i.e., International Justice Mission). Many have worked to fight for religious freedom nationally and internationally (i.e., Barnabas Fund). We might say that because of our call to inner freedom, we are called to fight for outer freedom—against injustice, wherever we see it in personal and public life.

Freedom from the bondage to sin, the law, death, and lies about reality will inevitably push further and further out, until it leads to freedom in all areas of life. Inner freedom often has led to outer freedom.

In summary, here are the basic attributes of freedom:

- Freedom is not autonomy or doing what you feel like doing without any constraints.
- Freedom involves structure. Bondage to Christ allows us to be free to be what we are created to be.
- Freedom is within the context of law. We are not under obedience to the law as a condition of salvation, but the moral law and Christ's commands give us a guide to know how to live and love.
- We are truly free when we know the truth about ourselves and the world. This means throwing off the lies and deceptions to which we are so often captive.
- Salvation is not primarily political liberation (as in some theologies). But God often intervened when his people were oppressed by unjust totalitarian leaders (Exodus, Judges).
- Inner renewal often leads to outer consequences and renewal of the land.
- The Bible doesn't prescribe one type of government, but freedom (political, economic, and religious) is consistent with, not contradictory to, the Bible.
- Inner freedom inevitably drives toward outer freedom. You can have political (economic and religious) freedom and still be in bondage to sin. You can have inner freedom in an oppressed situation. But having both inner and outer freedoms is the most ideal state for humans (Mic. 4:4).

Biblical Freedom as Foundational for Political, Economic, and Religious Freedom

As I have shown, the biblical view of freedom drives from the inside out. Inner freedom yearns for outer freedom to pursue life without undue obstruction. The biblical perspective is conducive to political, economic, and religious freedom. The rest of this chapter will show why this is so and why all three are necessary for a flourishing society. The interrelationships between the three freedoms can be described as a three-legged stool.

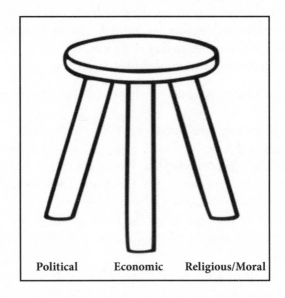

Political   Economic   Religious/Moral

If you damage or eliminate one of the legs of the stool, society becomes unstable, falls over, and fails to flourish. Without political freedom, economic freedom is precarious. It may be maintained for a while, but it is always in danger of being controlled at the whim of the ruling elite. Without economic freedom, a society will not flourish.

A nation will not be stable or flourish without political, economic, and religious freedom. When we lack political, economic, and religious freedom, we experience bondage and slavery in whole or in part. When we are not free to fulfill our calling, frustration results. When millions of people are not free (in whole or in part) to fulfill their callings, there is poverty.

The Three-Legged Stool: Political, Economic, and Religious Freedom Working Together

Political Freedom

The first leg of the stool is political freedom. Political freedom means, at least, as Abraham Lincoln said in the Gettysburg Address, "government of the people, by the people, for the people"—a democratic but representative government. The alternative to political freedom is a totalitarian dictator or a ruling elite. We see many examples of such societies throughout history, right up to this present time. Thomas Aquinas argued in *On Kingship* that an all-powerful king could be the best of all governments as long as that king were perfectly good and wise. However, he also argued that this could be the worst of all governments if that king were corrupt and evil.[6] Lord Acton's famous statement that "power corrupts, and absolute power corrupts absolutely"[7] seems to apply to all of history. This is because the power of the fall into sin corrupts all. C. S. Lewis argues in the *Abolition of Man* that there is no example of a dictator given absolute power who used it for benevolent ends.[8]

C. S. Lewis writes about losing freedom due to the wrong kind of progress. In the late 1950s, he was asked by *The Observer* newspaper to contribute to the series "Is Progress Possible?" His contribution was titled "Is Progress Possible? Willing Slaves of the Welfare State" (1958).[9] In his essay, he warns about an increasing loss of freedom and submitting more and more to government control.

He also encourages progress in "increasing goodness and happiness of individual lives." He adds, however, "Progress means movement in a desired direction and we do not all desire the same things for our species."

Lewis was particularly concerned about the tendencies in the U.K. during World Wars I and II to give up liberty for security. He says we have grown, "though apparently grudgingly, accustomed to our chains." He warns that once

---

[6] St. Thomas Aquinas, *On Kingship: To the King of Cyprus* (Toronto: Pontifical Institute of Mediaeval Studies, Department of Publications, 1949), 14.

[7] Lord Acton, "Acton-Creighton Correspondence [1887]," Online Library of Liberty, accessed February 20, 2019, http://oll.libertyfund.org/titles/acton-acton-creighton-correspondence#lf1524_label_010.

[8] C. S. Lewis, *The Abolition of Man* (New York: Macmillan, 1955), 78.

[9] C. S. Lewis, "Is Progress Possible? Willing Slaves of the Welfare State," *The Observer*, July 20, 1958, accessed February 20, 2019, http://liberty-tree.ca/research/willing_slaves_of_the_welfare_state.

government encroaches on our freedom, every concession makes it more difficult for us to "retrace our steps." Perhaps the most striking quotation from this
essay is the one on the nature of the happiness that he would like to see. Lewis
says,

> I believe a man is happier, and happy in a richer way, if he has "the free-
> born mind." But I doubt whether he can have this without economic
> independence, which the new society is abolishing. For independence
> allows an education not controlled by Government; and in adult life it is
> the man who needs and asks nothing of Government who can criticize
> its acts and snap his fingers at its ideology. Read Montaigne; that's the
> voice of a man with his legs under his own table, eating the mutton and
> turnips raised on his own land. Who will talk like that when the State is
> everyone's schoolmaster and employer?

Note Lewis's desire for freedom, economic and political. This economic "independence" allows free people to eat their own "mutton and turnips." This echoes the classic passage in Micah 4:4 that says, "Each of them will sit under his
vine and under his fig tree, with no one to make them afraid."

Lewis is especially concerned about the advent of a worldwide welfare
state and sees the enticement to accept it. Giving up freedom for security is a
"terrible bargain" that is so tempting that "we cannot blame men for making
it. We can hardly wish them not to. Yet we can hardly bear that they should."
Despite the temptation, if people do make this bargain, the loss of freedom
will lead to "total frustration" and "disastrous results, both moral and
psychological."

The temptation to turn our destiny over to the state often ignores the reali-
zation that some will take charge of others. These will simply be men and
women, "none perfect; some greedy, cruel, and dishonest." The more that people in government control our lives, the more we have to ask, as Lewis did,
"Why, this time, power should not corrupt as it has done before?"[10]

In light of the many who are pressing for socialism or democratic socialism
(a large welfare state), we need to note Lewis's observations.

Economic Freedom

Economic freedom is the second leg of the stool. Economic freedom is the
degree to which the laws and institutions of a country allow people to open

---

[10] Lewis, "Is Progress Possible?"

businesses, pursue work, and freely exercise their creativity. More specifically, this breaks down into limited government, established rule of law and property rights, sound currency, freedom to trade, and modest regulation not corrupted by special interests.[11] As Lewis observes in the previous section, a loss of political freedom imperils "economic independence" because the enlarged government restricts or regulates what we can do in our businesses. Without economic freedom, a society will not flourish.

How do we define *flourishing*? Generally speaking, it means to thrive or grow on many levels. *Merriam-Webster* defines *flourish* as "to grow luxuriantly, to prosper, or reach a height of development or influence."[12] A biblical definition of flourishing goes further and incorporates the concept of *shalom*—salvation, wholeness, integrity, soundness, community, connectedness, righteousness, justice, and well-being.[13] Shalom means "flourishing in every direction." Worldly measures of flourishing certainly incorporate some of these biblical ideas as well.

And, in the ways the world typically measures flourishing, there is a demonstrable, positive relationship between economic freedom and life expectancy, infant mortality, the quality of health care, poverty rates, corruption levels, clean environment, civil liberties, income levels, income of the poor, happiness, child labor, and unemployment.[14] The more economically free a society is, the better it performs in all these areas. Another way of saying this is that socialism and Marxism are demonstrably always bad for the poor. This insight from Michael Novak's book *The Spirit of Democratic Capitalism* is revolutionary. There are now extensive yearly reports that demonstrate the relationship between economic freedom and its outcomes, giving detailed surveys of every country in the world, such as the "Economic Freedom of the World Report" and the "Heritage Freedom Index." As these reports indicate, political freedom and economic freedom lead to a flourishing society.[15]

---

[11] Joe Connors and Anne Bradley, "Economic Freedom and the Path to Flourishing," Institute for Faith, Work & Economics website, accessed February 25, 2019, https://tifwe.org/wp-content/uploads/2013/10/Economic-Freedom-and-the-Path_Revised.pdf.

[12] *Merriam-Webster*, "flourish," https://www.merriam-webster.com/dictionary/flourishing.

[13] Hugh Whelchel, "What Is Flourishing?" Institute for Faith, Work & Economics blog, May 20, 2013, accessed February 20, 2019, https://tifwe.org/what-is-flourishing.

[14] Connors and Bradley, "Economic Freedom and Path to Flourishing."

[15] See Chapter Eight, which develops the connection between religious freedom and economic freedom more full, and also Michael Novak, *The Spirit of Democratic Capitalism* (Lanham, MD: Madison Books, 1990), 333–58.

Religious Freedom

The third leg of the stool, religiously based moral values—particularly biblical values, for all the reasons examined in the first section of this chapter—are essential and foundational for a flourishing society. Religious freedom includes the inalienable rights of freedom of belief, freedom of speech or expression, and freedom from fear of persecution. It is the right to lead a life according to our faith and religious moral code not only in places of worship but also in our homes, the workplace, and in the public square.

Without religious freedom, we are not free to be informed by our consciences and, thereby, transformed inwardly and outwardly. Being transformed inwardly and understanding what outward freedom and flourishing look like allow us to champion economic and political freedom. A society will eventually crumble without a solid, religiously based moral foundation. Political freedom could become anarchy, or a majority of people and their representatives could somehow inexplicably vote for something evil. A politically free nation can rise only as high as the character of those involved. Economic freedom without a religiously based moral foundation could also be harmful if it is not checked by the rule of law and the informed consciences of those who do business. A lack of religious freedom could lead to a society that refuses to allow the prophetic input of religiously based moral values. Richard Neuhaus argues, in his classic book *The Naked Public Square,* that such a society could be a disaster.[16]

Our culture was founded on morals rooted in the Bible. Without a belief in God, there is no secure basis to uphold objective evil or good.[17] An article in the *Wall Street Journal,* "In Europe God Is (Not) Dead," notes a prominent thinker's observation:

> Jürgen Habermas, influential German intellectual, member of the originally Marxist Frankfurt School of philosophy and self-described "methodical atheist," has revised his view that modernization inevitably leads to secularization. In a 2004 book, *Time of Transitions,* he hailed Christianity as the bedrock of Western values: "Christianity, and nothing else, is the ultimate foundation of liberty, conscience, human

---

[16] Richard John Neuhaus, *The Naked Public Square: Religion and Democracy in America* (Grand Rapids, MI: Eerdmans, 1988).

[17] Art Lindsley, *True Truth: Defending Absolute Truth in a Relativistic World* (Downers Grove, IL: IVP, 2004), 171. The entirety of *True Truth* is an extended argument on the premise that unless God exists, there's no objective evil or good.

rights, and democracy, the benchmarks of Western civilization. To this day, we have no other options [than Christianity]. We continue to nourish ourselves from this source. Everything else is postmodern chatter."[18]

So many Christians and non-Christians alike recognize these virtues are uniquely grounded in a biblical framework. It is easy to criticize political and economic freedom, but it is important to note that any criticism of political or economic freedom is inadequate unless it takes into consideration the religious/moral leg of the stool. It provides checks and balances on any abuses in the political or economic realm. These freedoms do not exist in a vacuum but are grounded in the soil of religiously based moral values (i.e., biblical values).

Austin Hill and Scott Rae argue in their book *The Virtues of Capitalism* that there are five core values underlying a market economy: creativity, initiative, cooperation, civility, and responsibility. All five are deeply grounded in biblical roots. Without these virtues, markets cannot flourish.[19]

Similarly, Wayne Grudem and Barry Asmus, in their book *The Poverty of Nations*, list thirty-five biblically based moral virtues that are encouraged by the free enterprise system and, in turn, help it function. Central to these virtues are honesty and truthfulness, which allow trust to be formed. If a society is so corrupt that people lose trust and almost every financial contract is violated, then the court system will become clogged and people will become reluctant or unwilling to do business.

Grudem and Asmus also list a cluster of biblical virtues that are necessary for work and productivity. These virtues include being thrifty with time and money (Eph. 5:16; Ps. 90:12), doing excellent work (as unto the Lord—Eph. 6:7), using one's creativity to serve others, and developing innovative ways to unlock the potential of God's creation (Gen. 1:28).

The biblical worldview teaches that time is linear, meaning that we can learn from the past and have hope for the future. Time is a valuable resource that should not be wasted. We can humbly learn from other countries and will eventually worship God with others from every tribe, tongue, people, and nation (Rev. 7:9).[20]

---

[18] Andrew Higgins, "In Europe God Is (Not) Dead," *Wall Street Journal*, accessed February 20, 2019, July 14, 2007, http://www.wsj.com/articles/SB118434936941966055.

[19] Austin Hill and Scott Rae, *The Virtues of Capitalism: A Moral Case for Free Markets* (Chicago, IL: Northfield Publishing, 2010), 41–55.

[20] Barry Asmus and Wayne Grudem, *The Poverty of Nations: A Sustainable Solution* (Wheaton, IL: Crossway, 2013), 322–24.

By emphasizing such values, the Bible provides the foundation essential to free enterprise. Markets viewed from this angle are not "unfettered" or "unbridled." Unless these moral values are deeply rooted in people's conscience and character, free enterprise moves slowly or grinds to a halt. Some have called this capitalism with a conscience, while others have argued for a triple bottom line—people, planet, profit. You might add a fourth value—purpose for the individual worker. Likewise, religiously (biblically) based morality is the only sure foundation for society in general and politics in particular. Peter Kreeft argues the following:

> Even in a secular society like America it's still true that religion is the firmest support for morality. There has never been a popular secular morality that's lasted and worked in holding a society together. Society has always needed morality, and morality has always needed religion. Destroy religion, you destroy morality; destroy morality, you destroy society. That's history's bottom line.[21]

In Defense of Religious Freedom for All

In light of the foundational role of religious freedom in experiencing economic and political freedom and flourishing, Christians have good reasons to be at the forefront of defending religious freedom.

First, many of the first settlers in this country left England because their religious liberty was being threatened. You could call religious liberty and tolerance America's first freedom.

Second, Christians do not believe that you can or ought to physically coerce someone else into religious belief, such as what occurred during the Inquisition. We can defend people's legal rights to freedom of conscience even when we believe them to be wrong. Scripture upholds a right to freedom of conscience even when people's views are misguided (Rom. 14:23).

Third, Christians have good reason for desiring the nonestablishment of religion. Generally, where religion has been established, it has become diluted and weak (see Anne Bradley's chapter). Where it has been allowed freedom, it has thrived. Just look at the dwindling established churches (with a few exceptions) in Europe, England, and Scandinavia. Contrast this

---

[21] Peter Kreeft, *A Refutation of Moral Relativism: Interviews with an Absolutist* (San Francisco, CA: Ignatius Press, 1999), 162.

situation with the vitality (despite many imperfections) of nonestablished Christian churches in America. At the founding of this country (in 1790), about 10 percent of people attended church once a week.[22] Today, roughly 40 percent attend church in a given week.[23] When there is full freedom to persuade, the most attractive options gain the most adherents. There is a free market of beliefs and ideas.

Lastly, the best way to retain our own freedoms as Christians is to be defenders of freedom for others. Lesslie Newbigin said,

> If we acknowledge the God of the Bible, we are committed to struggle for justice in society, justice means giving to each his due. Our problem (as seen in light of the gospel) is that each of us overestimates what is due to him as compared with what is due to his neighbor. . . . If I do not acknowledge a justice which judges the justice for which I fight, I am an agent, not of justice, but of lawless tyranny.[24]

Unless Christians become foremost defenders of religious freedom for others as well as for themselves, they will not be readily heard when they proclaim the gospel. A precondition for recovering culture is that we are for justice, not "just us."[25]

Conclusion

Freedom needs to grow out of a faith-based moral foundation. Political and economic freedom can be preserved only when they are rooted in virtue. Just as a relationship can rise only as high as the characters of those involved, so a nation can rise only as high as the characters and institutions of those involved. If honesty, trustworthiness, cooperation, love, creativity, initiative, responsibility, and other virtues are not encouraged, society will decline. As Peter Kreeft (quoted earlier) argues, "Destroy religion, you destroy morality; destroy

---

[22] Mark C. Carnes, John A. Garrety, and Patrick Williams, *Mapping America's Past: A Historical Atlas* (New York: Henry Holt, 1996), 50.

[23] Frank Newport, "In U.S., Four in 10 Report Attending Church Last Week," Gallup, December 24, 2013, accessed February 20, 2019, http://www.gallup.com/poll/166613/four-report-attending-church-last-week.aspx.

[24] Lesslie Newbigin, *The Open Secret: Sketches for a Missionary Theology* (Grand Rapids, MI: Eerdmans, 1978), 124.

[25] Lindsley, *True Truth*, 23–33.

morality, you destroy society." In other words, freedom requires virtue, and virtue requires faith.[26]

Freedom from virtue and faith—the "freedom from (restraints)" view—is insufficient to support society, because under it, all three legs of the stool grow weaker. Instead, we need to be "free to" serve under the structure of the reality God has created. The only way to stability and flourishing is the foundation of faith-based moral values applied to our political, economic, and religious spheres.

[26] Os Guinness, *A Free People's Suicide: Sustainable Freedom and the American Future* (Downers Grove, IL: IVP, 2012), 99.

Chapter 8

The Bricks and Mortar of Civil Society: An Empirical Analysis of Economic and Religious Freedoms

Joseph Connors and Anne R. Bradley
Assistant Professor of Economics, Southern College;
Vice President of Economic Initiatives, IFWE

"The more government takes the place of associations, the more will individuals lose the idea of forming associations and need the government to come to their help. That is a vicious circle of cause and effect."

—Alexis de Tocqueville

"Coercion may thus sometimes be avoidable only because a high degree of voluntary conformity exists which thus may be a condition of freedom. It is indeed a truth, which all the great apostles of freedom outside the rationalistic school have never tired of emphasizing, that freedom has never worked without deeply ingrained moral beliefs, and that coercion can be reduced to a minimum only where the individuals can be expected as a rule to conform voluntarily to certain principles."

— F. A. Hayek, 1958

"For centuries now, people have come to this country from every corner of the world to share in the blessing of religious freedom. Our Constitution promises that they may worship in their own way, without fear of penalty or danger, and that in itself is a momentous offering. Yet our Constitution makes a commitment still more remarkable—that however those individuals worship, they will count as full and equal American citizens. A Christian, a Jew, a Muslim (and so forth)—each stands in the same relationship with her country, with her state and local communities, and with every level and body of government. So that when each person performs the duties or seeks the benefits of citizenship, she does so not as an adherent to one or another religion, but simply as an American."

—Justice Kagan dissenting opinion, *Petitioner v. Susan Galloway et al.*, May, 5, 2014

Modern economic and political thought has a tendency to view the three human freedoms—economic freedom, political freedom, and religious freedom—as separate and distinct. For example, China has been pursuing policies that promote economic freedom while at the same time limiting political and religious freedom. Singapore is one of the highest rated countries in terms of economic freedom but has much less political freedom. Those in favor of social democracy argue that political freedom (i.e., democracy) can be combined with a socialist-style economic system, which would limit economic freedom.[1] While it is true that economic, political, and religious freedom each have different manifestations, it is a mistake to see them as separate and distinct. In the struggle for human freedom, each of these freedoms has been inextricably linked. From the Magna Carta to the U.S. civil rights movement, each freedom has been expanded. Thus, a suppression of one aspect of freedom necessarily limits the others.[2]

Today, the United States has a wonderful inheritance as it enjoys a large degree of each of these freedoms. However, there is a growing view that prefers to see religious freedom strictly as the freedom of religious belief. This view argues that people should be free to have religious beliefs in the privacy of their own home but not free to bring those beliefs into the public sphere.[3] This view, while masquerading as religious freedom, necessarily requires a reduction of religious freedom. Freedom, in all its forms, necessarily involves the freedom to choose and the freedom to act, as long as the acts do not violate the reciprocal rights of others. Blocking religious beliefs from the public sphere limits religious freedom because it limits the ability of people to live out their faith. In a

---

[1] Giddens, *The Third Way: The Renewal of Social Democracy* (Malden: Polity Press, 1998).

[2] Ludwig von Mises, *Economic Freedom and Interventionism* (Atlanta: Foundation for Economic Education, 1990).

[3] For example, see Nick Jackson's 2007 interview with Simon Blackburn, "Against the Grain: Religion Should Be Kept Out of Politics," (https://www.independent.co.uk/news/education/higher/against-the-grain-religion-should-be-kept-out-of-politics-5332691.html) or Phil Zuckerman's 2017 interview of Monica Miller, "Fighting for the Separation of Church and State." https://www.psychologytoday.com/nz/blog/the-secular-life/201711/fighting-the-separation-church-and-state?amp

2006 speech, then Senator Obama eloquently expressed the importance of this broader view of religious freedom.

> But what I am suggesting is this—secularists are wrong when they ask believers to leave their religion at the door before entering into the public square. Frederick Douglas, Abraham Lincoln, Williams Jennings Bryan, Dorothy Day, Martin Luther King—indeed, the majority of great Reformers in American history—not only were motivated by faith but also repeatedly used religious language to argue for their cause. So to say that men and women should not inject their "personal morality" into public policy debates is a practical absurdity. Our law is, by definition, a codification of morality, much of it grounded in the Judeo-Christian tradition.[4]

The aim of this chapter is, first, to emphasize the importance of this broader conception of religious freedom—to choose and to act—and, second, to emphasize the fundamental role that religious freedom plays and has played in supporting economic and political freedom through a healthy and robust civil society. The analysis provided here will use recent data on religious freedom from the Pew Foundation and the Institutional Profiles Database (IPD) of the French government. These data help to illustrate the important role religious freedom plays in support of civil society and a flourishing people.

The Origins of Religious Freedom

In the span and scope of human history, religious freedom and its codification into law and culture is a relatively new phenomenon. At a time in the not-too-distant past, kings were born of divine right with all the power and fortune that accords. With no separation between what the state governed and what religious law governed, the power battles among kings and priests were typical and bloody. The idea that religions of varied and often contradictory views about human life and anthropology should be organically and freely adopted by the free will of ordinary human beings would have been shocking not long ago.

It is easy to understand that each religion would want freedom for their views, but it's also easy to understand that they would desire to use the state to impose those views on everyone. State imposition of religious authority

---

[4] Then Senator Obama's keynote address at the Call to Renewal's conference, Building a Covenant for a New America, June 28, 2006, https://www.nytimes.com/2006/06/28/us/politics/2006obamaspeech.html.

begets power and fortune, and this at a time when most people lived short lives that were very poor. One can see how the vying for religion to be a codified institution of the state was predictable and lasting. Thus, the codification of religious autonomy and competing religious views that would later occur outside the confines of the state, originating in Europe, was a profound move in the direction of personal liberty, human agency, and freedom—for ordinary people.

The notion of religious liberty spawns from Judeo-Christian origins and can be traced back to the human anthropology that is so clearly revealed through Scripture and natural law (see Chapter Five). Human beings are created in God's image and likeness (Gen. 1: 26–28) and given dominion over God's creation; we are *imago dei*. From this, emanates profound implications, for both us and our purpose. We are created, by God, to be creators. We cannot create in the same way that God does—we are fallible, finite, and face scarce resources. Yet, we are called to create nonetheless, and in creating and cultivating God's earth, we are enabled to serve one another. We are told that God put man in the garden to "work it and care for it" (Gen. 2:15). The Hebrew word for "work it" is *abad*, which means "to serve."

Our human anthropology is to serve each other because we need each other. We cannot create alone. We are different yet the same. As humans, we share many similar physiological traits, yet we are all unique and uniquely our own. We have different ideas, perceptions, attitudes, skills, and talents. God divinely created us this way, and in doing so, he created an order in which we must come together and work with one another. All of this means that humans have purpose and dignity and that we can choose and decide. This key aspect of free will and purposeful choice, which is anthropological, is the truth from which the concept of religious liberty stems. The truth is, objectively, the truth. Yet we must freely choose, which means that the truth cannot be imposed upon us by a government but rather revealed through nature and Scripture.

This truth is written on the heart of every person and, as such, must be discovered through reason and discourse. For each person to have the possibility of discovering truth and employing it in their daily lives, religion must be free from the coercive power of the state. In the United States, among other Western societies, sovereignty has been extended to the state where it hadn't been before, and this tends to crowd out the voluntary institutions that allow people to live out their different faiths in a peaceful and cooperative manner. The consequences of this will be discussed in detail in a later section.

One of the first historical experiments with legally codifying religious liberty, which would fracture the omnipotent power of state-as-church and church-as-state, can be found in the Magna Carta, written in 1215.[5] The Magna Carta was not a document that extended religious freedom to all in society, but it did create an avenue by which some in society gained religious autonomy, which was unprecedented. The Magna Carta was drafted by the archbishop of Canterbury to ease tensions between King John of England and resident barons, and, among other things, it included the protection of church rights.[6] The charter was later annulled by Pope Innocent III, because neither side was living up to their promises as written. The charter was reissued by Henry III in 1216, although not in its original form.[7] The Magna Carta became an important document and aspect of English political and legal history and was used to object to the formerly pervasive belief in the divine right of kings, even though it went through many different phases of use and adjustments in its language.[8]

The Magna Carta serves as a lesson about the nature of man, the nature of the state, and the relationship between man and state. Authorities have vested incentives to limit freedom of all types; it constrains their power and their ability to acquire resources. The battle for religious freedom has been long fought and continues globally today. The ethos of individual freedom and the pursuit of conscience in the quest for truth are necessary components of sustaining any of our cherished freedoms. Religious freedom provides a platform for people to seek truth. The quest for truth and adoption of ideas that are lived out voluntarily and peacefully are key components of human flourishing.

Spontaneous Order and Civil Society

Alexis de Tocqueville observed that society flourishes through voluntary choices and associations, a process that Nobel-prize-winning economist F. A. Hayek called spontaneous order. Tocqueville, a scholar of the French Revolution and an observer of early nineteenth-century American life, praised this spontaneous order in U.S. civil society when it was a young republic. He noted that families, churches, and local communities formed the backbone of a prosperous and free United States of America.[9]

---

5 "Magna Carta," Oxford English Dictionary, accessed March 11, 2019.

6 Sean McGlynn, *Blood Cries Afar: The Forgotten Invasion of England, 1216* (London: Spellmount, 2013).

7 Danny Danziger and John Gillingham, *1215: The Year of Magna Carta* (London: Hodder Paperbacks, 2004).

8 G. R. C. Davis, *Magna Carta* (London: The British Library Publishing Division, 1963); Claire Breay, *Magna Carta: Manuscripts and Myths* (London: The British Library, 2010).

9 Alexis de Tocqueville, *Democracy in America*, trans. Henry Reeve, ed. Francis Bowen, vol. 1 (1838, repr., Cambridge: Sever and Francis, 1876).

Hayek, a great admirer of Tocqueville's work, emphasized that civil society and government itself ought to emerge organically rather than through social engineering and collectivized experimentation. No one person is smart enough, wise enough, calculating enough, and benevolent enough to plan or comprehend the complexity of human society and the extended (and desired) voluntary cooperation of individuals. Rather, choice starts with individuals because humans are purposeful.[10] This purpose, driven by subjective value, emerges as conscious choice. Moreover, the knowledge that we need to plan our lives is local and decentralized and often conflicting.[11]

In economics, subjective value is the premise that individuals assign value to things based on their desired preferences and their own self-interest. [12] This differential and highly personal value system is the platform for human choices, and it means that each of us chooses differently. We have different preferences at our grocery stores, bookstores, and retail stores, and even our charitable activities are guided by our unique ordering of preferences. The social implications that come from this are profound. We are each different and want different things, and only we know our preferences and desires, which means that commerce and exchange, which are driven by these intimate preferences, must be organic. Society and market exchange, then, work best when manifested through the spontaneous order that comes through individual exchange guided by individual reason. No one person can "design" a society that will be best and most productive for all of its members. Societies that are emergent, rather than designed, satisfy the most preferences possible. Moreover, a market economy is part of this emergent order and produces the added benefit of wealth creation, which is not possible in a "top-down," centrally designed society.

Spontaneous orders are not planned; hence, the spontaneity is characterized by order rather than chaos. Societies plagued by chaos, strife, and conflict cannot support the strong civil society in which we see people organizing outside both the market economy and the state to form cooperative ventures with one another—from barn-raisings to church-run hospitals. Spontaneous orders are cooperative and provide a mechanism for divergent, and perhaps even contradictory, preferences and value systems to coexist. Spontaneous orders are not planned but are in no way arbitrary because individuals are intentionally

---

[10] Ludwig von Mises, *Human Action. A Treatise on Economics* (New Haven, Yale University Press, 1949)

[11] F. A. Hayek, *Individualism and Economic Order* (Chicago: The University of Chicago Press, 1948).

[12] Carl Menger, *Principles of Economics* (Arlington, VA: The Institute for Humane Studies, 1976).

planning and deciding. In short, there is planning, but the planning is left to the individuals and not government.

However, as Adam Smith,[13] Hayek,[14] and others have observed, an orderly society is achieved through a free society. This "order" is what we want because it eschews chaos and provides for predictability—something humans require—but it cannot be planned through government action. In fact, central planning of social orders necessarily results in chaos and plunder, and in a constrained or entirely lacking civility in social relations. Moreover, the history of Nazism and communism teaches us that when governments restrict human freedom, religious freedom is usually first on the chopping block. Marx famously derided religion by describing it as the "opium of the people."[15] Lenin, the founder of the Soviet Union was also critical of religious beliefs. Moreover, he saw them as being intimately linked with economic institutions. For Lenin, religious beliefs sustained a market economy. Consequently, religion wasn't needed in a socialist/communist society.[16] Adolf Hitler persecuted both Jews and Catholics in his takeover of the German government. Mao Zedong banned all practice of religion once gaining power in China. Today, religious persecution is still a prominent feature of China's government. Thus, human flourishing, which we all desire, can only be achieved when people are left to freely choose civility through shared norms and values that provide a lubricant for commercial exchange among strangers and a prophylactic against government power and the rent-seeking it necessarily entails.

Religious and Economic Freedoms

Both Tocqueville and Hayek noted that we must be free to choose our own set of values. We do this through our voluntary institutions, which include our

---

[13] Adam Smith, *An Inquiry into the Nature and Causes of the Wealth of Nations*, ed. Edwin Cannan, Fifth edition (1789; rept., 1904).

[14] F. A. Hayek, *The Collected Works,* ed. Bruce Caldwell, vol. 2 *The Road to Serfdom* (1944; rept., University of Chicago Press, 2007); Hayek, "The Use of Knowledge in Society," *American Economic Review* 35, no. 4 (September 1945): 519–30.

[15] Karl Marx, *Critique of Hegel's 'Philosophy of Right'* (Cambridge, UK: Cambridge University Press, 1977).

[16] "It would be bourgeois narrow-mindedness to forget that the yoke of religion that weighs upon mankind is merely a product and reflection of the economic yoke within society. No number of pamphlets and no amount of preaching can enlighten the proletariat, if it is not enlightened by its own struggle against the dark forces of capitalism. Unity in this really revolutionary struggle of the oppressed class for the creation of a paradise on earth is more important to us than unity of proletarian opinion on paradise in heaven." V. I. Lenin, *Collected Works: Vol. 33.* (Moscow: Progress Publishers, 1964).

churches and faith. Faithfulness to religion and God is necessarily personal and voluntary. While individuals will surely disagree on religious truth, a society characterized by the emergent nature of spontaneous ordering will mute the historical hostility that allows accompanied religious dispute. In a society characterized by religious freedom, each person, guided by his or her faith, is free to pursue that faith in the public square. With religious and economic freedom present, this process is peaceful; the outcome is possible only when religion is free from the state. Through this outcome, we achieve another important social outcome: people create and rely on local intermediating institutions, through which they solve community problems and serve (*abad*) each other.

No one can plan or comprehend the complexity of human society, yet spontaneous order exists, and human flourishing is the outcome of spontaneous order. Spontaneous order needs freedom. It can occur only if each individual (or family) is free to choose. Religious freedom allows for a spontaneous order in all the things that religion cares about; that is, the engagement of people with others in their community and the ability to worship freely and practice their faith in all dimensions of life. This ordering takes many forms: church groups, civic groups, sporting groups, and charitable groups. We know that the outcome of the spontaneous order of free people is human flourishing; thus, restriction of religious freedom necessarily limits this flourishing.

Economic freedom interacts with and is related to religious freedom. While the latter pertains to the voluntary belief system that an individual commits to and that informs his or her daily behavior, economic freedom provides the institutional platform for which people can live out their competing and often contradictory religious beliefs. When religious beliefs are freely adopted and voluntarily chosen, and when that choice sits outside of the state, there is less of an associated power struggle, because the choices are local, personal, and free from coercion.

An interesting aspect of economic life is that we often forget how much of our life is lived in the economic sphere. All the choices we make regarding how we use our time—where we live, eat, work, and go to school—are economic. These choices are fundamental to the way we live our lives. This is why economic freedom is a key aspect of human freedom. A society that boasts of high levels of economic freedom is one where people are free to make economic decisions so long as they do not impose on the economic decisions or violate the rights of others. Thus, economic freedom goes hand in hand with religious freedom. For example, in a world with economic freedom, an entrepreneur could decide that she will prohibit the sale of alcohol in a restaurant because alcohol consumption violates her religious beliefs; consumers are then free to choose to eat there or choose to eat somewhere where alcohol is freely served.

The most widely used measure of economic freedom is the Economic Freedom of the World (EFW) Index, published annually by the Fraser Institute.[17] This index categorizes the level of economic freedom in a country in five areas: (1) the size of government, (2) the legal system and security of property rights, (3) sound money, (4) the freedom to trade internationally, and (5) regulation of credit, labor, and business.

The measure of the size of government captures whether economic decisions over resources in a country are made by individuals or by those in power. When individuals have freedom and are able to make their own decisions, the size of government will be smaller. Government is capable of obtaining revenue in only three ways: it can tax, borrow, or inflate. Thus, government revenue, by definition, is acquired through either coercive taxation, theft through monetary inflation, or borrowing against the future. Therefore, a government is limited in its activity by how much revenue it generates through these means. To increase its activities, it must have more revenue. Increasing taxes reduces the freedom individuals have in choosing how to use their financial resources. Inflation reduces the freedom individuals have by reducing the effective amount of resources they have to use and make decisions over. Borrowing reduces the freedom individuals have over their resources in the future, as taxes will necessarily increase to pay off the debt.

All of this necessitates a limit to the size and scope of the state. A government that is too large in spending and consumption will not be able to finance those expenditures in the long run because the resources to do so crowd out other entrepreneurial activities in the market sector. This reduces economic freedom, human creativity, and cooperation and service through commerce. Lastly, a large government will tend to crowd out the productive intermediary institutions of civil society. In praising these institutions, Tocqueville also provided warnings about what civil society loses when these institutions are coercively replaced by government.

Economic freedom is meaningless without private property rights, rule of law, and a legal system that implements laws in a fair and even-handed manner. It is necessary here to make an important point about the nature of economic freedom, religious freedom and even political freedom. They are not wholly separate, as Milton Friedman suggested.[18] When we talk about

---

[17] James Gwartney et al., Economic Freedom of the World: 2018 Annual Report, The Fraser Institute, accessed March 17, 2019, https://www.fraserinstitute.org/studies/economic-freedom-of-the-world-2018-annual-report.

[18] M. Friedman, "Preface," in Economic Freedom of the World: 2002 Annual Report, ed. J. Gwartney and R. Lawson (Vancouver: Fraser Institute, 2002), xvii–xxi.

religious and economic freedom, we are necessarily talking, to some extent, about the size and scope of the state. When the state is expansive in its consumption and expenditures, it necessarily limits these other spheres of freedom. Thus, to have a thriving civil society in which religious and economic freedom flourish, the state necessarily must be limited. This requires that the leaders of a country submit themselves to the rule of law and that the law not be usurped by political power, and it implies egalitarianism in the courts and the laws. This, too, ensures an environment of trust and predictability, which is essential not only for wealth creation but for the functioning of civil society.

Money of sound value is central to exchange and commerce. In order for free people to plan their lives, the value of a currency cannot fluctuate wildly. When a currency is soundly maintained by the central bank, it signals a commitment to low levels of inflation and constraint by the government. This allows predictability in commerce and ensures an environment where entrepreneurship can flourish and where long-term investments can and will be made.

The freedom to trade internationally is important because it allows entrepreneurs the freedom to serve customers all over the world; in turn, it allows people all over the world to be served by those entrepreneurs. Moreover, it allows for the specialization and sharing of ideas that Adam Smith praised over two hundred years ago.

Regulations of credit, labor, and business necessarily restrict human freedom. We can all debate the merits of these regulations; however, their implementation always reduces freedom. These regulations typically affect the ability of businesspeople to obtain loans and titles and to open and maintain their own businesses, all key aspects of entrepreneurship and the unleashing of human creativity. If ordinary people are burdened by a corrupt and excessive regulatory regime, human creativity is stymied, economic growth is constrained, and human flourishing suffers. Moreover, in this environment, greed and "takings" are institutionalized. The rich and powerful get richer because they control the regulatory apparatus. A society that is overly regulated is one where trust dissipates and the quest for wealth tends toward a zero-sum or "winners and losers" game. When freedom is reduced through regulation, resources are wasted in the creation of the regulation in the first place and then in all the wasted activity that the regulation requires for compliance in the marketplace, resulting in higher taxes and higher costs to meet consumers' needs.

The EFW Index measures the extent of economic freedom in these five areas using forty-two different variables for 162 countries. The total measure of freedom is compiled into a summary index that ranges from 0 to 10 with 10 indicating a high level of economic freedom. These ranges are meant to be ideals. No country has ever achieved a score of either 0 or 10. In the latest report, Hong Kong achieved the highest rating of economic freedom with an 8.97, while Venezuela achieved the lowest with a rating of 2.88. There are two notable countries that would most likely rank below Venezuela. They are North Korea and Cuba. However, the EFW Index is an objective and transparent index and does not create or impute any of the data. Thus, because these two countries are totalitarian states, reliable data does not exist and they are not included in the index.

The mountain of recent research using the EFW Index loudly proclaims one clear result: human flourishing occurs only in societies with a great deal of economic freedom.[19] Compared to people who live in the least economically free countries of the world, people in the most economically free countries have income levels that are more than seven times higher, a life expectancy that is fifteen years longer, an infant mortality rate that is 6.5 times lower, much higher civil and political liberties, less gender inequality, and higher levels of happiness.[20] The body of research has illustrated the benefits of economic freedom for human flourishing that are too numerous to list here. In short, however one examines the data, the evidence in support of the benefits of economic freedom is compelling.

Excluded from this analysis of the benefits of economic freedom is an appreciation of the role of religious freedom. These economically free institutions are supported and maintained by a healthy civil society. Thus, the existence and importance of religious freedom is fundamental for an economically free society. If one thinks of economic freedom as a fundamental building block of a flourishing society, then religious freedom is the mortar that holds everything together. The following section will use data to examine religious freedom throughout the world. The supportive relationship that religious freedom plays in maintaining a civil society can be observed through some basic analysis of the data.

---

[19] For an excellent survey of this literature, see Beggren "On the Benefits of Economic Freedom: A Survey," 2003. Other key papers are James D. Guartney, Robert A. Lawson, and Randall G. Holcombe, "Economic Freedom and the Environment for Economic Growth," *Journal of Institutional and Theoretical Economics* 155, no. 4 (1999): 643–63. http://www.jstor.org/stable/40752161; Daron Acemoglu, Simon Johnson, and James A. Robinson, "The Colonial Origins of Comparative Development: An Empirical Investigation," *The American Economic Review* 91, no. 5 (December, 2001): 1369–1401.
[20] See Gwartney et al., *Economic Freedom of the World: 2018 Annual Report*, exhibits 1.5 through 1.13.

Religious Freedom

The quest to measure religious freedom internationally is in its infancy. One approach is to measure the degree to which communities can establish and operate a church or religious organization. This is the approach of the Institutional Profiles Database (IPD), which is compiled by the government of France and attempts to measure certain institutional characteristics of countries. The database covers 144 countries and measures a wide variety of indicators. Two of these indicators are used in our analysis. The first measures the ease of establishing a religious organization (0—very difficult, 4—very easy). The second uses the same scale and measures the ease of running a religious organization. These two measures only exist for the years 2009 and 2012.

The second approach measures the hostility that people of faith face either from their government or from society at large. This dataset is compiled by the Pew Research Center and results in two variables: social hostility and government hostility. Each variable is scaled from 0 to 10, with 10 indicating a high degree of hostility toward religious groups. These data from Pew are annual and cover the years 2007–2012.

While these data are relatively new, research utilizing the data has already established a link between religious freedom and economic growth. Researchers Brian Grim, Greg Clark, and Robert Snyder found that businesses in countries with more religious freedom were more competitive than companies in less free countries. Moreover, this impact spilled over into the growth rates of the country's economy. Countries with less religious freedom exhibited lower overall growth rates.[21] This result is consistent with the ideas of Tocqueville and Hayek that were discussed earlier: namely, that the spontaneous interactions of free people lead to greater levels of human flourishing.

Given the benefits of religious freedom on economic growth, what can these data also tell us about the impact of religious freedom on civil society? Economic and political freedom depend upon a robust civil society that limits the encroachment of the government on the rights of people. Does the data support the hypothesis that religious freedom and a robust civil society go hand in hand?

Figure 1 gives an overview of religious freedom around the world. This map averages the French IPD data regarding the ability of individuals within

---

[21] Brian J. Grim, Greg Clark, and Robert E. Snyder, "Is Religious Freedom Good for Business?: A Conceptual and Empirical Analysis," *Interdisciplinary Journal of Research on Religion* 10, 2014. http://www.religjournal.com/pdf/ijrr10004.pdf

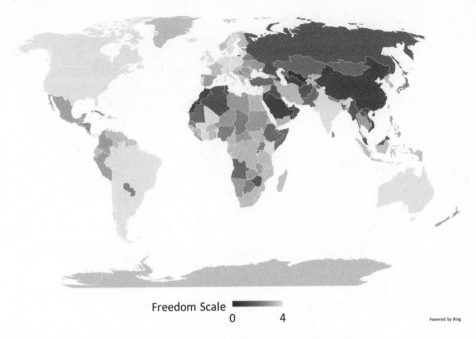

Freedom Scale

0   4

Powered by Bing

Figure 1: Freedom to Establish and Operate a Religious Organization

countries to establish and operate religious organizations into a composite measure of religious freedom. Figure 2 provides a similar global map using the Pew data on government hostility toward religion. The same exercise was constructed for the Pew data regarding social hostility toward religion, and it was almost identical to Figure 1. In both figures, the data are color-coded so that lighter colors indicate more religious freedom and darker colors indicate less.

A pattern begins to emerge from this global overview. First, religious freedom is lacking in the countries touched by socialism/communism. The former Soviet countries and China lack religious freedom. This should not be surprising as state-enforced atheism has always been a fundamental tenet of socialism/communism. As mentioned, Marx understood the power religion has in affirming human dignity—a notion very dangerous to authoritarians. He put it this way:

> Religious distress is at the same time the expression of real distress and the protest against real distress. Religion is the sigh of the oppressed creature, the heart of a heartless world, just as it is the spirit of a spiritless situation. It is the opium of the people. The abolition of religion as the illusory happiness of the people is required for their real happiness.

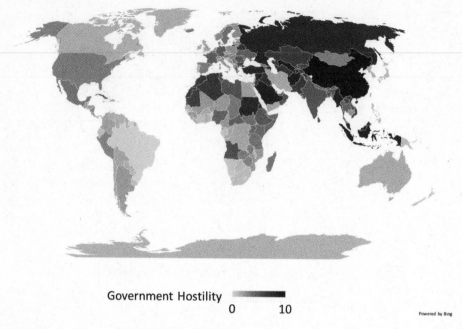

Government Hostility
0   10

Powered by Bing

Figure 2: Government Hostility toward Religious Freedom

The demand to give up the illusion about its condition is the demand to give up a condition which needs illusions. [22]

The stamping out of religious beliefs has always accompanied the imposition of Communism.[23] The individual must surrender her values to the value of the state itself.[24] The state becomes god and we direct our activities and loyalty to it accordingly—this gives the state moral power over the people. Thus, a lack of religious freedom is a fundamental aspect of socialism and Communism in theory and practice.

Second, majority Muslim countries also display a lack of religious freedom. Again, this should not be surprising, as Islamic culture generally punishes converting from Islam to other faiths and preaching beliefs contrary to Islam. A recent case illustrates this point. The Christian pastor Andrew Brunson was

---

[22] Marx, *Critique of Hegel's "Philosophy of Right."*

[23] Glen Fairman, "Socialism as Religion," *American Thinker*, November 2012, accessed March 31, 2019, https://www.americanthinker.com/articles/2012/11/socialism_as_religion.html.

[24] F. A. Hayek, *The Road to Serfdom: Fiftieth Anniversary Edition* (Chicago: University of Chicago Press, 1994).

arrested in Turkey and held for several years before finally being released and allowed to return to the United States.[25]

There is an additional aspect of religious freedom that can be observed in these data. In the Judeo-Christian political tradition, the separation of church and state power evolved over time. However, this cultural aspect of distinct church and state power does not exist in many countries today. The interesting thing about this is that, often, authoritarian power is wrapped up with religious power.

Illustrating this point, Figure 3 uses data from the World Values Survey to examine the importance of religious faith. The data are grouped into quartiles (four groups) based on whether a strong religious faith is an important quality to instill in a child. The figure indicates that there is a distinctive trend toward instilling a strong faith in countries with the least amount of religious freedom. On average, 55 percent of adults in the least religiously free countries felt that religious faith in a child was important, while only a quarter of adults in countries with the most religious freedom thought that way. This indicates that countries without religious freedom tend to be places where a religious majority dominates and controls state power.

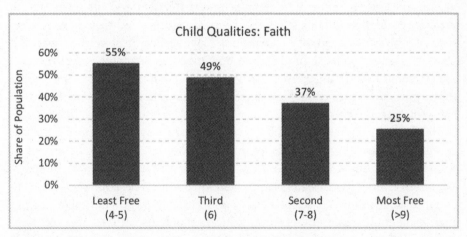

Figure 3: Religious Freedom and Whether Religious Faith Is Important for a Child

The regions of the world that lack religious freedom are also regions of the world that lack economic and political freedom. Returning to the ideas of

---

[25] This *New York Times* article discusses Andrew Brunson's release from Turkey: https://www.nytimes.com/2018/10/12/world/europe/turkey-us-pastor-andrew-brunson.html.

Hayek and Tocqueville helps to illustrate why this is the case. Economic freedom depends upon a robust civil society. And a robust civil society depends upon free association of individuals and religious groups. The graphs and figures in the following section help illustrate this point.

Religious Freedom and Civil Society

The foundation of a free and flourishing society rests upon the voluntary interaction of individuals, families, churches, and communities. Data contained in the World Values Survey now allows us to examine the formation of these groups in countries throughout the world.

The World Values Survey is a survey started by social science researchers to measure different aspects of the values of individuals in countries throughout the world. These surveys were conducted in waves, beginning with several countries in the early 1980s and expanding thereafter.

Currently, six waves of the study have been conducted, and the seventh is underway. Included in these surveys are questions relating to one's participation in a variety of social groups. The following figures use these data in order to examine the relationship between religious freedom and the formation of various types of social and religious groups. Keep in mind that these data on social groups are an important barometer of the health of civil society. Put another way, they offer a glimpse into how much spontaneous order exists in societies that have religious freedom. At first blush, it might not appear that a sports group or an art group have much to do with religious freedom. However, many of these groups are formed out of church communities. Whether it is youth football, basketball, baseball, volleyball, or any other sport, religious communities are always intimately involved. And let's not forget those of us who are older but still young enough at heart that we participate in sports leagues in church gymnasiums before and after work. The same connection to religious communities permeates arts and crafts groups, charitable groups, environmental groups, professional groups, and many others. In short, one does not have to look far in order to see the rich involvement of religious people in these voluntary aspects of civil society.

Before looking at specific social groups, Figure 4 starts by examining the overall participation in social groups based on religious freedom. As in Figure 3, countries are divided into quartiles of religious freedom. For these graphs, the Pew government hostilities data is used as the measure of religious freedom. The groups included in this figure are church, sports, art, labor, political-party affiliated, environmental, professional, charity, and others. Using these data, we

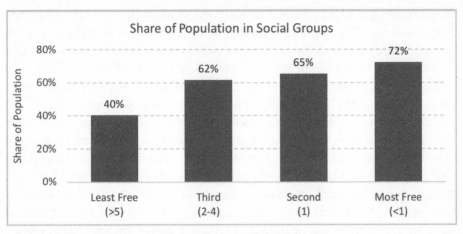

Figure 4: Religious Freedom and Participation in All Social Groups

see a clear pattern emerge. In the least religiously free countries, 40 percent of the people surveyed participated in social groups, which means that 60 percent of the people in that country did not participate in any social groups. Compare that to the individuals in the most religiously free countries. They had a 72 percent participation rate in social groups. Comparing the two extremes indicates that while 60 percent of people are socially detached in the least religiously free countries only 28 percent were in the most free countries. The progression of all four quartile groups in the figure makes it clear that the more religious freedom in a country, the higher the participation in social groups.

This same pattern emerges when each of the group categories are examined individually. Figure 5 presents the data on participation in church groups (e.g.,

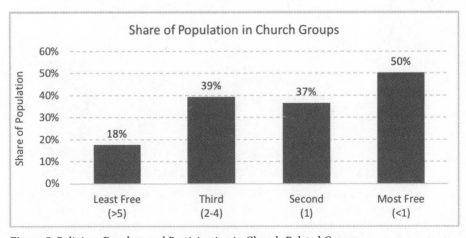

Figure 5: Religious Freedom and Participation in Church-Related Groups

Bible studies and small groups) and religious freedom. In the most religiously free countries, 50 percent of respondents indicated that they participate in groups relating to their church. Respondents living in the least religiously free countries had an 18 percent participation rate in church-related activities. Two aspects of this graph are interesting. First, this graph is very supportive of the ideas of Tocqueville and Hayek. When people are free to make their own choices, they will spontaneously form into groups. Here, we see free people with a desire to form church-based groups. Second, this figure stands in stark contrast to Figure 3. Using data from the same individuals, Figure 3 illustrates that religiously authoritarian governments value instilling a religious faith in their children. The implication of Figures 3 and 5 together is that an imposed faith appears to be weak, because the children (whose parents want to instill faith in them) grow up to have very little involvement in church-related activities.

Alexis de Tocqueville also marveled at the willingness of people in American society to come together in charitable activity. To this day, this remains a hallmark of U.S. culture. When it comes to private charitable giving and activity, the United States dwarfs all other countries. No other country comes close to matching the charitable instinct of the United States. Figure 6 indicates that this is also associated with a religiously free society. These figures do not include charitable giving; they merely measure the participation of an individual in charitable groups. Not surprisingly, the trend observed earlier remains: people living in religiously free countries have higher levels of

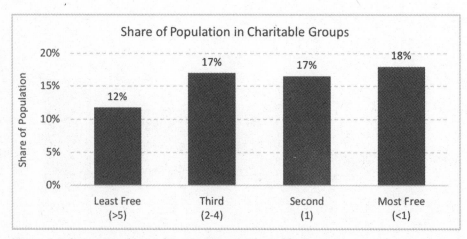

Figure 6: Religious Freedom and Participation in Charitable Groups

participation in charitable groups than those living in less religiously free countries.

Figures 7–10 examine several of the other subgroups in the "social group" category. In each case, we observe the same pattern: countries with a greater degree of religious freedom have more participation in sports, the arts, professional groups and societies, and political parties. More rigorous regression analysis using these data yields results that are consistent with Figures 1–10. Using the Pew social hostility data and controlling for age, gender, employment status, marital status, and a host of other personal characteristics, people living

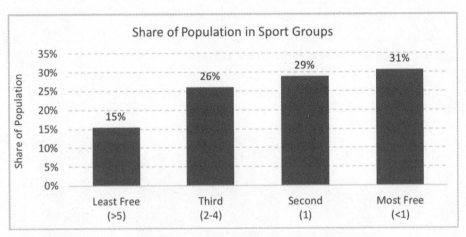

Figure 7: Religious Freedom and Participation in All Social Groups

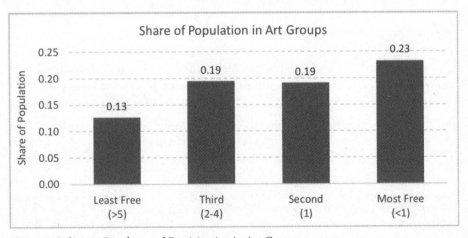

Figure 8: Religious Freedom and Participation in Art Groups

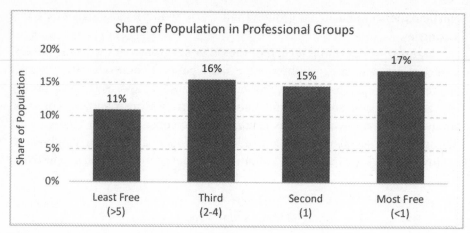

Figure 9: Religious Freedom and Participation in Professional Groups

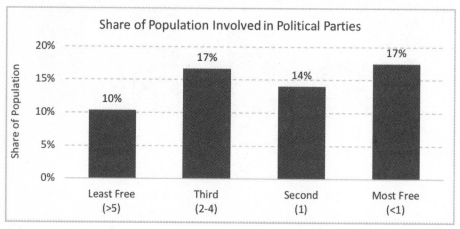

Figure 10: Religious Freedom and Participation in Political Parties

in less religiously free countries had significantly fewer years of schooling.[26] Regressions using the social group data in Figures 4–10 found these relationships to be statistically significant with regard to religious freedom. For example, between a low- and high-religious-freedom country, there was a 16-percentage-point statistical difference in participation in all social groups. The difference was 23 percentage points for participation in church groups,

---

[26] In regressions using the Pew social hostility data, the World Values Survey data, and ethnolinguistic fractionalization data, the average years of schooling in a country rises by 1.5 years when comparing the most to the least religiously free countries. This result was significant at the 1-percent level. Source for ethnolinguistic fractionalization data: K. Desmet, I. Ortuño-Ortin, and R. Wacziarg, "The Political Economy of Ethnolinguistic Cleavages," NBER Working Paper #15360, September 2009.

28 percentage points in charitable groups, and 21 percentage points in labor organizations.[27] These are the very groups that form the backbone of civil society. Still more regressions, examining measures of life satisfaction and life control, yielded similar results. People actively involved in the various social groups of civil society reported significantly higher levels of life satisfaction and a sense of control over their lives.[28]

These data directly measure the active participation of a society in social life. A healthy civil society has always been the foundation of a free and flourishing society. It is the reason Communists target those who can most influence this aspect of a society; under Lenin and Stalin, for example, priests, teachers, intellectuals, musicians, and artists were rounded up and imprisoned. It is also the reason Jews became scapegoats in Nazi Germany. Those who exert an influence over civil society are always targeted by authoritarian regimes. Thus, the ability of civil society to keep governmental power confined to its proper sphere is paramount. And religious freedom is an essential ingredient for a flourishing civil society.

Conclusion

There are two aspects of religious freedom that are important to the history of liberty and human freedom. The first is the disentangling of church power and government power. For most of human history, these two powers resided in the same body or person. Whether it was the pharaohs of Egypt, the kings of Israel, the caesars of Rome, the caliphs of the Middle Eastern kingdoms, or the kings and queens of Europe, each ruler who claimed both political and religious power tended to restrict the free exercise of both. However, over time, in the Western tradition, there grew a delineation between the exercise of church power and government power. With this delineation arose the second important aspect of religious freedom—namely, an increase in political, economic, and religious freedom. Much research has already examined the benefits and impact of political and economic freedom; however, the essential role that religious freedom plays has been overlooked. The glue of economic and political freedom is the civil society in which they are embedded. The foundation of a flourishing civil society is the free association of people from all walks of life. Religious freedom is a fundamental aspect of human freedom and civil society.

---

[27] These regressions used the IPD religious freedom data in addition to the other datasets.
[28] This analysis used the IPD data and the World Values Survey data and found a statistically significant higher level of life satisfaction for those living in religiously free countries.

This aspect of religious freedom is easiest to observe by examining the diversity of institutions around the world. In doing this, we observe that free people engage in the spontaneous order that Tocqueville and Hayek wrote about. They form a variety of voluntary groups and professional organizations, and foremost among these are religious and charitable groups. In countries that limit religious freedom, we observe lower participation in all of the social groups that make up a healthy civil society. People, on average, achieve lower levels of schooling, and people left out of social groups are generally less happy and feel they have less control over their lives. Thus, these data help to illustrate the important role that religious freedom plays in maintaining a flourishing civil society and an economically and politically free people.

In this capacity, religious freedom serves as a bulwark against the authoritarian and coercive powers of government. It is no coincidence that the maps in this chapter show a positive association between authoritarianism and a lack of religious freedom. When free people form groups to solve local problems and deal with issues, this obviates the need for intrusive government power. However, where civil society is absent, all problems become political, and, thus, all problems become government problems to solve. Religious freedom is not a freedom that is less necessary than economic or political freedom. The three are intertwined and the three are foundational. A free and flourishing society is sustained, supported, and protected by a free people who are allowed to worship and live their vocation in the public sphere.

Why Is Religious Freedom at Risk in Today's Culture and What Can Be Done about It?

Chapter 9

Preserving Religious Freedom, Pursuing the Common Good

Jennifer Marshall Patterson

Senior Visiting Fellow, Institute for Family, Community, and Opportunity, the Heritage Foundation

Following the U.S. Supreme Court's 2015 decision requiring government recognition of same-sex marriage, religious believers in wedding-related industries, like bakers, florists, and photographers, increasingly faced challenges related to their convictions about marriage.

The most well-known of these stories, to date, is the 2018 Supreme Court case involving a Colorado baker named Jack Phillips. Jack's shop is called *Masterpiece* Cakeshop, not only because of the excellent artistry he strives to give each custom-made cake but also because of his conviction to serve one Lord and master, Jesus Christ, in his work.

He's happy to serve all customers but cannot express all messages, so he declined to create a custom cake celebrating a same-sex marriage. The state's civil rights commission charged him with discrimination on the basis of sexual orientation, and the case went all the way to the Supreme Court.

In June 2018, the court issued an opinion protecting Jack's freedom and rejecting the civil rights commission's argument that he had been motivated by wrongful discrimination. Despite that victory at the U.S. Supreme Court, a new charge was brought against Jack for declining a request for another custom cake—this time, it was to be blue on the inside and pink on the outside to celebrate a gender transition. Before the year was over, Jack was once again back in court to defend his freedom to pursue his professional calling in a way that was consistent with his faith.

But challenges today are not limited to wedding vendors and creative professionals like Jack. Changing views of the foundational institution of marriage and shifting sexual mores in an increasingly pluralistic culture present a general challenge to those who look to the Bible for guidance about these issues. Points of friction are emerging across professional fields, and these will no doubt increase if new policy on sexual orientation and gender identity—the kind of policy used in the Jack Phillips case—becomes more common.

These conflicts are likely to confront Christians and other religious believers who sincerely seek to integrate their faith in everything they do—whether they work in medicine, counseling, child welfare, law, public service, education, or any other calling. Now is the time to work to prevent such problems; they are not inevitable, and they are not in anyone's best interest.

To address these challenges, we need to recognize the pattern of problems already appearing across numerous professions. Protecting the common good includes protecting the freedom of religious believers to work in their many callings.

Medicine

Expanding government regulation into numerous areas of daily life has created more conflicts of conscience. Over the last decade, this expansion has included new mandates about what health insurance must cover and what services healthcare professionals must provide. Much has been written about the mandate concerning insurance coverage of contraception, which forced Hobby Lobby and the Little Sisters of the Poor all the way to the U.S. Supreme Court. Less well known is a 2016 regulation filed by the U.S. Department of Health and Human Services at the very end of the Obama administration, which redefined "sex" as "gender identity" and required relevant healthcare professionals to provide gender-transition treatments and surgeries. A judge's injunction prevented the policy from going into effect, and in May 2019 the Trump administration announced a rule change to reverse the policy.

Had the rule been enforced, it would have required a surgeon who provides hysterectomies for women suffering from cancer to also perform surgeries on women seeking gender transition. The mandate would have applied regardless of whether the physician had religious or moral objections or whether the doctor simply concluded that removing a healthy and well-functioning organ was not medically indicated. In other words, the policy failed to respect medical professionals' expertise and moral convictions about how best to treat a person experiencing gender dysphoria, coercing their participation in these controversial treatments.

Counseling

A similar example emerged earlier in the field of counseling. Julea Ward was a counseling student at Eastern Michigan University. During an internship, she was asked to counsel someone about a same-sex relationship.

Julea had a conscientious objection to counseling a client about *any* sexual relationship outside of marriage, so she knew this assignment would pose a personal conflict. So she consulted with her supervisor and then, consistent with her course teachings and the ethical rules on resolving values conflicts, referred the client to another counselor before they ever met, as counselors sometimes do in other cases.

Despite her professional handling of the case, the school expelled her, saying that she "imposed her values" on the client.

With the help of the Alliance Defending Freedom, Julea Ward took her case to court. Eventually, a federal appeals court decided in her favor, ruling that "discriminating against the religious views of a student is not a legitimate end of a public school."[1]

Social Services—Adoption and Foster Care

In recent years, policy in several cities and states has forced religious agencies providing foster and adoptive homes to place children with same-sex couples. This began after the redefinition of marriage in Massachusetts law in 2003, which, in conjunction with state policy regarding sexual orientation, forced a Boston organization, Catholic Charities, to violate Catholic teaching in order to obey the law. The group subsequently announced that it would have to end its work in foster care and adoption, after more than a century of such service to children and families in the city. Faith-based child-welfare agencies in other jurisdictions faced similar challenges in the years that followed.

For example, in 2018, the city of Philadelphia announced it would no longer work with Catholic Social Services on foster care. Government is the gatekeeper for groups to participate in the foster care network, so the decision effectively barred the religious agency from further serving children in need.

Ironically, before the city announced it wouldn't work with Catholic Social Services, city officials had just issued a recruiting call for 300 additional families to take in more of the 6,000 children in the city's foster care system. The need had grown especially acute because of the impact of the opioid crisis on the city. In September 2015, more than half of the 16,000 children in Pennsylvania foster care had been removed from their homes because of parents' drug

---

[1] Ward v. Polite (6th Cir. 2012).

abuse. In 2016, Philadelphia County had the second highest death rate due to drug overdose among the forty-four largest counties in the country.[2]

Catholic Social Services was well-positioned to help drive response to that recruiting appeal. In 2017, the agency had placed more than 250 children in foster families, thanks to a network built over fifty years as it worked with the city of Philadelphia. The agency was rated second out of twenty-nine foster care agencies in the city's own rankings.

With more than 400,000 children in foster care across the country, the need for loving families is great—and attrition among parents who start the process is high. Faith-based networks offer the support families need to persevere through a system fraught with frustration and often heartache, so that the families, in turn, can provide the security and stability their foster children desperately need.

Same-sex couples in Philadelphia are free to foster or adopt children through many agencies. Catholic Social Services had never gotten a complaint from a same-sex couple. In spite of that, city officials' actions signaled intolerance because of the group's religious convictions concerning marriage and family. Needy children lost out as a result.

Since then, attorneys at Becket Law, a religious-liberty litigation group, have gone to court to maintain the constitutional right to religious liberty for Catholic Social Services in Philadelphia. In addition, faith-based foster care and adoption agencies have faced similar situations in Boston, Washington, DC, San Francisco, and the state of Illinois.

Law

In 2016, the American Bar Association (ABA) adopted a model rule as part of its code of professional conduct for attorneys, which many fear would have a chilling effect on freedom of speech about social or religious perspectives that diverged from majority opinion. UCLA School of Law professor and legal scholar Eugene Volokh described the ABA policy as a speech code for lawyers.[3]

---

[2] Larry Eichel and Meagan Pharis, "Philadelphia's Drug Overdose Death Rate Among Highest in Nation," Pew Charitable Trusts, www.pewtrusts.org/en/research-and-analysis/articles/2018/02/15/philadelphias-drug-overdose-death-rate-among-highest-in-nation.

[3] Eugene Volokh, "A Speech Code for Lawyers: Banning Viewpoints that Express 'Bias,' Including in Law Related Social Activities," *The Washington Post*, August 10, 2016, www.washingtonpost.com/news/volokh-conspiracy/wp/2016/08/10/a-speech-code-for-lawyers-banning-viewpoints-that-express-bias-including-in-law-related-social-activities-2/?utm_term=.8a5274dc2f00.

The model rule says it is professional misconduct to discriminate on the basis of race, sex, religion, and a number of other characteristics, including sexual orientation and gender identity. The trouble is that it includes "verbal conduct"—in other words, speech—and extends beyond what an attorney does in the course of representing a client, to include a wide scope of activities like "participating in bar association, business or social activities in connection with the practice of law."[4] This broad range means the rule could apply, for example, to casual conversation at a reception of a legal professional group. It could include comments a lawyer makes in his or her capacity as a board member of a religious organization. What concerns leading legal scholars analyzing the rule is how it might be applied to viewpoints about contested issues like same-sex marriage or bathroom policy that, given the ever-changing standards of political correctness, someone might characterize as "discriminatory."

Violating the rule could result in being publicly reprimanded or suspended by the state bar association, or even losing one's bar license. The bottom line is that it would have a chilling effect on attorneys' freedom to speak their minds about contested issues.

The ABA has called on state supreme courts to follow suit in adopting its model rule. To date, only the State of Vermont has such a broad policy in place. The Christian Legal Society and many others have weighed in to oppose the policy, and they have urged members to monitor the issue closely in each state.[5]

More recently, religious views have figured in the confirmation hearings, before the U.S. Senate Judiciary Committee, of a string of nominees to serve as judges in federal courts. Despite the Constitution's prohibition of religious tests for officeholders in the United States, senators have harangued nominees about their religious beliefs and affiliations. In 2017, Senator Dianne Feinstein (D-CA) declared disparagingly of nominee Amy Coney Barrett's Catholic faith that the "dogma lives loudly in you." The implication of her remarks was that serious religious faith is incompatible with judicial service.

Late in 2018, Senator Mazie Hirono (D-HI) sent federal district court nominee Brian Buescher a questionnaire asking about the likelihood of his impartiality as a judge given his affiliation with a Catholic service organization, the Knights of Columbus. "The Knights of Columbus has taken a number of

---

[4] American Bar Association Model Rule 8.4(g), comment 4, https://www.americanbar.org/groups/professional_responsibility/publications/model_rules_of_professional_conduct/rule_8_4_misconduct/comment_on_rule_8_4/.

[5] Christian Legal Society, "The Pitfalls in the New ABA Model Rule 8.4(g)," February 2017, accessed July 24, 2019, www.clsnet.org/document.doc?id=996.

extreme positions," wrote Senator Hirono. "For example, it was reportedly one of the top contributors to California's Proposition 8 campaign to ban same-sex marriage."[6] Proposition 8 was a question on the 2008 ballot in California asking voters whether marriage should be defined as one man and one woman in the state constitution. More than 52 percent of voters affirmed the historic understanding of marriage. Ten years later, some seek to make anathema an affiliation with an organization whose views aligned with the majority of Californians just a decade ago. But most serious was Senator Hirono's suggestion that a judge should have to disavow affiliation with a religious group.

February 2019 brought another such instance when Senator Cory Booker (D-NJ) grilled Neomi Rao, a nominee for the vacancy left on the DC Circuit Court of Appeals when Justice Brett Kavanaugh was confirmed to serve on the U.S. Supreme Court. The object of Senator Booker's interrogation was Rao's views on whether same-sex relationships "are a sin." As his fellow committee member Senator Ted Cruz (R-TX) subsequently noted, the Senate Judiciary Committee is not a "theological court of inquisition," and the U.S. Constitution does not permit religious tests for office.[7]

Public Service

In 2015, Kelvin Cochran, fire chief of the City of Atlanta, was terminated for having written a men's devotional book on his own time, which included a few sentences about a biblical view of marriage and sexuality.

Chief Cochran was highly successful in his field—President Obama had named him to the post of fire administrator of the United States before the mayor of Atlanta recruited him back to his city. Chief Cochran is an African American who, early in his career, overcame discriminatory conditions and made it his practice to treat everyone with respect.

After several years in court, Chief Cochran's case was finally resolved in 2018. A federal district court determined that city policy was unconstitutional in allowing city officials to restrict nonwork speech with which they disagreed.

---

[6] Andrew O'Reilly, "Dems Challenge Trump Judicial Nominee over Knights of Columbus Membership," *Fox News,* December 24 2018, https://www.foxnews.com/politics/harris-and-hirono-question-federal-judicial-nominee-over-knights-of-columbus-membership.

[7] Tim Hains, "Ted Cruz Slams Cory Booker for 'Theological Inquisition' of Trump Nominee: Democrats Hostile to Faith," *RealClearPolitics,* February 5, 2019, www.realclearpolitics.com/video/2019/02/05/ted_cruz_slams_cory_booker_for_theological_inquisition_of_trump_judicial_nominee.html.

Chief Cochran was ultimately awarded $1.2 million in a settlement with the City of Atlanta.

Education

In early December 2018, a school board in Virginia voted unanimously to fire a teacher who would not go along with an administrator's demand to use masculine pronouns for a female student.

For teacher Peter Vlaming, it was a matter of Christian conviction about biblical anthropology. He believes God creates human beings as male or female. He treated the student with respect and tried not to make an issue by avoiding the use of pronouns and simply referring to the student by name. But when an administrator insisted on the use of the student's preferred masculine pronouns, Mr. Vlaming could not comply, and the school board fired him from his teaching post.

This followed the development in which the Obama administration directed public schools to permit students to use the bathrooms of their preferred gender rather than of their biological sex. In other words, biological males were to be given access to girls' locker rooms and showers.

Rather than allowing local schools to develop solutions, like creating individual-use facilities, the administration forced everyone to adopt a new transgender ideology. Subsequently, the Trump administration rescinded the policy guidance, removing federal pressure—for the time being.

These examples highlight how individuals across a wide variety of fields have experienced coercion to embrace new views about marriage, sexuality, and gender—or face professional peril. This is starkly at odds with the free speech and ideological liberty Americans have historically enjoyed. The coercion is aimed at silencing reasonable debate about highly contested recent premises about sex and gender. It is intolerant of dissent rooted in religious conviction and disregards our heritage of religious liberty.

The negative repercussions of such illiberalism will spread far beyond the religious believers who find themselves in the kinds of situations mentioned here, however. It will have implications for everyone's freedom of speech, privacy and safety, and conscience rights. To avoid these outcomes, we need to recover an understanding of why religious freedom matters and how it is linked to all Americans' freedom generally. This begins with developing a sense of responsibility for preserving and protecting religious freedom in an increasingly pluralistic culture. This is a matter of stewardship for the Christian citizen. It is a way to love and serve our neighbors by treating them with dignity and seeking the common good of the communities in which we live.

Religious Freedom for the Common Good

(1) *Religious freedom goes hand in hand with other freedoms.*

The religious freedom enjoyed in the United States is admired around the world. One of the ways that our country can advance religious freedom abroad is by making sure that this lamp of liberty continues to burn bright for the rest of the world to see.

Some U.S. leaders have, in recent years, referred to "freedom of worship" rather than "religious freedom." That might seem unimportant, but it is actually very significant. The freedom to worship is the freedom to practice religion in one's home or house of worship, privately.

But the free exercise of religion guaranteed by the First Amendment to the Constitution is much broader. The free exercise of religion is the freedom to speak and to act in public on the basis of one's beliefs. It is the freedom to share one's faith and even to invite others to it. Free exercise means that we don't have to leave our faith outside when we enter the schoolhouse or the workplace.

Religious freedom is closely related to freedom of speech. This connection explains why even some supporters of same-sex marriage have called attention to the dangers of compelling creative professionals to use their talents to express views with which they disagree. Peter Tatchell is a British gay-rights activist who supported the freedom of the Christian family operating Ashers bakery in Belfast who, like Jack Phillips, declined to create a cake communicating support for same-sex marriage. When Britain's highest court issued a unanimous decision in favor of the bakers' freedom, Tatchell hailed the verdict as "a victory for freedom of expression." He explained,

> As well as meaning that Ashers cannot be legally forced to aid the promotion of same-sex marriage, it also means that gay bakers cannot be compelled by law to decorate cakes with anti-gay marriage slogans. Businesses can now lawfully refuse a customer's request to emblazon a political message if they have a conscientious objection to it. This includes the right to refuse messages that are sexist, xenophobic or antigay, which is a good thing. Although I profoundly disagree with Ashers opposition to marriage equality, in a free society neither they nor anyone else should be forced to facilitate a political idea that they oppose.[8]

---

[8] Peter Tatchell, "Ashers 'Gay Cake' Verdict is a Victory for Freedom of Expression," Peter Tatchell Foundation, October 10, 2018, https://www.petertatchellfoundation.org/ashers-gay-cake-verdict-is-victory-for-freedom-of-expression/.

Freedom of speech and religious freedom are fundamental liberties guaranteed by our U.S. Constitution . . . for all—majority and minority. By definition, most people will *not* agree with a minority viewpoint. But that doesn't mean that government should be able to force people with a minority view to express the majority viewpoint—or to be silent. In too many cases, that has been the choice government has presented religious believers.

(2) *We need religious freedom to be able to reason together.*

Reasoning together is one of the most important ways that we acknowledge and respect each other's dignity. But the kinds of challenges to religious liberty we've seen in the United States in recent years are shutting down our ability to reason together about the common good. Religiously informed speech and action have been and should remain an important aspect of that deliberative process in American society. All citizens bring along beliefs about the good when they engage in conversations about public issues. For many Americans, those views are shaped by their religious convictions. Others' outlooks are informed by philosophical and moral ideas that are not explicitly religious. Whether religious or philosophical, these foundational perspectives expressed in speech and action are and ought to remain a part of public life in a free society.

Consider how this has played out in the course of the marriage debate: throughout history, societies have understood that it takes a man and a woman to bring a child into the world and that children need a mom and a dad. The institution of marriage was set apart in law as the unique relationship that recognized these realities about human existence.

It was only in 2015 that the Supreme Court refused to acknowledge that historic understanding as a reasonable argument, mandating that all states issue marriage licenses to same-sex couples. How quickly things have changed. Now we're having to defend the freedom *even to speak and to act* consistently with the conviction that marriage is the union of a man and a woman. We're having to protect the freedom to live by the conviction that there is a difference between a mom and a dad and that children need both. We're having to stand up for the freedom to recognize that sex is a biological reality that does not change.

Even in the years leading up to the Supreme Court's 2015 same-sex marriage decision in *Obergefell*, it was alarming to see the hostility toward those holding historic beliefs about marriage simply because they took part in public dialogue. Two examples serve to illustrate this. In 2012, Angela McCaskill, associate provost for diversity and inclusion at Gallaudet University for the deaf in Washington, DC, was put on administrative leave. What was her offense? She had merely signed a petition, along with 200,000 other people, to put a referendum on the Maryland ballot so that citizens could vote on a same-sex marriage law passed by the state legislature. Simply participating in the political process was enough to cause such treatment of Dr. McCaskill, who was the first black, deaf woman to earn a PhD from Gallaudet and was a twenty-year veteran of the staff.

Similarly, Brendan Eich was ousted from his post as CEO of Mozilla (the company behind Firefox) in 2014. His transgression was a donation six years earlier to the Prop 8 campaign to define marriage as the union of a man and a woman in the California state constitution. Events like these, in which individuals who were simply participating in the political process were professionally punished for it, have a chilling effect on other people's willingness to stand up for what they believe.

Earlier still, in 2011, was a turning point, which had to do with the legal representation of the traditional view of marriage, which was at the time being challenged in court. Attorney Paul Clement was representing members of the U.S. House of Representatives to defend the 1996 congressional statute defining marriage in federal law as being between one man and one woman. When the law, known as the Defense of Marriage Act (DOMA), was challenged in federal court, the law firm of King & Spalding, at which Clement was a partner, had agreed to defend the law. Following protests, however, the firm announced in the spring of 2011 that it was dropping the case. In order to continue defending his client, Clement was forced to resign and join a new law firm, Bancroft LLC. As he wrote in his letter of resignation, "I resign out of the firmly held belief that a representation should not be abandoned because the client's legal position is extremely unpopular in certain quarters."[9]

Of course, the law firm was—just as other businesses and other private organizations are—legally free to take such action. But that does not make it the right thing to do to advance the common good. As citizens, we need to engage each other in reasoned debate as we seek to pursue the good of society. This also means that we should expect and call on others—even those who oppose us—to use reason, and not coercion or intimidation, to make their points. Coercion and intimidation seek to silence rather than to settle debate.

(3)   Concern for those in need is reason to care about religious freedom.

For countless Christian ministries serving the poor, providing food and shelter to the homeless, mentoring children, and restoring neighborhoods, their good

---

[9] John Hudson, "After Law Firm Quits DOMA Case, Partner Resigns in Protest," *The Atlantic*, April 25, 2011, https://www.theatlantic.com/politics/archive/2011/04/law-firm-withdraws-doma-case-senior-partner-resigns/349967/.

works and their faith go hand in hand. Those seeking to help people overcome drug addiction emphasize that they rely on the transforming power of prayer and Scripture in their work. Those who serve in faith-based outreach to prisoners point to God's work to set men and women spiritually free even as they remain behind bars. The Christian worldview lived out in these ministries defines who these groups are and what they do.

But new policies are being proposed that would undermine that religious identity. These policies would not allow those ministries that seek social justice by serving people at risk to live according to their biblical understanding of the truth about marriage and sexuality. That's not tolerance. And it will end up hurting those in need.

A situation in 2018 at the Downtown Hope Center in Anchorage, Alaska, shows how this can happen. For over thirty years, the Hope Center has offered homeless men and women free food and laundry service and job training. It also provides women—many who are victims of abuse and trafficking—with an overnight shelter. The Hope Center is a nonprofit Christian ministry "inspired by the love of Jesus."

In January 2018, a biological male presenting himself as a female sought to enter the women's shelter. He was injured and drunk. The Hope Center paid for a cab to take him to a local hospital rather than admit him to the shelter, where changing rooms, showers, and sleeping quarters were restricted to provide a safe place for women. A complaint against the Hope Center was subsequently filed with the Anchorage Equal Rights Commission. As a result, the ministry has had to go to court to defend its freedom to serve battered women in a way that is consistent with its mission.

When intolerance lashes out at religious ministries like the Hope Center, it hurts the most vulnerable. Concern for fighting poverty and helping victims of abuse should give us all reason to stand for religious liberty. Religious freedom matters for the needs of our neighbors and for the common good of the communities in which we live.

(4)   Religious freedom is about true tolerance for diversity. It's a way for us to treat each other with dignity and respect in spite of our differences.

The mere fact of one's own existence presents each human being with questions of ultimate significance. We must be free to pursue answers to those deepest questions and to live by the answers that we find. That's what religious freedom is all about. The fact that these fundamental questions confront every human being shows why religious freedom is not a special-interest demand but an essential freedom for all.

One of the most important ways that we can treat each other with dignity and respect, despite our deep differences, is through religious freedom. Religious freedom is about true tolerance for diversity, in view of the existential reality we all face and the ultimate questions that confront everyone. As citizens, we need to engage each other reasonably as we seek to pursue the common good. Incivility denies the dignity of those directly involved and the surrounding community.

Christians should continue to speak and to act and to reason in ways consistent with biblical truth about marriage and sexuality. Reasoning together does not require erasing disagreements. Instead, it involves the commitment to find ways to live together despite our deep differences.

What Can Be Done?

The public controversy over these issues can give the impression that we live in a hopelessly divided society with incompatible differences. That's wrong. We should continue to seek sound policy that advances the common good for all without forcing religious citizens to seek exemptions in order to preserve their fundamental freedoms. When conflicts arise, we have constitutional and policy-based tools to navigate public life together, despite our deep differences. The broad balancing test of the Religious Freedom Restoration Act, a law enacted a quarter of a century ago, remains an important foundation in law that has preserved liberty, particularly in instances of challenges to minority religious practice. Meanwhile, more specific policy tools have been proposed to address the kinds of emerging conflicts mentioned above.

Policy Tools

The first policy response must be to seek laws that advance the common good and resist bad policy that forces citizens to seek exemptions to preserve fundamental freedoms. Policymakers should pursue sound policy in health care, education, and family, and in the broad range of other issues that shape society. When healthcare reform created problems for the Little Sisters of the Poor—as Obamacare did in requiring nearly all insurance plans to include contraceptive coverage—it was clear something was wrong with the underlying statute. Good law takes religious freedom and freedom of speech into account from the outset.

The Religious Freedom Restoration Act (RFRA) is a law that helps to balance competing concerns in our pluralistic society. When conflicts emerge between government policy and religious belief, RFRA enables those competing interests to be weighed in court according to clear criteria. That explains why it passed Congress nearly unanimously and was signed by President Clinton in 1993 with the support of a broad coalition that included organizations from the Southern Baptists to the ACLU. The House bill was introduced by then-Rep. Chuck Schumer (D-NY).

Sadly, today some of those original supporters want to argue that RFRA does not apply to dissenting views with respect to sexual orientation/gender identity (SOGI) nondiscrimination. For example, the Equality Act (discussed below) proposed by some in Congress would explicitly trump RFRA. With respect to the new SOGI policy that the Equality Act would establish, RFRA could not be used as a defense in the event of conflicts with religious liberty. But protecting religious individuals and groups from coercion takes nothing away from anyone. It simply recognizes their freedom to live in a way that is consistent with their convictions.

In addition to RFRA, specific policy mechanisms responding to emerging challenges have been developed and enacted in several states. The First Amendment Defense Act represents one such approach. This is a bill proposed in Congress—and similar state policy has been developed—that would prohibit government from discriminating against those who believe that marriage is the union of a man and a woman. For example, the federal government could not deny tax-exempt status to a group if it happens to disagree with the government's policy on marriage. This protection should also be extended to disagreements concerning gender identity.

A similar policy tool is the Child Welfare Provider Inclusion Act. The Inclusion Act would protect religious foster care and adoption agencies from state discrimination because of their convictions about placing children with a mom and a dad. The policy has been proposed at the federal level, and several states have enacted something similar.

A number of other specific policy protections can and should be pursued to help us navigate these challenging issues. For example, no medical professional should be forced to participate in gender-transition treatments in violation of his or her conscience. No one who believes that human beings are created by God as male and female should be coerced to use a pronoun that is inconsistent with biological reality. Christians and other concerned citizens should be a part of seeking out the facts about existing policy and legal accommodations, and they should pursue new proposals that can help resolve the tensions. We should seek to secure the comprehensive common good, of which religious freedom is an essential component.

For the Common Good

To safeguard religious freedom in this way is not a special pleading for religious individuals and groups; nor does it take anything away from anyone. Indeed, the protections mentioned above should also cover those who, for nonreligious reasons, share a moral understanding about the nature of marriage and sex as a biological reality.

After all, religious freedom is just one aspect of the common good. Christians and other religious believers should be concerned about the safety, privacy, and equality of women and girls threatened by new gender-identity policy that has allowed biological males into women's restrooms and girls' sports competitions. Religious individuals should defend medical professionals—whether or not they are religious—whose consciences are violated by mandates to participate in gender-transition treatments that they do not believe best serve their patients. Believers must also stand with parents whose commitment and responsibility to care for their minor children suffering from gender dysphoria are abrogated by new policies that could cut them out of radical treatment decisions. Advocates of religious freedom must be committed to these aspects of the common good as well.

These challenges to religious freedom, the safety and equality of women, medical-conscience rights, and parental rights are coming, in particular, from SOGI policies that have been adopted in a number of states and cities. Such policies elevate SOGI to the status of a protected class in law. Nondiscrimination policies should be "shields, not swords," as author and Heritage Foundation scholar Ryan Anderson has helpfully put it.[10] Nondiscrimination policy of the civil rights era was used in just that way—as a shield against systemic injustice. But today's SOGI nondiscrimination policies have been used as swords: as tools of coercion against those who happen to dissent. Or, as LGBT activist Tim Gill has put it, "to punish the wicked."[11]

So far, SOGI policies are in a patchwork of states and cities, but advocates want to extend these policies nationwide through federal legislation. They've proposed the Equality Act, which would add sexual orientation and gender identity to the list of protected characteristics, like race, under federal law. As seen from the kinds of conflicts just named, such a law would be used to stamp out disagreement on issues related to marriage, sexuality, and gender. It would

---

[10] Ryan T. Anderson, "Shields, Not Swords," *National Affairs*, Spring 2018, https://nationalaffairs.com/publications/detail/shields-not-swords.

[11] Andy Kroll, "Meet the Megadonor behind the LGBTQ Rights Movement," *Rolling Stone*, June 23, 2017, https://www.rollingstone.com/politics/politics-features/meet-the-megadonor-behind-the-lgbtq-rights-movement-193996.

coerce Americans to embrace transgender policies for bathroom access, pronoun use, and health care—among many other areas.

Advocates of SOGI policies claim they are necessary because of discrimination against those who identify as LGBT. But—as seen in the examples earlier in this chapter—the charge is made in many instances against those who, because of sincere convictions, simply *disagree* with evolving government policies and cultural trends on these matters.

"Disagreement is not always discrimination," writes Anderson.[12] Even President Obama, when he publicly endorsed same-sex marriage in 2012, acknowledged that there are people of good will on both sides of the debate. Justice Anthony Kennedy made a similar statement even as he drafted the majority opinion for the Supreme Court decision in *Obergefell v. Hodges* on same-sex-marriage. But SOGI laws regard legitimate dissent as discrimination.

Another variation on SOGI proposals would establish policy and then try to mitigate it through exceptions. In this version, some have proposed SOGI laws with religious exemptions and labeled the combined policy Fairness for All. The Fairness for All proposal would create SOGI policies and then carve out exemptions for some religious groups, but they would do nothing to protect the privacy of public schoolchildren in showers and locker rooms or doctors with conscience objections to performing gender-reassignment surgeries. Setting bad policy and then creating exemptions from it for some is no way to pursue the common good or love our neighbors. This is not "fairness for all."

An important test of any proposed policy should be whether it would preserve Americans' freedom to speak and act consistently with their religious convictions and to express reasonable differences about matters related to marriage, sexuality, and gender. Any new policy proposals should protect, for example, the privacy of schoolgirls, the conscience rights of healthcare workers, and freedom of speech for Americans in all kinds of public contexts. Protecting these concerns and preserving religious liberty is essential for protecting the common good.

Cultural Engagement

The effort to protect religious liberty and promote the common good must go well beyond public policy. Today's religious liberty challenges require clearer

---

[12] Ryan T. Anderson, "Disagreement Is Not Always Discrimination: On Masterpiece Cakeshop and the Analogy to Interracial Marriage," *The Georgetown Journal of Law & Public Policy*, 16 (2018): 123–45, www.law.georgetown.edu/public-policy-journal/wp-content/uploads/sites/23/2018/05/16-1-Disagreement-Is-Not-Always-Discrimination.pdf.

articulation of how faith transforms individuals and communities and why we should protect the freedom to exercise that faith for the good of society as a whole. Religious freedom is not a special pleading on behalf of an interest group; it is the condition necessary for all humans to pursue answers to the ultimate questions presented by our very existence and the world around us, and to speak and act according to our convictions. It is a critical aspect of the common good.

Ultimately, religious liberty is about the freedom to tell the story of how God has made human beings to flourish in relation to Him. And it's the freedom to pursue service to that end, for the good of our neighbor.

One of the most pressing tasks before Christians in the twenty-first century is to articulate how faith transforms individuals and communities and why we should protect the freedom to exercise that faith for the good of society as a whole. Innovative individuals across many professions can help restore a cultural understanding of what it means to be made in the image of God, male and female, and made for each other, both in community and through marriage.

Conclusion

Professional challenges like the ones named above are likely to confront those who confess biblical views of marriage and sexuality and gender at odds with new cultural trends. Now is the time to prepare and to work to face them. That will require a sense of responsibility for preserving religious liberty, as a matter of stewardship and of commitment to the common good of all.

We have a wonderful heritage of religious freedom in America . . . and that may have led us to take it for granted. It's time for us to take personal responsibility for preserving and protecting what we have been given.

Standing up for religious freedom and testifying to the truth about marriage, sexuality, and gender will determine the freedom to speak and act consistently with biblical convictions in the future. It's a matter of stewardship, serving our neighbors, pursuing the common good, and ultimately, about loving God.

Chapter 10

Religious Accommodations and the Common Good

Mark David Hall
Professor of Politics, George Fox University

The United States has a long history of accommodating citizens who find their religious convictions at odds with government laws, regulations, and mandates. Starting in the colonial era, legislators, statesmen, and jurists have crafted accommodations to protect people of faith from neutral, generally applicable laws that nevertheless burden the free exercise of religion, even in such areas of extreme importance as national defense, education, drug use, health care, and civil rights.

The explosive growth of government at both the state and national levels in the twentieth century has made accommodations even more important for protecting religious citizens. Because religious liberty has been highly valued by both Democrats and Republicans, legislatures have routinely crafted accommodations to protect religious individuals. By one count from the early 1990s, there were approximately two thousand federal or state laws that accommodated religious citizens.[1]

In virtually all of these cases, there is little evidence that such accommodations create significant harm to other individuals or keep either states or the nation from meeting policy objectives. America's laudable history of protecting religious citizens from otherwise valid laws makes it clear not only that protecting "the sacred rights of conscience" and promoting the common good possible, but also that religious accommodations *themselves* promote the common good.

Why Accommodations?

Virtually every civic leader in the American Founding agreed that governments, in the words of James Madison, should not compel "men to worship

---

[1] James E. Ryan, "Smith and the Religious Freedom Restoration Act: An Iconoclastic Assessment," *Virginia Law Review* 78 (September 1992): 1445.

God in any manner contrary to their conscience."[2] By the late twentieth century, it was a rare legislative body that would even consider explicitly dictating or banning a religious practice.

In one of these extraordinary cases, the town of Hialeah, Florida, banned the slaughter of animals in religious ceremonies but not for other purposes. Members of the Church of Santeria, whose religious practices include animal sacrifices, were prosecuted under this statute. In 1993, the Supreme Court of the United States held unanimously that the law violated the free exercise clause of the First Amendment.[3]

For at least the past sixty years, the chief threats to religious liberty in America have come from general laws or policies aimed at advancing the common good, which unintentionally burden religious actors. These statutes rarely mention specific religions or religious practices, but they nonetheless prevent some citizens from acting on their religious convictions (or make it very costly for them to do so).

For example, a state may determine that beards can be used to conceal contraband or help prisoners escape and so ban inmates from growing them. Yet this neutral, generally applicable rule would keep Muslim prisoners, whose faith requires them to grow beards, from following the dictates of their religion. What should be done? One possibility would be to abolish the regulation altogether, but assuming that the policy advances its intended goals, such a solution detracts from the common good. Alternatively, the religious convictions of Muslim prisoners could simply be ignored.

At their best, Americans have opted for a third way. In this situation, many states voluntarily create accommodations to allow prisoners to grow very short beards, if required to do so by their faith.[4] Arkansas did not, but the U.S. Supreme Court ruled unanimously that Congress's Religious Land Use and

---

[2] Daniel L. Dreisbach and Mark David Hall, ed. *The Sacred Rights of Conscience: Selected Readings on Religious Liberty and Church-State Relations in the American Founding* (Indianapolis: Liberty Fund Press, 2009), 427.

[3] Justice Kennedy did note in his majority opinion that a law banning a religious practice would be constitutional if "it is justified by a compelling interest and is narrowly tailored to advance that interest." See *Church of the Lukumi Babalu Aye, Inc. v. Hialeah*, 508 U.S. 520, 533 (1993). It is difficult to find contemporary examples of such a statute, although one possibility might be Kentucky's law against handling "any kind of reptile in connection with any religious service." Revised Statutes of Kentucky, 437.060.

[4] Brief for the United States as *amicus curiae* supporting petitioner in *Holt v. Hobbes*, May 2014, 28–29.

Institutionalized Persons Act of 2000 required such an outcome.[5] One major purpose of this act, which was passed without objection in both houses of Congress, was to ensure that the religious convictions of prisoners were accommodated whenever possible.

Of course, not all religious practices should be accommodated. Religious liberty is not an absolute trump card that empowers citizens to disregard laws. State and national governments have sometimes refused to protect religious citizens or have even withdrawn protections when they determine that the actions in question are extremely damaging to the common good. In 1878, for instance, the Supreme Court refused to recognize a First Amendment right to engage in polygamy for religious reasons,[6] and in the twentieth century, many states accommodated parents who had religious objections to providing medical treatment for their children and then abolished these accommodations when it became evident that children were dying from illnesses that medical advances had rendered easily treatable.

Ultimately, there is no theoretical answer to the question of which actions dictated by religious convictions should be protected and which should not. This is a practical question to be decided prudentially on a case-by-case basis. In deliberating about any such case, civic leaders and jurists must balance a concern for securing the common good with a mindfulness of the duties that citizens believe they have to God and the importance of allowing them to discharge such duties. Civic friendship would also suggest that religious objectors be accommodated so long as doing so does not imperil the common good.[7]

In the later part of the twentieth century, the Supreme Court developed a framework for thinking through when to accommodate religious objectors to general laws. In 1963, under the leadership of liberal Justice William J. Brennan, the Court adopted the principle that government actions that burden a religious practice must be justified by a compelling state interest.[8] Later, the Court added the requirement that this interest must be pursued in the least restrictive manner possible.

In other words, citizens should not be forced to violate their religious beliefs unless necessary. Whenever possible, an accommodation should be found.

---

[5] Holt v. Hobbes, 574 U.S. ___ (2015).

[6] Reynolds v. United States, 98 U.S. 145 (1878).

[7] On similar grounds, one could argue for the protection of nonreligious convictions that are at odds with the law. Legislatures and courts have become better at doing this, but historically, religion has been specially protected in America.

[8] *Sherbert v. Verner*, 374 U.S. 398 (1963).

Although this test was developed to help jurists interpret the First Amendment's free exercise clause, it is also a useful guide for legislatively crafted accommodations.[9]

When a majority of Supreme Court justices repudiated this test with respect to interpreting the free exercise clause in the 1990 case of *Oregon v. Smith* (involving the use of an illegal drug in religious rituals), Congress enacted the Religious Freedom Restoration Act (RFRA) of 1993 to restore it.[10] It is noteworthy that the bill was passed in the House without a dissenting vote, was approved 97 to 3 by the Senate, and was signed into law by President Bill Clinton.

RFRA stipulates that "Government shall not substantially burden a person's exercise of religion even if the burden results from a rule of general applicability" except "if it demonstrates that application of the burden to the person" is "in furtherance of a compelling governmental interest" and "is the least restrictive means of furthering that compelling governmental interest."[11] The law was meant to apply to all levels of government, but in 1996, the Supreme Court ruled that it could not be applied to the states. In response, twenty-one states have enacted RFRA laws of their own.[12]

Historically, there has been broad consensus that religious citizens should be protected against otherwise valid laws unless the state has a compelling interest. Alas, this consensus may be unraveling. Robert P. George, McCormick Professor of Jurisprudence at Princeton University, observed in 2012 that there

---

[9] There is an extensive scholarly debate over whether America's Founders intended the free exercise clause to require accommodations. See, for instance, Michael W. McConnell, "The Origins and Historical Understanding of Free Exercise of Religion," *Harvard Law Review* 103 (May 1990): 1409–517; Philip A. Hamburger, "A Constitutional Right of Religious Exemption: An Historical Perspective," *George Washington Law Review* 60 (April 1992): 915–48; Ellis M. West, "The Right to Religion-Based Exemptions in Early America: The Case of Conscientious Objectors to Conscription," *Journal of Law and Religion* 10 (June 1993): 367–401; and Douglas Laycock, "The Religious Exemption Debate," *Rutgers Journal of Law & Religion* 11 (Fall 2009): 152–54. I take no position on this debate here.

[10] See *Employment Division, Department of Human Resources of Oregon v. Smith*, 494 U.S. 872 (1990).

[11] Religious Freedom Restoration Act of 1993, accessed December 13, 2018, https://www.govtrack.us/congress/bills/103/hr1308/text.

[12] *City of Boerne v. Flores*, 521 U.S. 507 (1997). Other states have not enacted such laws because, in some cases, courts in these states continue to interpret their state constitutions as requiring strict scrutiny of laws restricting religious activities. For a helpful compilation of state RFRAs, see National Conference of State Legislatures, "State Religious Freedom Restoration Acts," accessed December 14, 2018, http://www.ncsl.org/research/civil-and-criminal-justice/state-rfra-statutes.aspx.

is "a massive assault on religious liberty going on in this country right now."[13] Although most civic leaders and jurists remain committed to religious liberty in the abstract, support for protecting citizens from neutral laws that infringe upon religious convictions has deteriorated.[14]

In the 1990s, Republicans and Democrats were able to come together to protect religious liberty. But since the turn of the century, some jurists, politicians, scholars, and activists have abandoned the founders' commitment to accommodating religious citizens.[15] In the academy, professors such as Marci Hamilton, Brian Leiter, John Corvino, Richard Schragger, and Micah Schwartzman have made well-publicized arguments attacking the logic and substance of accommodations that protect (or should protect) religious citizens from neutral, generally applicable laws.[16] Others have contended that religious accommodations (or at least some of them) violate the establishment clause.[17] The Supreme Court has regularly rejected this argument, and legislators have seldom found it persuasive.[18]

---

[13] Quoted in Brian Tashman, "Robert George Warns of Obama's 'Massive Assault on Religious Liberty,'" People for the American Way, Right Wing Watch, February 15, 2012, accessed December 13, 2018, http://www.rightwingwatch.org/content/robert-george-warns-obamas-massive-assault-religious-liberty.

[14] See American Civil Liberties Union, "Using Religion to Discriminate," accessed December 13, 2018, https://www.aclu.org/feature/using-religion-discriminate, and Americans United for Separation of Church and State, "Protect Thy Neighbor," accessed December 13, 2018, http://www.protectthyneighbor.org/.

[15] I discuss the founders' view of religious liberty and the contemporary rejection of their views in greater detail in *Did America Have a Christian Founding?: Separating Modern Myth from Historical Fact* (Nashville: Thomas Nelson, 2019).

[16] Marci Hamilton, *God vs. the Gavel: Religion and the Rule of Law*, 2nd rev. ed. (New York: Cambridge University Press, 2015); Brian Leiter, *Why Tolerate Religion?* (Princeton: Princeton University Press, 2013); John Corvino, Ryan T. Anderson, and Sherif Girgis, *Debating Religious Liberty and Discrimination* (New York: Oxford University Press, 2017) (Corvino's chapters); Richard Schragger and Micah Schwarzman, "Against Religious Institutionalism," *Virginia Law Review* 99 (2013): 917–85.

[17] See, for instance, Frederick Mark Gedicks and Rebecca G. Van Tassell, "RFRA Exceptions from the Contraception Mandate: An Unconstitutional Accommodation of Religion," *Harvard Civil Rights–Civil Liberties Law Review* 49 (Summer 2014), 343–84.

[18] The one exception to this rule is *Estate of Thornton v. Caldor, Inc.*, 472 U.S. 703 (1985). For further discussion, see Laycock, "The Religious Exemption Debate," 152–54, and Carl H. Esbeck, "Third-Party Burdens, Congressional Accommodations for Religion, and the Establishment Clause," testimony before the Subcommittee on the Constitution and Civil Justice, Committee on the Judiciary, U.S. House of Representatives, February 13, 2015, accessed December 13, 2018, http://clsnet.org/document.doc?id=829.

In the political arena, the Obama administration showed little concern for religious liberty when it required businesses to provide contraceptives and abortifacients to employees, even when the business owners had religious convictions against doing so.[19] In 2016, the U.S. Commission on Civil Rights issued a report that said religious accommodations should be virtually nonexistent. The commission's chair, Martin R. Castro, remarked in in his personal statement:

> The phrases "religious liberty" and "religious freedom" will stand for nothing except hypocrisy so long as they remain code words for discrimination, intolerance, racism, sexism, homophobia, Islamophobia, Christian supremacy or any form of intolerance.[20]

At the state level, some small-business owners who have religious objections to participating in same-sex marriage ceremonies have been prosecuted for declining to do so. Courts in these states have given little weight to arguments that the religious liberty provisions of state or national constitutions protect these photographers, florists, and bakers.[21] When Indiana and Arkansas considered bills similar to the national RFRA, at least in part to help protect such citizens, a virtual firestorm erupted.

In some states, civil rights commissions charged with enforcing the law have been openly hostile to people of faith. The Colorado Civil Rights Commission displayed such clear animus toward a Christian baker whose religious convictions did not permit him to bake a cake celebrating a same-sex wedding. The U.S. Supreme Court justices ruled 7–2 in his favor in *Masterpiece Cakeshop v. Colorado Civil Rights Commission* (2018). This victory is important, but it may be short-lived, as antireligious civil rights commissioners may simply hide their animus in the future.[22]

The Trump administration has been friendlier to religious citizens than its predecessor, but cause for concern remains. President Trump's 2017 executive

---

[19] *Burwell v. Hobby Lobby Stores*, 573 U.S. ___ (2014).

[20] *Peaceful Coexistence: Reconciling Nondiscrimination Principles with Civil Liberties*, 20, accessed June 17, 2018, https://www.usccr.gov/pubs/Peaceful-Coexistence-09-07-16.PDF.

[21] See, for instance, *Elane Photography, L.L.C v. Willock*, 2013-NMSC-040, 309 P.3d 53 (concerning a photographer in New Mexico); *In the Matter of Melissa Elaine Klein, Interim Order, Commissioner of the Bureau of Labor and Industries*, case nos. 44–14 and 45–14, January 29, 2015 (concerning bakers in Oregon); and *State of Washington v. Arlene's Flowers*, No. 13-2-008715 (February 18, 2015) (concerning a florist in Washington State).

[22] For a discussion of this case and its impact, see my essay "A Missed Opportunity: *Masterpiece Cakeshop v. Colorado Civil Rights Commission*," accessed December 15, 2018, http://www.libertylawsite.org/2018/06/06/masterpiece-cakeshop-v-colorado-civil-rights-commission.

order aimed at better protecting religious liberty was described by ACLU director Anthony Romero as "an elaborate photo-op with no discernible policy outcome." He went on to say that his organization would not bother to challenge it.[23] Since then, the Trump administration has taken additional steps to better protect religious liberty, but these measures can be repealed by a subsequent administration.[24] Religious liberty should not depend on who is president.

Citizens, civic leaders, and jurists interested in good public policy should look to history as a guide to the impact of laws and constitutional provisions aimed at protecting religious citizens. This chapter shows that American civic leaders and jurists, at both the national and state levels, have long created significant protections for religious Americans who object to neutral, generally applicable laws. Consideration of a range of policy areas reveals that Americans, at their best, have agreed that governments should not force individuals to violate their sincerely held religious convictions unless they have compelling reasons for doing so. Moreover, the nation and the states have still been able to achieve important policy objectives in spite of these accommodations.

Military Service

Among the civil government's roles, few are as important as national security. Virtually no one disputes that governments have an obligation to protect their citizens from external threats. In the modern era, states and nations have regularly relied upon compulsory militia service or conscription to raise armies. Religious pacifists often ask to be excused from such service, but some countries have rejected their pleas.

Most American colonies required adult males to serve in the militia. Members of the Society of Friends, better known as Quakers, were often pacifists who refused to do so. As early as the 1670s, a few colonies began excusing Quakers from military service, provided they perform an alternative service, pay a fine, or hire a substitute.[25] All colonies did so by the mid-eighteenth century, often expanding accommodations to include other religious citizens.

---

[23] "ACLU Statement on the So-Called 'Religious Freedom' Executive Order," accessed May 31, 2018, https://www.aclu.org/news/aclu-statement-so-called-religious-freedom-executive-order.

[24] See https://www.whitehouse.gov/briefings-statements/president-trump-champion-religious-freedom (accessed May 31, 2018). Although this is hardly an unbiased list, it references easily verifiable executive orders and actions.

[25] See, for instance, Rhode Island's 1673 statute, available in *Records of the Colony of Rhode Island and Providence Plantations*, ed. John Russell Bartlett (Providence: Greene & Brother, 1857), 2: 497–98.

During the War for Independence, the Continental Congress supported these accommodations with the following July 18, 1775, resolution:

> As there are some people, who, from religious principles, cannot bear arms in any case, this Congress intend no violence to their consciences, but earnestly recommend it to them, to contribute liberally in this time of universal calamity, to the relief of their distressed brethren in the several colonies, and to do all other services to their oppressed Country, which they can consistently with their religious principles.[26]

Fourteen years later, during the debates in the First Federal Congress over the Bill of Rights, James Madison proposed a version of what became the Second Amendment that stipulated that "no person religiously scrupulous, shall be compelled to bear arms."[27] Although largely forgotten today, this provision provoked almost as much recorded debate as the First Amendment's religion provisions. James Jackson, a representative from Georgia, insisted that if such an accommodation were made, then those accommodated should be required to hire a substitute.

According to newspaper accounts, Connecticut's Roger Sherman objected that it "is well-known that those who are religiously scrupulous of bearing arms, are equally scrupulous of getting substitutes or paying an equivalent; many of them would rather die than do either one or the other." Sherman, however, did not see an absolute necessity for a clause of this kind. "We do not live under an arbitrary government," he said, "and the states respectively will have the government of the militia, unless when called into actual service."[28] Sherman was sympathetic to the plight of pacifists, but he preferred to rely on state and federal legislatures to protect them rather than make it a constitutional principle.

Madison's proposal was approved by the House but rejected by the Senate and did not make it into the final text of what would become the Second Amendment. Madison and Sherman returned to the issue two months later, when representatives debated a bill regulating the militia when called into national service. Madison offered an amendment to protect from militia

---

[26] Worthington Chauncey Ford, ed., *Journals of the Continental Congress, 1774–1779* (Washington, DC: U.S. Government Printing Office, 1906), 5:189.
[27] Quoted in Mark David Hall, *Roger Sherman and the Creation of the American Republic* (New York: Oxford University Press, 2013), 139.
[28] Hall, *Roger Sherman*, 139.

service "persons conscientiously scrupulous of bearing arms." According to a newspaper account, Madison argued the following:

> *It is the glory of our country, said he, that a more sacred regard to the rights of mankind is preserved, than has heretofore been known.* The Quaker merits some attention on this delicate point, liberty of conscience: they had it in their own power to establish their religion by law, they did not. He was disposed to make the exception gratuitous, but supposed it impracticable.[29]

Sherman immediately supported Madison's amendment, contending that

> [T]he exemption of persons conscientiously scrupulous of bearing arms [is] necessary and proper. He was well convinced that there was no possibility of making such persons bear arms, they would rather suffer death than commit what appeared to them a moral evil—though it might happen that the thing itself was not a moral evil; yet their opinion served them as proof. As to their being obliged to pay an equivalent, gentlemen might see that this was as disagreeable to their consciences as the other, he therefore thought it advisable to exempt them as to both at present.[30]

The amended bill eventually was passed, although with the requirement that conscientious objectors hire a substitute.[31]

Few men were as influential in crafting the U.S. Constitution and Bill of Rights as Madison and Sherman. Their commitment to protecting religious citizens in this situation is surely praiseworthy, even if practical concerns that such accommodations could undermine national security are understandable. Throughout the nineteenth century, states often accommodated religious pacifists by permitting them to hire a substitute or pay a fine instead of performing military service.

Because states were the main source of soldiers for America's wars into the twentieth century, religious pacifists were well, if not perfectly, protected. The nation's first conscription law in the twentieth century, the Selective Draft Act of 1917, exempted from combat service the members of "any well-recognized religious sect or organization at present organized and existing whose creed or

---

29 Hall, *Roger Sherman*, 145 (emphasis added).
30 Hall, *Roger Sherman*, 144–45.
31 Hall, *Roger Sherman*, 145.

principles forbid its members to participate in war in any form."[32] Instead of fighting, Quakers, Mennonites, Brethren, and members of other historic peace churches were required to perform noncombat duties. If they refused to do so, which some did as a matter of conscience, they were jailed.

A serious objection to the religious accommodation in the Selective Draft Act of 1917 is that it protected members of historic peace churches but not pacifists from other traditions. In 1918, the Supreme Court rejected the argument that this violated the establishment clause in *Arver v. United States*.[33] To the relief of other religious pacifists, Congress broadened the accommodation in the Selective Training and Service Act of 1940 to include anyone "who, by reason of religious training and belief, is conscientiously opposed to participation to war in any form."[34] Congress rejected arguments that nonreligious pacifists be accommodated as well, and in 1948 defined the phrase "religious training and belief" to mean "an individual's belief in a relation to a Supreme Being involving duties superior to those arising from any human relations, but [not including] essentially political, sociological, or philosophical views or merely personal moral code."[35]

The exercise of religion is specially protected by the U.S. Constitution, and it is not unreasonable for Congress or state legislatures to accommodate religious citizens. Yet it is also reasonable to insist that nonreligious individuals who have similar convictions be given similar accommodations. Congress has refused to do this with respect to military service, but the Supreme Court creatively read the Selective Service Act to require such accommodations in *United States v. Seeger*[36] and *Welsh v. United States*.[37] To this day, however, the U.S. Code limits conscientious-objector status to religious pacifists:

> Nothing contained in this title shall be construed to require any person to be subject to combatant training and service in the armed forces of the United States who, by reason of religious training and belief, is conscientiously opposed to participation in war in any form. As used in this subsection, the term "religious training and belief" does not include

---

[32] Robert Miller and Ronald Flowers, *Towards Benevolent Neutrality: Church, State, and the Supreme Court*, 5th ed. (Waco: Baylor University Press, 1996), 2: 642.

[33] Arver v. United States, 245 U.S. 366 (1918).

[34] Miller and Flowers, *Towards Benevolent Neutrality*, 2: 644.

[35] Miller and Flowers, *Towards Benevolent Neutrality*, 2: 645.

[36] *United States v. Seeger*, 380 U.S. 163 (1965).

[37] Welsh v. United States, 398 U.S. 333 (1970).

essentially political, sociological, or philosophical views, or a merely personal moral code.[38]

Not every religious conviction should be accommodated, and it is worth noting that Congress never created an accommodation for selective conscientious objectors (individuals who object to a particular war but not all wars). In *Gillette v. United States*,[39] the Supreme Court ruled that the free exercise clause did not require an accommodation for such citizens. Similarly, Congress and the Supreme Court have refused to exempt religious pacifists from paying the portion of their taxes that supports the military.[40]

The United States has a significant interest in ensuring that personnel needs are met during a time of war and that the burdens of conscription are shared fairly. Military requirements were great in World War I and World War II, yet Congress saw fit to exempt religious pacifists from military service, and the United States, along with her allies, was able to win both conflicts.[41] Personnel needs were met more easily in the Korean and Vietnam Wars as the nation was far from full mobilization. If the United States did not win these wars, it was not due to accommodations granted to religious pacifists.

Swearing Oaths

Historically, oaths have been seen as essential for ensuring the loyalty and fidelity of citizens and elected officials. They were also viewed as critically important for the effective functioning of judicial systems. In his famous farewell address, President George Washington observed,

> Of all the dispositions and habits which lead to political prosperity, Religion and morality are indisputable supports. . . . A volume could not trace all their connections with private and public felicity. Let it simply be asked where is the security for property, for reputation, for life, if the sense of religious obligation *desert* the oaths, which are the instruments of investigation in Courts of Justice?[42]

---

[38] 50 U.S.C. App. § 456(j).

[39] Gillette v. United States, 401 U.S. 437 (1971).

[40] U.S. v. American Friends Service Committee, 419 U.S. 7 (1974).

[41] Mulford Q. Sibley and Philip E. Jacob, *Conscription of Conscience: The American State and the Conscientious Objector, 1940–1947* (Ithaca: Cornell University Press, 1952). This book focuses on the Second World War, but the authors also discuss and provide data on conscription in the First World War.

[42] Dreisbach and Hall, *Sacred Rights of Conscience*, 468 (emphasis in original).

In the Christian West, oaths usually invoke God as the witness of the oath-taker's veracity; written oaths often end with the phrase "so help me God." The state obviously has an interest both in the loyalty of its citizens and elected officials and in having a reliable judicial system.

Members of the Society of Friends objected to taking oaths as early as the 1650s. Simply put, they took (and take) such biblical passages as Matt. 5:33–5:37 literally, where Jesus says, "Swear not at all. . . . But let your communication be, Yea, yea; Nay, nay: for whatsoever is more than these cometh of evil." They interpret these passages to the letter, refusing to "swear" oaths but willing to "affirm" or otherwise assent to them.

In England, Quakers were routinely jailed for failing to swear oaths in courts and, after the Glorious Revolution of 1688, refusing to swear loyalty to the new regime. In 1696, Parliament passed a law known as the Quaker Act, which allowed Friends in England, in some cases, to offer a "Solemn Affirmation or Declaration that 'I A.B. do declare in the Presence of Almighty God the Witness of the Truth of what I say,'" but they still faced numerous disabilities. For instance, they were not permitted to be witnesses in criminal cases or to hold civic offices because of their unwillingness to swear oaths. In spite of these advances, in England, Quakers and others with conscientious scruples against swearing were not able to testify in criminal trials until 1828 or become members of Parliament until 1832.[43]

American colonial governments were not originally bound by the Quaker Act, but many voluntarily accommodated Quakers and others who objected to swearing oaths. Notably, in 1647—almost half a century before Parliament passed the law—Rhode Island enacted a statute to protect the "consciences of sundry men" who "may scruple the giving or taking of an oath." Instead of swearing, these individuals were permitted to offer a "solemn profession or testimony in a court of record" so that they could hold office or give testimony.[44] This remarkably generous accommodation was available to anyone (not just Quakers). It is all the more striking because the colony's founder, Roger Williams, detested Quakers.[45]

Most colonies voluntarily accommodated Quakers and others who had objections to swearing oaths by the early eighteenth century, and as the century progressed, Parliament and royal officials sometimes encouraged or even

---

[43] A research note in "Reconsideration of the Sworn Testimony Requirement: Securing Truth in the Twentieth Century," *Michigan Law Review* 75 (1977): 1692.

[44] *Records of the Colony of Rhode Island and Providence Plantations*, 1:181–82.

[45] See, for instance, Williams' *George Fox Digged out of his Burrowes* (1672).

required them to do so. After America broke with Great Britain, state governments could have revoked these laws and policies, but none of them did so. When America's founders gathered in Philadelphia to draft a new constitution, they wove accommodations into the nation's fundamental law. Articles I, II, and VI permit individuals to either swear *or affirm* oaths. The best known of these provisions is Article II, Section 1, which reads, "Before he [the president] enter on the execution of his office, he shall take the following oath or affirmation: 'I do solemnly swear, (or affirm,) that I will faithfully execute . . . '" Of course, one does not need to be religious to take advantage of these provisions, but in the context in which they were written, there is little doubt that these accommodations were intended for citizens who had religious objections to taking oaths.

There is no reason to believe that exempting Quakers and others from oath requirements has had a detrimental effect on the judicial system at either the state or national levels. Nor is there evidence that these citizens have been less loyal to America than other groups. Indeed, in the eighteenth century, many Quakers became very successful merchants, in part because they were known to be particularly trustworthy in spite of their unwillingness to take oaths.

Mandatory School Attendance

In the nineteenth century, civic leaders in many states advocated for compulsory education laws and the creation of public school systems. One motivation behind this movement was the desire for children to learn basic skills such as reading, writing, and arithmetic. Today, there is broad agreement that education is one of the most important services provided by government. Some critics of public schools argue that the government should fund private education as well, but virtually no one contends that states should revoke compulsory attendance laws or eliminate funding for education.

Many nineteenth-century reformers wanted public education not only to teach basic skills but also to help turn the large waves of immigrants into good, democratic, Protestant Americans. When Catholics objected to requirements that they send their children to what were effectively Protestant schools, they were charged with being "sectarian," and Protestant civic leaders were not amused by Catholic attempts to receive a share of state-education funding.[46]

As biased as public schools tended to be toward Protestantism in the nineteenth century, it was rare for states to require Catholics and other dissenters to

---

[46] Philip Hamburger, *Separation of Church and State* (Cambridge: Harvard University Press, 2002), 191–284.

attend them. Oregon famously attempted to achieve such an outcome by banning all private schools in 1922. Although the initiative did not specifically prohibit Catholic schools, virtually every private school in the state was Roman Catholic. In 1925, the U.S. Supreme Court declared the law to be a violation of the right of parents to control their children's education.[47]

Public schools became noticeably less Protestant (or, for that matter, less religious) with the advent of the Supreme Court's modern establishment clause jurisprudence. Notably, teacher-led prayer was declared to be unconstitutional in 1962,[48] as was devotional Bible reading in 1963.[49] Parents who wanted to send their children to religious schools were free to do so, provided they could afford private school tuition. In some cases, states attempted to aid these schools, but much of this aid was declared unconstitutional in the 1970s and 1980s.[50] Because the licensing of private schools was often onerous, and home-schooling was rare at this time, parents who desired a religious education for their children were often unable to provide one.

Included among these parents were a group of Amish who lived in New Glarus, Wisconsin. These families did not object to sending their children to public schools through the eighth grade, but they refused to send them to the public high school. Although Amish generally do not go to court to resolve disputes, an attorney acting on their behalf objected that the free exercise clause required the state to exempt them from the state's compulsory attendance law. In 1972, a unanimous Supreme Court (with a partial dissent by Justice William O. Douglas) agreed.[51]

Since 1972, states have liberalized their compulsory attendance laws and made it easier to run private schools and teach children at home. Accordingly, it is far easier to remove children from public schools. Moreover, the Supreme Court has allowed states to increase aid to the private schools, making them more affordable.[52] These laws were changed for a complex set of reasons, but among them was the desire of legislators to accommodate citizens who desired a faith-based education for their children.

---

[47] Pierce v. Society of Sisters, 268 U.S. 510 (1925).

[48] Engel v. Vitale, 370 U.S. 421 (1962).

[49] Abington v. Schempp, 374 U.S. 203 (1963).

[50] See, for instance, Lemon v. Kurtzman, 403 U.S. 602 (1971); Meek v. Pittenger, 421 U.S. 349 (1975); and School District of Grand Rapids v. Ball, 473 U.S. 373 (1985).

[51] Wisconsin v. Yoder, 406 U.S. 205 (1972).

[52] See, for instance, Zelman v. Simmons-Harris, 536 U.S. 639 (2002), which upheld Ohio's school voucher program.

States have a powerful interest in ensuring that children are educated. Yet, since the early 1980s, they have been increasingly willing to craft exemptions from compulsory attendance laws. Because students educated at home or in private schools often outperform students in public schools, it seems reasonable to conclude that such accommodations have not had a detrimental effect on the quality of education in these states.[53]

Laws Requiring "Religious" Acts

Ever since the advent of the Supreme Court's modern establishment clause jurisprudence in 1947, it has been almost impossible to think that a state would require individuals to support a religious institution or conduct a religious exercise. This was not always the case.

In the early American colonies, from north to south, many civic leaders believed that the state should favor a particular denomination and/or encourage Christianity. States with established churches often required everyone, including nonadherents, to fund them. In the eighteenth century, colonial governments began to craft accommodations that allowed dissenters to support their own churches rather than the established church, but independence from Great Britain raised the possibility that states could revoke these exemptions. Fortunately for religious dissenters, by this time, even many supporters of establishments had come to the conclusion that individuals should not be required to support churches to which they did not belong.[54]

For instance, Patrick Henry's famous 1784 Bill for Establishing a Provision for Teachers of the Christian Religion would have required individuals to support their own churches while exempting the Quakers and Mennonites (who objected to any state involvement) from this requirement. When Connecticut revised its statutes in 1783, the state continued to favor the Congregationalists, but dissenting Protestants were permitted to direct their ecclesiastical taxes to their own churches (a provision that was unfair to non-Protestants, of which there were virtually none in the state, but useful to the Anglicans, Baptists, and

---

[53] Joseph Murphy, *Homeschooling in America: Capturing and Assessing the Movement* (Thousand Oaks: Corwin, 2012); Jason Bedrick, "Yes, Private Schools Beat Public Schools," March 28, 2014, accessed December 13, 2018, https://www.cato.org/publications/commentary/yes-private-schools-beat-public-schools.

[54] Of course, many civic leaders had come to oppose establishments altogether. See, for instance, Dreisbach and Hall, *Sacred Rights of Conscience*, 250–52 and 307–13.

Quakers who resided there).[55] In each case, supporters believed that establishments promoted the common good but were willing to accommodate most (if not all) religious dissenters.

Yet these accommodations did not satisfy all dissenters. Many believers considered supporting their clergy and houses of worship a religious duty. For the government to involve itself in such matters, even if the state merely required people to support their own churches, was considered by some as a violation to their right to religious liberty.[56] Eventually, debates on these matters were mooted when states voluntarily abolished their religious establishments.

Over the past 150 years, states have rarely passed statutes explicitly requiring individuals to participate in religious acts, but several states did so inadvertently as the United States headed into the Second World War.[57] In order to promote national unity, a number of states enacted laws requiring schoolchildren to salute and pledge allegiance to the American flag. Most Americans have no objection to these practices, but Jehovah's Witnesses believe that they violate the Bible's command not to worship graven images (e.g., Exod. 20:4–5). In 1940, eight Justices ruled that the states' interest in promoting national unity permitted them to override these objections.[58]

Three years later, the Supreme Court returned to this issue. In a stunning reversal, six justices concluded that states could not compel Jehovah's Witnesses to engage in these acts. In oft-quoted words, Justice Robert H. Jackson averred,

> The very purpose of a Bill of Rights was to withdraw certain subjects from the vicissitudes of political controversy, to place them beyond the reach of majorities and officials and to establish them as legal principles to be applied by the courts. One's right to life, liberty, and property, to free speech, a free press, freedom of worship and assembly, and other fundamental rights may not be submitted to vote; they depend on the outcome of no elections.[59]

---

[55] Dreisbach and Hall, *Sacred Rights of Conscience* 252–53 and 246–47; Hall, *Roger Sherman and the Creation of the American Republic*, 83–90.

[56] See, for instance, Isaac Backus, "An Appeal to the Public for Religious Liberty," and John Leland, "The Rights of Conscience Inalienable," in *Sacred Rights of Conscience*, ed. Dreisbach and Hall, (1791), 204–11 and 335–45.

[57] This movement started earlier, but it accelerated as the United States approached the war. For an excellent overview, see Richard J. Ellis, *To the Flag: The Unlikely History of the Pledge of Allegiance* (Lawrence: University Press of Kansas, 2005).

[58] Minersville School District v. Gobitis, 310 U.S. 586 (1940).

[59] West Virginia State Board of Education v. Barnette, 319 U.S. 624, 638 (1943).

After considering the state's interest in forcing students to salute the flag, Jackson concluded,

> If there is any fixed star in our constitutional constellation, it is that no official, high or petty, can prescribe what shall be orthodox in politics, nationalism, religion, or other matters of opinion, or force citizens to confess by word or act their faith therein. If there are any circumstances which permit an exception, they do not now occur to us.[60]

Justice Jackson's opinion relies on multiple provisions from the Bill of Rights and can certainly be read to protect both religious and nonreligious citizens, but his argument is particularly compelling with respect to state laws that command people to participate in what they consider to be religious actions with which they disagree. That most Americans do not view saluting the flag and pledging allegiance to it as equivalent to worshiping a graven image was properly determined by the Court to be completely irrelevant. Religious liberty protects the ability of citizens to worship or not worship according to the dictates of their own consciences, not the consciences of others.

Laws Banning Alcohol and Drug Use

The abuse of alcohol and drugs has led to untold problems throughout American history. Colonial Americans sought to regulate alcohol, and in the nineteenth century, a powerful movement arose to ban it altogether. In 1919, the U.S. Constitution was amended to prohibit "the manufacture, sale, or transportation of intoxicating liquours." Congress passed the Volstead Act the same year to implement this amendment. For our purposes, of particular interest is Congress's approach to the issue of sacramental wine.

Sensitive to traditional religious belief that wine should be used for the Eucharist (also known as Communion) and other ceremonies, Congress crafted an exemption to the Volstead Act. The language of Title II, Section 6 of this law alludes to two major religious traditions but is broad enough to cover others. It begins,

> Nothing in this title shall be held to apply to the manufacture, sale, transportation, importation, possession, or distribution of wine for sacramental purposes, or like religious rites. . . . No person to whom a

---

[60] *West Virginia State Board of Education v. Barnette*, 642.

permit may be issued to manufacture, transport, import, or sell wines for sacramental purposes or like religious rites shall sell, barter, exchange, or furnish any such to any person not a rabbi, minister of the gospel, priest, or an officer duly authorized for the purpose by any church or congregation, nor to any such except upon an application duly subscribed by him, which application, authenticated as regulations may prescribe, shall be filed and preserved by the seller.[61]

The text of the bill makes it clear that Congress was committed to protecting religious beliefs held by large denominations (e.g., Roman Catholics) and small religious bodies (e.g., Jews) that believed that sacramental wine should be used in religious ceremonies.[62]

Far more difficult for legislators and courts have been the claims of citizens who contend that the use of other regulated substances is part of their religious practices. Particularly well-known is the case of Native Americans who use peyote in religious ceremonies. Although peyote is a controlled substance, the national government recognized its legitimate use in "bona fide religious ceremonies of the Native American Church" in 1966.[63] Some states adopted similar accommodations, but Oregon did not.

In *Oregon v. Smith*, the Supreme Court ruled that the First Amendment does not shield Native Americans or others who use peyote in religious ceremonies from neutral, generally applicable laws. Shortly after *Smith* was decided, Oregon passed a statute protecting the right of individuals (not just Native Americans) to use peyote in religious ceremonies. In 1994, without any recorded objections, Congress amended the American Indian Religious Freedom Act to protect Native Americans in the twenty-two states that did not already permit them to use peyote in religious ceremonies.

As noted, the abuse of drugs and alcohol has caused a great deal of damage throughout American history. At different times and in different ways, the national and state governments have attempted to prohibit alcohol and certain drugs. There have been extensive debates about the efficacy of these endeavors, but there is no reason to believe that accommodations crafted by legislatures to

---

[61] Public Law 66–66, National Prohibition Act (Volstead Act), 66th Cong., 1st Sess., October 28, 1919, accessed December 13, 2018, http://www.legisworks.org/congress/66/publaw-66.pdf.

[62] Many states continue to exempt sacramental wine from general laws prohibiting adults (other than parents or guardians) from serving alcohol to minors. See, for instance, Oregon Revised Statutes 471.430.

[63] 31 Fed. Reg. 4679 (1966); 21 C.F.R. § 1307.31.

permit the sacramental use of wine, peyote, or other controlled substances[64] by religious citizens have been detrimental to public health. From a historical perspective, these accommodations fit well with similar laws crafted to protect religious practitioners.

Laws Requiring Medical Treatment

Traditionally, states and the national government have deferred to individuals and families to make their own medical decisions. As medical knowledge improved during the nineteenth century, it became evident that the decisions of some individuals could have an impact on others. Particularly contested in the late nineteenth and early twentieth centuries were laws mandating vaccinations.

Advocates of vaccinations contended that they are necessary both for the health of the individuals vaccinated and for the well-being of others. If some individuals and families refuse vaccinations, the argument went, others would suffer from the spread of disease. In 1905, the Supreme Court ruled that the government's interest in protecting the "health and safety of the people" was sufficiently weighty to override the liberty of citizens to refuse a vaccine.[65]

Today, all fifty states have laws requiring specified vaccines for students. States usually require vaccination as a prerequisite to attending school, but forty-five states grant exemptions for parents who have religious convictions against immunizations. Fiftteen states also allow philosophical exemptions for those who object to immunizations because of personal, moral, or other beliefs.[66]

The health and safety of citizens is a vital state interest, yet there is little reason to believe that accommodating citizens who have religious objections to vaccinations has caused significant harm. However, a 2015 spike in measles cases in California linked to unvaccinated adults and children clearly caused *some* harm. In response to several outbreaks, state legislators revoked the

---

[64] See, for instance, *Gonzales v. O Centro Espirita Beneficente União do Vegetal*, 546 U.S. 418 (2006), in regard to protecting the ability of members of the Brazilian church União do Vegetal to use hallucinogenic tea.

[65] *Jacobson v. Massachusetts*, 197 U.S. 11 (1905).

[66] See National Conference of State Legislatures, "States with Religious and Philosophical Exemptions from School Immunization Requirements," June 14, 2019, accessed July 18, 2019, http://www.ncsl.org/research/health/school-immunization-exemption-state-laws.aspx.

religious and philosophical exemptions to California's vaccination require-ment.[67] Reconsidering previously granted accommodations is certainly appro-priate, but a better option might have been to remove only the philosophical exemption and make the religious one more difficult to obtain. This would have protected both California's interest in public health and the religious liberty of the relatively few citizens who have sincere religious objections to vaccination requirements. An added benefit is that it would prevent some families from withdrawing their children from schools so that they would not have to vacci-nate them.

As has been repeatedly stipulated, not all religious convictions should be accommodated. In the early to mid-twentieth century, followers of Mary Baker Eddy, commonly known as Christian Scientists, lobbied successfully for exemp-tions from state laws that required parents to provide medical treatment for their children. Tragically, hundreds of children died because of easily treatable diseases. As a result, many states properly repealed these exceptions.[68]

Medical Providers

Perhaps the most contentious and difficult political/moral/legal issue over the past half-century has been abortion. Large numbers of Americans consider it tantamount to murder, whereas others insist that access to the procedure is a fundamental constitutional right. Some activists believe that the state or private employers should be able to force medical providers to perform abortions even if they have sincere religious beliefs against doing so. The advent of emergency contraceptives/abortifacients such as Plan B and Ella raise similar issues with respect to pharmacists filling prescriptions.

In 1973, shortly after *Roe v. Wade* was decided, Congress passed the Church Amendment to protect healthcare professionals. The legislation prohibits any court or public official from using the receipt of federal aid to require a person or institution to perform an abortion or sterilization contrary to their "religious

---

[67] See, for instance, Rosanna Xia, Rong-Gong Lin II, and Sandra Poindexter, "Fewer California Parents Refuse to Vaccinate Children," *Los Angeles Times*, January 23, 2015, accessed September 1, 2015, http://www.latimes.com/local/california/la-me-immunization-data-20150123-story .html; Kristin A. Feemster, "Eliminate Vaccine Exemptions," *The New York Times*, March 23, 2014, accessed September 1, 2015, http://www.nytimes.com/roomfordebate/2014/03/23/mak-ing-vaccination-mandatory-for-all-children/eliminate-vaccine-exemptions; California SB 277, June 30, 2015.
[68] Alan Rogers, *The Child Cases: How America's Religious Exemption Laws Harm Children* (Amherst: University of Massachusetts Press, 2014); Hamilton, *God vs. The Gavel*, 38–83.

beliefs or moral convictions."[69] The amendment also makes it illegal for health-care organizations to discriminate against individuals who refuse to perform these procedures. In arguing in favor of these protections, Senator Frank Church (D-ID) remarked,

> [N]othing is more fundamental to our national birthright than freedom of religion. Religious belief must remain above the reach of secular authority. It is the duty of Congress to fashion the law in such a manner that no Federal funding of hospitals, medical research, or medical care may be conditioned upon the violation of religious precepts.[70]

Subsequent Congresses expanded these protections. For instance, in 1996, Congress passed the Danforth Amendment, according to which,

> [T]he federal, state, and local governments [were prohibited] from dis-criminating against healthcare entities that refuse to (1) undergo abor-tion training, (2) provide such training, (3) perform abortions, or (4) provide referrals for training or abortions. Specifically, it protected doc-tors, medical students, and health training programs from being denied federal financial assistance, certifications, or licenses they would other-wise receive but for their refusal.[71]

While not limited to institutions that oppose these practices for religious rea-sons, there is little doubt that an important motivation behind this act was pro-tecting religious citizens.

Like Congress, numerous states protect healthcare providers who have objections to performing certain procedures. According to the National Abor-tion Rights Action League (NARAL), "47 states and the District of Columbia [have] passed laws that permit certain medical personnel, health facilities, and/or institutions to refuse to provide abortion care."[72] It is noteworthy that many

---

[69] Quoted in Robin Fretwell Wilson, "Matters of Conscience: Lessons for Same-Sex Marriage from the Healthcare Context," in *Same-Sex Marriage and Religious Liberty*, ed. Douglas Laycock, Anthony R. Picarello Jr., and Robin Fretwell Wilson (Lanham: Rowman & Littlefield, 2008), 83.

[70] Quoted in Robin Fretwell Wilson, "When Governments Insulate Dissenters from Social Change: What *Hobby Lobby* and Abortion Conscience Clauses Teach About Specific Exemp-tions," *UC Davis Law Review* 48 (2014): 735.

[71] Wilson, "Matters of Conscience," 85.

[72] NARAL, "Refusal Laws: Dangerous for Women's Health" 1, http://www.prochoiceamerica.org/media/fact-sheets/abortion-refusal-clauses-dangerous.pdf (accessed September 1, 2015); *Cf.* Gutt-macher Institute, "An Overview of State Abortion Laws," December 1, 2018, https://www.gutt-macher.org/state-policy/explore/overview-abortion-laws (accessed December 15, 2018).

(but not all) states specify that their conscience clauses protect individuals who object to abortions on "moral or *religious* grounds."[73] Some of these statutes offer better protection for religious liberty than others, but overall, both the national and state governments have made significant efforts to protect the ability of healthcare professionals to act (or not act) according to their religious convictions in these policy areas.

At the national level, acting under the authority of the Patient Protection and Affordable Care Act of 2010 (the Affordable Care Act), the Department of Health and Human Services mandated that businesses cover a range of contraceptive devices, including several forms of emergency contraception, which some individuals believe may be used to cause abortions. Religious denominations and houses of worship were exempted from these requirements, but other religious organizations were not.

In response to significant outcry, the Obama administration issued regulations whereby insurance providers used by religious organizations would offer these drugs at no cost (in theory) to the religious organizations' employees. Some religious organizations were satisfied by this approach, but others believed they were still complicit in wrongdoing. For-profit businesses received no such protection, but in 2014, the Supreme Court held in *Burwell v. Hobby Lobby Stores, Inc.* that the Religious Freedom Restoration Act requires such accommodation for a closely held for-profit corporation.[74] As of this writing, the Trump administration is in the process of creating rules that will offer protection to a wide range of organizations that object to providing both birth control and emergency contraception, but these rules will be challenged in court and may be altered by a subsequent administration.[75]

There is no denying that protecting religious citizens who are licensed by the state to provide medical services is one of the most complicated policy areas in which religious citizens have been accommodated. In some instances, such as with emergency contraception, even the basic effects of the drug are debated. Even when they are not, the state's interest in regulating the provision of medical care, which can involve issues of life and death, is undoubtedly high. These cases are further complicated because they raise equal-protection issues and sometimes concern about what the Supreme Court has called a fundamental

---

[73] Wilson, "Matters of Conscience," 300 (emphasis added), and, generally, 299–310.
[74] *Burwell v. Hobby Lobby Stores, Inc.*, 573 U.S. ___ (2014).
[75] For details, see https://www.hhs.gov/about/news/2018/11/07/fact-sheet-final-rules-on-religious-and-moral-exemptions-and-accommodation-for-coverage-of-certain-preventive-services-under-affordable-care-act.html (accessed December 18, 2018).

right to abortion. It is telling that, despite these complications, the nation and many states have gone to great lengths to protect the moral and religious convictions of healthcare providers.

Time and experience may reveal that some of the accommodations mentioned in this section are harmful. Although some advocacy groups fear these accommodations will lead to great harm,[76] there is little reason to believe that this is the case.[77] If substantial evidence arises that shows some policies as being detrimental to the well-being of patients, legislatures may have to rethink existing accommodations. If such evidence does not surface, however, legislatures in states without accommodations should move quickly to protect the religious liberty of all citizens more effectively.

Civil Rights Laws

As we have seen, the national and state governments often create accommodations to protect religious individuals from neutral, generally applicable laws, but such accommodations—and many more that could be discussed—do not exhaust the state's interest in protecting religious citizens. For instance, legislators have passed laws to protect religious citizens from discrimination by both private and governmental entities.

Most prominently, Title VII of the Civil Rights Act of 1964, as amended, prohibits employers with more than fifteen employees from, among other things, firing or refusing to hire someone because of their religion or religious practices. The statute also requires private businesses to make "reasonable accommodations" for their employees' or potential employees' sincerely held religious convictions unless the accommodation would create an undue hardship for the employer.[78]

Religious Americans, especially religious minorities, have benefited from this law. In 2014, for example, Samantha Elauf, a Muslim woman who wore a

---

[76] Douglas NeJaime and Reva B. Siegel, "Religious Accommodation, and Its Limits, in a Pluralist Society," in *Religious Freedom, LGBT Rights, and the Prospects for the Common Good*, ed. William N. Eskridge Jr. and Robin Fretwell Wilson (New York: Cambridge University Press, 2019), 69–81.

[77] Luke W. Goodrich, "The Health Care and Conscience Debate," *Engage: The Journal of the Federalist Society's Practice Groups*, 12 (June 2011): 122–23.

[78] 42 U.S.C. § 2000e-2(a) (2000); 42 U.S.C. § 2000e(j) (2000). For a general overview of how Title VII protects religious Americans, see Equal Employment Opportunity Commission, "Section 12: Religious Discrimination," in *Compliance Manual*, 2008, accessed December 15, 2018, http://www.eeoc.gov/policy/docs/religion.html.

headscarf for religious reasons, applied for a job at the clothing store Abercrombie & Fitch but was not hired because her scarf violated the company's dress code. The Supreme Court ruled 8 to 1 that Title VII "prohibits a prospective employer from refusing to hire an applicant in order to avoid accommodating a religious practice that it could accommodate without undue hardship."[79]

Many Americans agree that employers should not be able to discriminate on the basis of religious practices such as wearing a headscarf, a yarmulke, or a turban. Yet the Congress that passed Title VII recognized that *some* religious discrimination is acceptable and protected by the First Amendment. Accordingly, it crafted an accommodation to Title VII that permits religious institutions to make employment decisions on the basis of religion. Specifically, "a religious corporation, association, educational institution, or society" is exempt "with respect to the employment of individuals of a particular religion to perform work connected with the carrying on by such corporation, association, educational institution, or society of its activities."[80]

As a result, the Roman Catholic Church can insist that only faithful Roman Catholics run its hospitals, an Evangelical college may require its employees to be committed Evangelicals, and a Jewish social service agency may decide to employ only orthodox Jews. To prohibit religious institutions from making such decisions, Congress reasoned, would constitute a grave threat to religious liberty.[81]

Today, it is not uncommon for activist organizations such as the American Civil Liberties Union to contend that religious individuals and institutions should rarely be exempted from neutral, generally applicable laws.[82] Fortunately, legislators in even the most secular of states often disagree. For instance, before the Supreme Court redefined marriage for the entire country, some states passed statutes recognizing same-sex marriage that also protected religious organizations from being compelled to participate if it violated their doctrine. Washington State's law recognizing same-sex marriage stipulates,

> (4) . . . No state agency or local government may base a decision to penalize, withhold benefits from, or refuse to contract with any religious organization on the refusal of a person associated with such religious organization to solemnize or recognize a marriage under this section.

---

[79] *Equal Employment Opportunity Commission v. Abercrombie & Fitch Stores Inc.*, 575 U.S. (2015).

[80] 42 U.S.C. § 2000e(1)(a) (2000).

[81] Religious liberty concerns prompted Congress similarly to carve out religious institutions from the mandates of the Fair Housing Act, the Americans with Disabilities Act, and Title IX of the Education Amendments Act of 1972.

[82] See, for instance, American Civil Liberties Union, "Using Religion to Discriminate."

(5) No religious organization is required to provide accommodations, facilities, advantages, privileges, services, or goods related to the solemnization or celebration of a marriage.

(6) A religious organization shall be immune from any civil claim or cause of action, including a claim pursuant to chapter 49.60 RCW, based on its refusal to provide accommodations, facilities, advantages, privileges, services, or goods related to the solemnization or celebration of a marriage.[83]

Washington State understands that it is unconscionable to compel religious organizations to participate in or lend their resources to "celebrations" when doing so would violate their religious convictions.

One shortcoming of the Washington statute is that it does not protect small-business owners who have sincere religious convictions that likewise prevent them from participating in same-sex wedding ceremonies. They should also be protected by carefully crafted accommodations. As we have seen, governments regularly create such accommodations and still manage to meet important policy objectives.

Conclusion

Religious liberty is a core American principle—not a Democratic or Republican one. Many of the accommodations discussed in this essay were passed with significant bipartisan support. Both conservative and liberal jurists have supported judicially created accommodations.

One significant lesson highlighted by this chapter is that religious exemptions do not prevent governments from meeting their policy objectives. As the nation and states address new threats to what the American founders called "the sacred right of conscience," they should carefully consider such lessons of the past as they make laws and policies for the future.

---

[83] RCW 26.04.010. Congress passed a similar provision to protect military chaplains. Section 544 of the National Defense Authorization Act for 2012 reads, "A military chaplain who, as a matter of conscience or moral principle, does not wish to perform a marriage, may not be required to do so." See "Section 544: Freedom of Conscience of Military Chaplains with Respect to the Performance of Marriages," H.R. 1540, National Defense Authorization Act for Fiscal Year 2012, accessed December 14, 2018, http://www.gpo.gov/fdsys/pkg/BILLS-112hr1540enr/pdf/BILLS-112hr1540enr.pdf.

Chapter 11

Free to Serve: Safeguarding Churches and Ministries as They Contribute to Justice and the Common Good

Stanley W. Carlson-Thies

Senior Director, Institutional Religious Freedom Alliance

The title of this chapter is likely to seem, in the minds of many, oxymoronic. After all, doesn't allowing religious freedom to churches and religious charities enable them to be, well, religious? That is, doesn't it enable them to be sectarian and thus undermine, not add to, the common good? The topic of *institutional* religious freedom—religious freedom as it applies to churches and other religious organizations—is full of paradoxes, too. Doesn't the concept "religious freedom" bring to mind not afflicted religious organizations but images of persecuted *individuals* (for instance, Egyptian Christians beheaded by ISIS for refusing to acknowledge Allah; a Muslim job applicant turned away because of her head covering; or a nurse compelled, despite her Catholic convictions, to assist in elective abortions)? And yet a typical and key aspect of religious communities is an array of faith-based *organizations*—houses of worship, religious schools, and religious charities that help the sick, the poor, and the elderly. There are also businesses with a faith angle—kosher delis, Christian radio stations, Islamic financial institutions.

It is true that much religious-freedom litigation involves individuals—that Muslim job applicant (who won a decision in the Supreme Court's *EEOC v. Abercrombie & Fitch*, 2015), the Catholic nurse (who won a changed policy in *Cenzon-DeCarlo v. The Mount Sinai Hospital*), the Kentucky wedding clerk who refused to assist same-sex marriage applicants (Kim Davis, August, 2015), the Jehovah's Witness students who challenged their school's requirement to salute the American flag as idolatrous (and who won the freedom not to salute in *West Virginia State Board of Education v. Barnette*, 1943). Yet, many high-profile U.S. Supreme Court cases concern the religious freedom of religious organizations: *Hosanna-Tabor v. EEOC* (in 2012, in which a unanimous decision was made to protect the right of religious organizations to select their religious leaders), *Trinity Lutheran v. Comer* (in 2017, in which it was decided that a state cannot exclude a church from participating in a government grant program), and *Everson v. Board of Education* (in 1947, which stressed a high "wall of separation between church and state" but allowed state funds to support the transportation of parochial school students). And, as this chapter will propose, institutional religious freedom—by protecting diverse, private, nongovernmental organizations—enables U.S. citizens, who hold varied and even conflicting religious and moral convictions, to live *together*; to be "*e pluribus Unum*," or one out of many.

Here are three other quick indicators of the importance of religious organizations and the institutional religious freedom that protects their religious beliefs and practices:

(1) A 2016 study estimates that houses of worship, religious charities, and faith-related businesses together contribute some $1.2 trillion annually to the American economy—more than the top ten high-tech companies combined.[1]

(2) When President George W. Bush decided early in his administration to create a major new federal program to provide expansive AIDS prevention and treatment services overseas, the program was designed specifically to extensively utilize grassroots groups, and in particular faith-based organizations, to deliver services. Why did PEPFAR (the President's Emergency Plan for AIDS Relief) look specifically to religious organizations in this contentious matter of preventing and treating HIV-AIDS? One reason is just how central religious organizations are in some nations—as many as 50 percent of health services in some African nations are provided through faith-based organizations. Another reason is precisely the moral sensitivity of HIV-AIDS: with some training, the U.S. Department of State concluded, faith-based grassroots groups "often design the most culturally appropriate and responsive interventions and have the legitimacy and authority to

---

[1] Brian J. Grim and Melissa E. Grim, "The Socio-Economic Contribution of Religion to American Society: An Empirical Analysis," *Interdisciplinary Journal of Research on Religion* 12, art. 3 (2016): 1–31; "The Socio-Economic Contributions of Religion to American Society: An Empirical Analysis," two-page summary of Grim and Grim, "Socio-Economic Contribution of Religion," accessed February 11, 2019, https://faithcounts.com//wp-content/uploads/Summary-Sheet.pdf.

implement successful programs that deal with normally sensitive subjects."[2]

(3) Although President Barack Obama's administration was often accused of misinterpreting religious freedom to mean only the narrower freedom of worship, the president was a strong supporter of the faith-based initiative, the federal commitment to the full inclusion of religious service organizations as partners in federally funded programs to address social problems. After all, he said, it is not possible for government to respond adequately to pressing social needs without an "all-hands-on-deck" approach.[3]

"All hands." Indeed, this is an illuminating way to characterize faith-based service organizations (houses of worship that offer help to their neighbors, specialized religious nonprofits, faith-shaped businesses). They are the "hands" of religions: their means and their structures for carrying out their commitments to the service of their neighbors in the world. Religious organizations do a tremendous amount of good. Their institutional religious freedom needs to be protected. They need to be "free to serve."[4]

Religious Organizations Advance Social Justice and Enlarge the Common Good

Houses of worship and religious service organizations such as schools, hospitals, and orphanages have served our society from the very beginnings of the American colonies. In doing so, they were continuing in the New World patterns of faith-based service developed in Europe.[5] In both New World and Old, these

---

[2] For a short discussion and the State Department quote, see Stanley W. Carlson-Thies, "Faith-Based Initiative 2.0: The Bush Faith-Based and Community Initiative," *Harvard Journal of Law and Public Policy* 32, no. 3 (2009), 931–47, http://www.harvard-jlpp.com/wp-content/uploads/2009/05/Carlson-ThiesFinal.pdf.

[3] Jeff Zeleny and Michael Luo, "Obama Seeks Bigger Role for Religious Groups," *New York Times*, July 2, 2008, accessed March 17, 2018, http://www.nytimes.com/2008/07/02/us/politics/02obama.html.

[4] Cf. Stephen V. Monsma and Stanley Carlson-Thies, *Free to Serve: Protecting the Religious Freedom of Faith-Based Organizations* (Grand Rapids, MI: BrazosPress, 2015).

[5] From a large literature, a scholarly study: James William Brodman, *Charity and Religion in Medieval Europe* (Washington, DC: Catholic University of America Press, 2009), and a study for a popular audience: Alvin J. Schmidt, *How Christianity Changed the World* (Grand Rapids, MI: Zondervan, 2004).

institutions and actions were, and are, responses to the mandates for service recorded in both the Old and New Testaments. For example, care for orphans is required in multiple passages; among them, Psalm 82:3, which says, "Defend the weak and the fatherless. . . ," and James 1:27—"Religion that God our Father accepts as pure and faultless is this: to look after orphans. . . ." These organizations have continued to serve even as federal, state, and local government programs have multiplied; indeed, they often partner with government programs. Religious institutions promote "pro-social" attitudes and behaviors, such as service to others and a strong commitment to family; they contribute extensively to the economic and social vitality of their communities; and they offer a large volume and diverse array of services to help the needy and to further develop society.

Snapshots of Religious Organizations in Action

Columbia Learning International Ministries. In poverty-stricken southeast Washington, DC, Apostle Angeloyd Fenrick refused the offer of more than $1 million for the apartment building she had bought with her retirement savings years before. Her faith-based mission of service—the mission of Columbia Learning International Ministries (CLIM)—she said, was not over. The apartment building is central to CLIM's work to assist the neighborhood's working homeless "in their transition to permanent housing," helping them "make and sustain changes that lead to balanced, healthy lives," and "encourag[ing] the restoration of family relationships." All of this started when Fenrick prayed for God to send someone to turn around the lives of the homeless men she witnessed gathering daily around a liquor store. The store sat across the street from the school where she worked as a school psychologist. That "someone" turned out to be her.[6]

The Chow Train. This faith-inspired nonprofit organization provides "restaurant-quality and healthy food" to homeless people in San Antonio, Texas. In 2015, its leader, Joan Cheever, received national attention—and a ticket—when she served meals from her pickup rather than the Chow Train's city-licensed food truck. Why the pickup truck? Because the food truck is too large to navigate through the alleys where she goes in search of those needing meals. In response to the officer writing her the ticket, she claimed a "legal right" to use

[6] Ashley Fisher, "The Role of Faith-Based Organizations in Addressing Homelessness in D.C.," blog for the Sacred Sector initiative of the Center for Public Justice, republished from the Shared Justice initiative of the Center for Public Justice, March 13, 2018, accessed February 9, 2019, https://www.sacredsector.org/sacred-stories/2018/3/13/the-role-of-faith-based-organizations-in-addressing-homelessness-in-dc.

the pickup—protection by the Texas Religious Freedom Restoration Act—for her faith-based acts of service.[7]

World Relief. World Relief, headquartered in Baltimore, Maryland, is an Evangelical relief and development organization that works with U.S. churches to resettle refugees from around the world. In February 2017, it announced that, as a consequence of a Trump administration decision to reduce the number of refugees who would be resettled in the United States it had to lay off more than one hundred forty staff members and close five local offices—offices that had together "resettled more than 25,000 refugees over the past four decades." But the organization remained undaunted. Tim Breene, its CEO, said, "The unfortunate truth is that[,] given the unprecedented nature of the global refugee crisis, there are simply more people than ever that need our support and our compassion. We are redoubling our efforts to find solutions to serve displaced peoples in the Middle East, sub-Saharan Africa, and elsewhere around the globe."[8]

Are some of the actions and views of these faith-based organizations troubling, manifesting disputed understandings of need, controversial concepts of social justice, or odd notions of the common good? By definition, in our society comprised of many religions, plural moral commitments, multiple ethnicities, varied philosophies of life, and diverse local cultures, many practices and beliefs precious to one group will be puzzling, sometimes even alarming, to other parts of the population. Indeed, these disagreements are the reason for the guarantee of religious freedom and for the other protections of the First Amendment. If we citizens agreed on everything important, there would be no need for specific protections, whether for the exercise of religion, for speech, or for the wide variety of associations people create.

Notice, this, too, about the three faith-based organizations: they serve others without regard to religion. They do this not because they do not care about

---

[7] Chelsea Langston, "Feeding the Homeless Requires Religious Freedom," blogpost at the Institutional Religious Freedom Alliance, June 18, 2015, accessed February 9, 2019, http://www.irfalliance.org/feeding-the-homeless-requires-religious-freedom/; David Martin Davies, "When Feeding the Homeless Runs Afoul of the Law," NPR story, June 13, 2015, accessed February 9, 2019, https://www.npr.org/2015/06/13/413988634/when-feeding-the-homeless-runs-afoul-of-the-law.

[8] "World Relief Announces the Layoff of 140+ Staff and Closure of Five Local Offices Due to the Trump administration's Reduction in Refugee Resettlements in the U.S.," World Relief press release, February 15, 2017, accessed February 9, 2019, https://worldrelief.org/press-releases/world-relief-announces-the-layoff-of-140-staff-and-closure-of-five-local-offices-due-to-the-trump-administrations-reduction-in-refugee-resettlements-in-the-us.

religious truth, but rather because the religious truths to which they respectively are committed compels them to see others as neighbors, not as foreign "others." Recall Jesus's story about the Good Samaritan—the traveler who is named "good" because he regarded whoever was in need as the one he should serve (Luke 10:25–37). Or, as a leader of the Archdiocese of Washington, DC, once put it: Our Catholic organizations serve whomever shows up not because *they* are Catholic but because *we* are Catholic.[9]

And notice, too, that these profiled organizations and their faith-based activity are not centered on "birth control, baking, or bathrooms," notwithstanding that the religious freedom of religious organizations is increasingly noticed and criticized because of our society's culture wars concerning various issues related to human sexuality. In truth, most of what faith-based organizations do involves not those charged issues but, instead, the provision of safe housing for the homeless, food for the hungry, day care for the children of busy families, treatment for the addicted, health care for the sick, aid for the ex-prisoners who want to get reestablished in society, and so on.[10]

"Many Sikh organizations and houses of worship provide charitable services to homeless persons and others, without regard to the homeless person's religion. In exchange, Sikh organizations and houses of worship often require such persons to abide by certain religious traditions of the Sikh faith. Those requirements take several forms: Persons may be asked to remove their shoes while in a house of worship, to cover their head, and to refrain from tobacco and alcohol."[11]

Institutional religious freedom protects the freedom of religious organizations to be true to the religious impulses and practices that are specific to their particular way of public service and to their particular contributions, both to the common good and to the advancement of social justice. Why do they need institutional religious freedom to make these contributions? Exactly because

---

[9] Kristen Hannum, "Why Social Justice? 'Because We're Catholic'," U.S. Catholic, July 2012, accessed February 11, 2019, https://www.uscatholic.org/church/2012/06/why-social-justice-'because-we're-catholic'.

[10] See the discussion by Chelsea Langston Bombino in "Religious Freedom and the Social Safety Net," Public Justice Review series, "Freedom to Serve the Vulnerable," vol. 6 (2017), accessed February 9, 2019, https://cpjustice.org/index.php/public/page/content/pjr_vol6no1_chelsea_bombino_freedom_safety_net.

[11] Amicus brief by The Sikh Coalition, presented in Intermountain Fair Housing Council v. Boise Rescue Mission (9th Cir. 2010).

we do not all agree about how best conduct our lives, serve others, contribute to the common good, or advance social justice.

"Pro-Social"

Religious organizations *do* a lot of good—they operate varied programs of service and also create economic benefits, as we will see in a moment. We should note, first, though, their important role of shaping people into positive contributors to society. This is a complex and relatively new area of inquiry,[12] but two examples show the argument and suggest the magnitude of the impact for good.

A dramatic example is in the area of criminal justice. Byron Johnson encapsulates the positive dynamic in the title of his recent book *More God, Less Crime*.[13] As he documents from the research literature, religious values and commitments, which are transmitted and sustained through the programs and teachings of religious organizations, can powerfully help people who have committed crimes turn toward a constructive pattern of life; that is a vital effect, given normally high rates of recidivism. But there is a powerful additional benefit of religion, less well studied and understood: guiding people away from criminal and destructive actions in the first place. For example, according to Johnson, research shows that "[y]outh who attend church frequently are less likely to engage in a variety of delinquent behaviors, including drug use, skipping school, fighting, and violent and nonviolent crimes. Indeed, youth exposure to religious and spiritual activities is a powerful inhibitor of juvenile delinquency and youth violence."[14]

Here's another example, which is dramatic in its own way. Robert Putnam and David Campbell, in their acclaimed study *American Grace: How Religion Divides and Unites Us*, document that America's religious communities shape their adherents to be especially generous donors and volunteers, not only to their own religious communities but also to secular causes and organizations.[15]

---

[12] For an overview of the early literature, see Byron R. Johnson, with Ralph Brett Tomplins and Derek Webb, *Objective Hope: Assessing the Effectiveness of Faith-Based Organizations: A Review of the Literature*, a 2002 report for the Center for Research on Religion and Urban Civil Society, University of Pennsylvania.

[13] Byron R. Johnson, *More God, Less Crime: Why Faith Matters and How it Could Matter More* (West Conshohocken, PA: Templeton Press, 2011).

[14] Johnson, *More God, Less Crime*, 175.

[15] Robert D. Putnam and David E. Campbell, *American Grace: How Religion Divides and Unites Us* (New York: Simon & Schuster, 2010), chap. 13.

In short, religions have the powerful effect of shaping people to be constructive in society (notwithstanding the controversy surrounding various beliefs and
actions and the undoubted ills that religions occasionally permit and may even
require). To play this constructive role, they need to be free to teach their views,
exemplify those views in their operations, and be guided by the views as they
serve their neighbors. They need institutional religious freedom.

The "Halo Effect"

Research into what is termed the "economic halo effect" documents the surprisingly large economic value of the operations and activities of churches and
other houses of worship. For example, a study of a sample of ninety congregations housed in historic buildings in Philadelphia, Fort Worth, and Chicago
calculated that they each, on average, generated more than $1.7 million annu-
ally in economic activity, conservatively assessed. Given the more than 1,750
historic churches, synagogues, and temples in those three cities—not counting
the multitudes of other (smaller, newer) houses of worship in the same cities—
that's an economic impact of more than $3 billion each year in those three loca-
tions alone.[16]

This value is generated by the payment of clergy and other salaries; the pur-
chase of utilities and supplies; purchases made at local shops, gas stations, and
restaurants by people who come to the building for religious services or other
activities; the operations of daycare centers and private elementary schools
often subsidized by congregations on behalf of low-income families; and the
activities and events of the many community organizations to which houses of
worship typically give low-cost or free space and thousands of volunteer
hours.[17]

Note this: nearly 90 percent of the weekly visits to these congregations were
for reasons other than worship, and nearly 90 percent of the beneficiaries of the
events and services staged in these historic buildings are not members of the

---

[16] "The Economic Halo Effect of Historic Sacred Places," report published in *Sacred Places: The Magazine of Partners for Sacred Places*, November 2016, accessed January 14, 2019, https://sacredplaces.org/uploads/files/16879092466251061-economic-halo-effect-of-historic-sa-cred-places.pdf. For similar studies in Canada, see the Cardus Social Cities website, accessed February 11, 2019, https://www.cardus.ca/research/social-cities/.

[17] "Economic Halo Effect," 4–5. The research did not even attempt to estimate the economic value of the consequences of the activities and programs provided by or housed in these historic congregations—the value of the "pro-social" behaviors, the positive contribution to society of children who receive better schooling than they otherwise might get or the good effects of the marriages that are strengthened and addictions overcome with the help of services offered.

respective congregations.[18] In short, these houses of worship extensively "bless" the economic and social life around them in very large and varied ways. As Partners for Sacred Places says, "Older churches, synagogues, temples, and meetinghouses should now be seen as engines of community health and vitality."[19] Zoning actions, tax policies, municipal redevelopment plans, and other government choices that hamper or help congregations, regardless of whether the decisions are identified as "religious freedom decisions," clearly have strong consequences for the good of society and the well-being of the many marginalized and lower-income persons and families who are positively affected by houses of worship of all sizes and faiths.

A Large Volume of Social Services

Religious organizations also make very specific positive contributions to society and on behalf of poor and marginalized people, families, and communities by providing a large number and wide range of social services. Churches maintain food pantries, and religious people organize faith-based food banks. Congregations offer job-prep and ESL classes, and believers create comprehensive faith-based employment service organizations. Houses of worship organize volunteers into jail ministries, and people of faith bring to life specialized criminal justice advocacy and service organizations. Synagogues, mosques, and churches offer emergency help to community members who are late in paying rent, and—either together with congregations or separately from them—religious people create specialized faith-based organizations, often in partnership with government, to construct and manage low-income housing. And much more.

One scholar has remarked that a person in an American urban area venturing out in the morning for a coffee will have passed, on average, more than twenty congregations before arriving at a Starbucks, and virtually every one of those congregations is providing a range of social and educational services, not only to its own members but also to unaffiliated people from the surrounding neighborhoods.[20] And, as just noted, in addition to the many such congregation-based services, America's extensive nonprofit sector is full of religious nonprofits: faith-based service organizations created specifically to develop, raise funding for, and provide a wide range of social service, educational, health, housing, financial, and community-development services. Brian Grim reported in 2016 that 40 percent

---

[18] "Economic Halo Effect," 4–5.
[19] "Economic Halo Effect," 4.
[20] Brian J. Grim, "Faith by the Numbers: The Socio-Economic Impact of Religion in the U.S.," YouTube video, accessed February 11, 2019, https://youtu.be/iTw0gzn633k.

of the fifty largest charities in the United States were faith-based, with a combined operating revenue of more than \$45 billion.[21]

There are no comprehensive numbers on the extent and societal impact of these services, but much is known. Services offered by congregations have been researched most creatively and intensively by Ram Cnaan. See, for example, the 2002 path-breaking work by Cnaan and colleagues, *The Invisible Caring Hand: American Congregations and the Provision of Welfare.*[22] However, there is no complete national list of congregations—researchers say that the only way to find them all is to walk down every street and alley in a community. And research to identify the range and extent of services they offer is hampered by the propensity of houses of worship to regard what they do as the carrying out of religious "ministries" rather than the provision of "social services" akin to those provided by specialized service organizations. Congregations tend not to measure and document their ministries, either, because their focus is relationships, spiritual formation, and personal transformation rather than units of service with associated impact metrics.[23]

Faith-based nonprofits are easier to study because they are organized specifically to offer services; and typically, though not always, they are organized under federal law as 501(c)(3) organizations and thus appear on lists of formal nonprofit organizations. However, there is no agreement on how to identify whether an organization is religious, secular, or only nominally religion-related (e.g., having evolved after being founded by a church decades ago).[24] There is no comprehensive account of how many faith-based service organizations exist,

---

[21] Grim, "Socio-Economic Contributions of Religion to American Society," 2.

[22] Ram A. Cnaan et al., *The Invisible Caring Hand: American Congregations and the Provision of Welfare* (New York: New York University Press, 2002).

[23] These and other challenges for understanding the roles and impact of religious institutions in society are discussed in various contributions to the three-report series prepared by Cardus, *Religion and the Good of the City* (Hamilton, Ontario: Cardus Social Cities, 2017) May, August, and October 2017, accessed February 12, 2019, https://www.cardus.ca/research/social-cities/reports/.

[24] Government does not require organizations to identify as religious lest its very definitions circumscribe—or "establish"—an official definition of religion. Classification efforts are hampered, too, by the propensity of researchers to assume that an organization is either a religious entity *or* a provider of some kind of social, health, or educational service, even though faith-based nonprofits typically are providers of faith-informed versions of such services. For an excellent discussion and typology of different ways that faith can be present in and shape social service organizations and programs, see Heidi Rolland Unruh and Ronald J. Sider, *Saving Souls, Serving Society: Understanding the Faith Factor in Church-Based Social Ministry* (New York: Oxford University Press, 2005), 103–28.

what they do, and how many people they assist, much less how effective their services are.

And yet their social contribution is undoubtedly very important. A 2016 review of research estimates the annual value of the services provided by faith-based health care, higher education, and other social service nonprofits to be about $303 billion.[25] Even focusing on a detail, such as the role of faith-based organizations in responding to the crisis of homelessness in contemporary America, shows the impact of such services. Research from Baylor University's Institute for Studies of Religion, assessing services in eleven cities, discovered that nearly 60 percent of the available beds in emergency shelters for the homeless—what some call "the safety net of all safety nets," as it is the most basic protective help—are provided by faith-based organizations. Moreover, those beds and the related services are mainly funded by private donations, not government dollars.[26]

Diverse Services for a Diverse Public

Religious organizations contribute strongly and widely to society not only through the volume of services they offer but also through their variety of offerings, as they often serve differently than their nonreligious peers. This different way of serving—for example, a Catholic hospital that, because of church teachings, does not offer elective abortions—is undoubtedly controversial to many, and yet the population that hospitals serve is diverse and includes many patients, Catholic or not, who are pro-life. As the U.S. Conference of Catholic Bishops notes, if all of the doctors and nurses who refused to participate in elective abortions were driven out, the medical profession could not serve the whole population of patients well, because "[m]any patients want access to physicians and other health care providers who do not see the taking of human life as part of a profession devoted to healing."[27]

---

[25] Grim and Grim, "Socio-Economic Contribution of Religion to American Society," 25.

[26] Byron R. Johnson and William H. Wubbenhorst, *Assessing the Faith-Based Response to Homelessness in America: Findings from Eleven Cities* (Waco, TX: Baylor Institute for Studies of Religion Case Study, 2016).

[27] Comment submitted by the Office of General Counsel of the United States Conference of Catholic Bishops to the Office of Public Health and Science, Department of Health and Human Services, concerning the department's proposed rescission of a 2008 conscience protection regulation, March 23, 2009, http://www.usccb.org/about/general-counsel/rulemaking/upload/comments-to-hss-on-conscience-2009–03.pdf.

In short, a vital aspect of the value added by religious organizations in the area of service delivery—an aspect specifically protected by institutional religious freedom—is that they often provide services differently: education that includes religious components; day care that incorporates religious stories and prayer time, and mirrors the values of parents of a particular faith; drug treatment that adds a spiritual dimension to medical treatment and psychological help; services for the homeless that not only provide emergency sleeping provisions, food, and job-search help but that also work creatively to reconnect homeless people with their families; and many others.

> "People don't become homeless when they run out of money, at least not right away. They become homeless when they run out of relationships. And this means that the solution to homelessness necessarily involves a reestablishment of relationships and community."
>
> —New City Initiative faith-based homeless shelter, Portland, Oregon[28]

Serving Together with, and Not Only Separate from, Government

As noted, many faith-based services for the homeless are privately funded, although many faith-based providers accept federal and other government funds to add to the support they raise themselves. This is the variegated pattern in American health care, education, and social services: some programs are privately funded, others wholly supported by government, and yet others funded by both private and government dollars.[29]

---

[28] From the website of New City Initiative, Portland, Oregon; quoted in Johnson and Wubbenhorst, *Assessing the Faith-Based Response to Homelessness*, 21.

[29] Critics of government partnerships with faith-based organizations sometimes ask how it can be right for government to give money to religious organizations. Yet partnerships with government may not enrich the organizations at all. Note this comment by Rev. Larry Snyder, then president of Catholic Charities USA and formerly head of Catholic Charities in Minneapolis: "I can say from my time in Minneapolis, the programs that we had that were contracted with the government, the government would pay somewhere between two-thirds and three-fourths of what we needed and we had to make up the rest. So we were subsidizing the government, if you will, by hundreds of thousands of dollars every year. We were happy to do that because it furthered our mission and the mission of the common good." Remarks made as a panelist at a symposium organized by the Brookings Institution, *Faith-Based and Neighborhood Partnerships in the Obama Era: Assessing the First Year and Looking Ahead* (February 18, 2010), uncorrected event transcript, accessed February 11, 2019, https://www.brookings.edu/events/faith-based-neighborhood-partnerships-in-the-obama-era-assessing-the-first-year-and-looking-ahead/.

Recall President Obama's declaration that America's social problems are too extensive to be addressed by government programs alone. Instead, an all-hands-on-deck approach is needed, he said. The final report of his advisory council stressed the same point and also underscored that faith-based organizations, with their distinctive approaches, are indispensable to the success of efforts to address the complex problem of entrenched poverty and extreme inequality. The report, *Strengthening Efforts to Increase Opportunity and End Poverty*, states that "[p]overty and extreme inequality are social ills with deep spiritual and communal implications" and not only economic problems. Those conditions "demean human dignity, crush the human spirit, and sever family and communal bonds. . . ." As such, solutions have to be similarly multidimensional and not only focused on economic need. While government resources and coordination are essential, the report says, government efforts have to be "channeled in a manner that encourages partnerships" at the local level, partnerships that include faith-based organizations and other neighborhood groups. The goal is "holistic solutions to well-being and success."[30]

Although it is impossible to document the full scope and value of the contributions, there is no doubt about the high importance of faith-based services and activities in shaping people toward the good, aiding those in difficult circumstances, and contributing to the positive social and economic health of communities.

The Religious Freedom that Religious Organizations Need

The United States is designed as a pro-freedom nation (albeit an imperfect design that is imperfectly implemented). It operates under constitutional principles and historic government-society relationship patterns that prioritize personal freedom and limit government regulation of private organizations. This bias for freedom, both in principle and in practice, accrues to the benefit of religious organizations whose modes of operation and fundamental beliefs are out of line with those of the majority culture. For instance, for businesses seeking to be religiously faithful, it is helpful that regulatory burdens on the business sector in general are comparatively light. Similarly, our principles and

---

[30] President's Advisory Council on Faith-Based and Neighborhood Partnerships, *Strengthening Efforts to Increase Opportunity and End Poverty: Recommendations of the President's Advisory Council for Faith-Based and Neighborhood Partnerships to Address Poverty and Inequality*, advisory report, October 27, 2016, 11–12, accessed August 31, 2018, https://obamawhitehouse. archives.gov/sites/default/files/docs/2017_advisory_council_report.pdf.

laws, which strongly support a thriving and diverse civil society (for instance, broad freedoms that allow for organizations of diverse visions and values to be created, to gain federal tax-exempt status, and to be eligible to solicit tax-deductible contributions) greatly benefit churches and religious nonprofit organizations.

However, religious organizations need and are accorded an additional, specialized, freedom: religious freedom. Religious freedom simply means that an organization (or a person) is legally free—within limits—to do things differently than the law generally requires, if the religious views involved require or forbid such different action.

Institutional Religious Freedom

Religious freedom for organizations is similar to religious freedom for individuals, yet it is, in some ways, distinct.[31] Institutional religious freedom can even, on occasion, appear to be in direct conflict with individual religious freedom. This is because, for an organization to be distinct in some way—for example, to stand consistently and strongly for animal rights—it may need every employee, or at least all key employees, to uphold that distinctive stance, with the result that persons with different views simply are not hired, even though they are otherwise well-qualified.

Indeed, that is PETA's employment policy. As an organization with "uncompromising stands on animal rights,"[32] it requires its media spokespersons, fundraisers, and the directors of its public campaigns to be consistently vegan.[33] This should be no surprise: why would anyone take seriously PETA's belief that it is morally wrong to eat animals if its prominent leaders dine at Ruth's Chris Steakhouse or Five Guys? Similarly, many religious organizations only hire people who profess and live consistently with the religious convictions that guide the organization: Catholics who follow church teachings about abortion, Evangelicals who accept the traditional teaching about marriage, Jews who observe kosher practices.

---

[31] On institutional religious freedom, see Monsma and Carlson-Thies, *Free to Serve*; Stanley W. Carlson-Thies, "Beyond the Right of Conscience to Freedom to Live Faithfully," *Regent University Law Review*, 24, no. 2 (2011): 351–68; Stanley Carlson-Thies, "Why We Need Institutions in Order to Be Faithful, and What Institutions Need so That They Can Be Faithful," *Pro Rege*, XLIV, no. 1 (2015): 1–10.

[32] "Uncompromising Stands on Animal Rights," PETA, accessed December 12, 2018, https://www.peta.org/about-peta/why-peta/.

[33] "Frequently Asked Questions about Working for PETA/FSA," PETA, accessed December 12, 2018, https://www.peta.org/about-peta/work-at-peta/jobs-faq/.

By being religiously selective—or "discriminatory"—in who they hire, these organizations ensure that their personnel embody, rather than conflict with, the organization's mission and message. They make it more likely for employees to approach planning and decision-making with common values. They even make it possible for the workplace itself to be a form of spiritual community. And while an organization with a religion-based (or vegan-based) employment policy certainly excludes some otherwise suitable employees, the existence of distinctive organizations is a positive good for both employees and people seeking services: when there are diverse organizations, diverse job-seekers are more likely to find a compatible workplace; and diverse customers, patients, and students are more likely to find the particular services and assistance they need and most value.

Protection for Faith-Based Organizations and Not Only Churches

Religious freedom certainly must at least protect the existence and activities of "steepled" religious organizations—the primary or core organizations of a religion: churches, temples, synagogues, mosques, gurdwaras (Sikh), and other worship bodies, as well as associated denominational headquarters, seminaries, monasteries, nunneries, and so on. In most religions, these are the core organizations through which religion is taught and worship is conducted: primary places where believers engage in acts of faith. But acts of faith are found far beyond worship. It is notable that, as we saw above, houses of worship very commonly not only host worship and religious instruction but also offer a range of ministries to others. In Christian terms, they observe both the first great commandment—to love God entirely—and the second, to love our neighbors as ourselves (Matt. 22:36–40).

And, as we have seen, faith-inspired and faith-shaped services are offered not only by houses of worship but also by specialized service organizations, which should make it no surprise that, in our nation, so much protects and encourages civil society organizations. These purpose-built organizations offer education, childcare, drug treatment, low-income housing, and other forms of assistance to the public. They are also engaged in the exercise of religion that must be safeguarded by religious freedom protections. Though they generally serve the surrounding community and not only their own members, and though they usually provide "secular" services (housing, education, health care, etc.) rather than worship- or evangelism-related services, just like houses of worship, they are engaged in religious acts. The various religions that inspire and guide their actions often require a way of operating and serving others than what the law prescribes (e.g., hiring by religion, offering a curriculum shaped by religious understandings). Thus, these faith-based organizations need institutional religious freedom, just as do "steepled" religious bodies.

Religious Freedom and Religion-Inspired Companies

Our laws and public opinion do not readily acknowledge that businesses can be religious organizations. Rather, the presumption seems to be that the only goal of a business is to make profit, which means no possibility of animation by a religion-based vision of service.[34] Yet many companies are influenced by religious, cultural, or social-justice inspirations, and some regard themselves to be religious entities. Religious publishers, bookstores, and broadcasters, among others, may, in order to be faithful to their missions, closely consider religion both when hiring and when deciding what they will sell or how they will serve (e.g., not broadcasting blasphemous or disrespectful shows, publishing only books that reflect the values of a particular religion).

More common are companies that do not have a specific religious focus but that may regard some particular legal requirement as conflicting with company commitments. An example is the Hobby Lobby company, whose challenge to the requirement that employee health insurance plans must include all FDA contraceptives, including abortifacients, was vindicated by the U.S. Supreme Court (*Burwell v. Hobby Lobby*, 2014). The company's owners, the Green family, did not claim that Hobby Lobby is a religious entity, although the family does operate the chain of stores in line with its religious and ethical beliefs (closing the stores on Sundays, paying more than the legal minimum, donating generously to charities). The court ruled that the company could exclude the challenged abortifacients from the health plan, not because Hobby Lobby stores were themselves religious organizations, but because permitting the exclusion was the way to uphold the constitutionally protected religious-exercise right of the owners.

What Does Institutional Religious Freedom Entail?

Institutional religious freedom is the freedom of an organization (church, religious nonprofit, religion-shaped business) to operate and serve consistently with the guidelines of the organization's religious commitments, despite laws that dictate they do otherwise.

---

[34] On how this idea of bare profits-only business operations is mistaken, see Ronald J. Colombo, *The First Amendment and the Business Corporation* (New York: Oxford University Press, 2015).

It is often said that personnel is policy: what an organization can and will do depends on the capabilities and values of its employees. Consistent with this, many religious organizations regard faith-based decisions about who to hire and fire as fundamental to being able to be faithful to their religious mission—similar to the human resources policy of PETA or the refusal of a Democratic senator's office to hire Trump supporters. Other operational policies are also of key concern: Must a health plan include abortifacients or pay for sex-change operations? Is having a nonreligious majority on the governing board a requirement for receiving a government grant? Can the company or nonprofit incorporate religious elements into staff meetings?

And decisions about what to offer or how to provide a service are also clearly important to organizations that intend to be faithful to some religious concept or mission: Will a pharmacy operated by Catholic owners decline to stock emergency contraceptives because the owners regard these to be abortifacients? Will a counseling service offer counseling informed by religious values, or will that wrongly impose views on its clients? Should a religious nonprofit serving immigrants, on account of its religious commitment to serving all marginalized people, disobey a government requirement to exclude undocumented immigrants?

Religious organizations, whether they focus on worship and evangelism or on creating jobs or helping addicts, seek to obey both of the great commandments: they seek to serve their neighbors in a way that reflects obedience to God. They understand the great good that is a stable system of laws and an orderly society. Yet their first duty is to be faithful, not law-abiding. When their religion tells their organizations to act, or not to act, in contradiction to the law, they seek protection of their institutional religious freedom.

Protections for, and Challenges to, Institutional Religious Freedom in Contemporary U.S. Society

Religious organizations—congregations, faith-based nonprofits, and religion-inspired businesses—many of whom maintain convictions and practices not popular in American society, would not play the large role they do if their freedom to be different was unprotected. But while U.S. law extensively protects institutional religious freedom, pressures to narrow those protections are strong and growing.

Extensive Protections

Examples of broad protections currently in force include the religious-staffing freedom, the liberty to operate religious private schools, and the level-playing field provisions of the federal faith-based initiative.

Religious staffing. The freedom of religious organizations to consider religion in their employment decisions has already been noted. Just as PETA needs to be able to insist that its key public representatives be consistently vegan, churches and many faith-based service organizations have to be able to rule a job applicant in or out based on religion. PETA can insist on its vegan requirement because our employment and civil rights laws do not protect an employee's right to eat meat. Religious staffing by religious organizations, in sharp contrast, is specifically and carefully protected by law.

In fact, religious staffing by religious organizations is protected exactly in the place—Title VII of the 1964 Civil Rights Act—where federal law prohibits religious job discrimination by secular employers.[35] Religious employers can assess the suitability of potential employees based on religious criteria such as religious affiliation, assent to religious beliefs, and faithfulness to religion-based moral standards, but secular employers may not inquire into any of those matters. What is more, in federal law, religious organizations can hire based on religion even when they receive taxpayer money to provide a service to the general public.[36]

This right to staff by religion was challenged by employees in a Mormon health club who were fired for not joining the Mormon church. Though their positions involved no explicitly "religious" duties and the employer was not a steepled religious organization, the U.S. Supreme Court unanimously upheld the firings and the expansive religious-staffing freedom.[37] It cannot be the legitimate task of government officials to tell religious organizations whether religious suitability is a legitimate qualification for any or all of its employees.

Nonpublic schools. The United States has a long tradition of "common schools": K-12 schools funded and managed by local public school districts, which are government entities.[38] Much of higher education is also public or

---

[35] Carl H. Esbeck, Stanley W. Carlson-Thies, and Ronald J. Sider, *The Freedom of Faith-Based Organizations to Staff on a Religious Basis* (Washington, DC: Center for Public Justice, 2004).

[36] This is true even in the relatively few federal programs with rules that explicitly ban religious and other forms of job discrimination. The Department of Justice has ruled that, faced with that employment nondiscrimination requirement, a religious organization has recourse to the Religious Freedom Restoration Act to have the employment restriction be lifted. Department of Justice, Office of Legal Counsel, "Application of the Religious Freedom Restoration Act to the Award of a Grant Pursuant to the Juvenile Justice and Delinquency Prevention Act," June 29, 2007, accessed February 12, 2019, https://www.justice.gov/file/451561/download. This Bush administration ruling has been confirmed by both the Obama and Trump administrations.

[37] *Corporation of the Presiding Bishop v. Amos* (1987).

[38] See Charles L. Glenn, *The Myth of the Common School* (Amherst: University of Massachusetts Press, 1988), for why those schools were less "common" in values than they purported to be.

governmental: state university systems, community colleges, land-grant colleges. But at both levels, there are also many private educational institutions, including many religious ones: Jewish day schools and Catholic universities, Catholic parochial schools and Protestant colleges, the Muslim liberal arts college Zaytuna, and many different kinds of Protestant K-12 schools.

These religious alternatives to secular, government-run institutions exist because religious communities have, and desire to pass on to new generations, distinctive and deeply valued convictions about life and the divine. Unless prevented by government force or a lack of resources, they will organize after-school supplemental religious training, Sunday School classes, religious schools, and even entire systems of religious schools at every level. And here in the United States, the law allows the operation of private religious educational institutions; it also allows and even supports fundraising for these and other civil society institutions.

Indeed, the law does not just "allow" private religious education: there is a U.S. Supreme Court case that upholds the right of private schools, including religious schools, to exist. In its 1924 ruling in *Pierce v. Society of Sisters* against the State of Oregon's requirement that all children attend public schools, the court proclaimed that children are not wards of government and that parents must be free to direct the education of their children. Other Supreme Court decisions have upheld the use of government scholarships at religious higher education institutions (*Witters v. Washington Department of Services for the Blind* [1986]); a state voucher program allowing parents to use the government-funded voucher to pay for schooling at religious schools (*Zelman v. Simmons-Harris* [2002]); and a state program giving tax credits to individuals and companies that donate to scholarships that can be used at religious as well as secular schools (*Arizona Christian School Tuition Organization v. Winn* [2011]).

Upon hearing about the planned closing in 2013 of Blessed Sacrament School in the Bronx, U.S. Supreme Court Justice Sonia Sotomayor, who was valedictorian of the school's class of 1968, said, "I am heartbroken. . . . You know how important those eight years were? It's symbolic of what it means for all our families, like my mother, who were dirt-poor. She watched what happened to my cousins in public school and worried if we went there, we might not get out. So she scrimped and saved. It was a road of opportunity for kids with no other alternative."[39]

[39] Quoted in David Gonzalez, "As Her Old School Faces the End, a Justice Reminisces," *New York Times*, January 25, 2013, https://www.nytimes.com/2013/01/26/nyregion/with-her-old-school-set-to-close-a-justice-reminisces.html.

Federal faith-based initiative. The faith-based initiative is another bright indicator and profound example of how U.S. political principles and practices strongly uphold institutional religious freedom. This is the federal initiative started by President George W. Bush to ensure that the federal government partners with, supports, and learns from faith- and community-based organizations that serve their neighbors.

The roots of the initiative go back to the Charitable Choice provision in the federal welfare-reform law signed by President Bill Clinton, a provision that requires states spending federal welfare funding to give religious providers of services the same opportunity as their secular cohorts to compete for government support. President Barack Obama and President Donald Trump have since maintained the goals of the initiative and, with some changes, the set of federal offices that promote those goals. Over these same years, various states and many municipalities have also experimented with ways to better engage with religious and community organizations.[40]

Why? These organizations, particularly the religious ones, understand and respond to social problems and marginalized and downtrodden people differently than large-scale and secularized service providers. Recall the report from the end of the Obama administration, which pointed out that entrenched poverty has many dimensions and requires a holistic response. Or consider the Access to Recovery (ATR) program started by the Bush administration. ATR provided additional federal drug-treatment funding to states and Native American tribes that created a voucher system. With vouchers, addicted people were given a choice of treatment options, including treatment that integrates religious teachings and activities.[41] Addictions, including opioid addiction, clearly

---

[40] Stanley W. Carlson-Thies, "Charitable Choice: Bringing Religion Back into American Welfare," in *Religion Returns to the Public Square: Faith and Policy in America*, ed. Hugh Heclo and Wilfred M. McClay (Washington, DC: Woodrow Wilson Center Press; Baltimore: Johns Hopkins University Press, 2003), 269–97; David Donaldson and Stanley W. Carlson-Thies, *A Revolution of Compassion: Faith-Based Groups as Full Partners in Fighting America's Social Problems* (Grand Rapids, MI: Baker Books, 2003); Carlson-Thies, "Faith-Based Initiative 2.0"; Lew Daly, *God's Economy: Faith-Based Initiatives and the Caring State* (Chicago: University of Chicago Press, 2009); John Chandler, *Faith-Based Policy: A Litmus Test for Understanding Contemporary America* (Lanham, MD: Lexington Books, 2014); Jay F. Hein, *The Quiet Revolution: An Active Faith that Transforms Lives and Communities* (n.p.: Waterfall Press, 2014); Stanley Carlson-Thies and Carl H. Esbeck, "Happy Birthday, Charitable Choice: Two Decades of Bipartisan Cooperation on Government Funding and Religion," blogpost at Institutional Religious Freedom Alliance, August 22, 2016, http://www.irfalliance.org/happy-birthday-charitable-choice-20-years-of-success/.

[41] Briefly described in Carlson-Thies, "Faith-Based Initiative 2.0," 940–41.

have a chemical-medical aspect, but also, it seems, a psychological and even spiritual dimension. For many, connecting with a "higher power," as the Twelve Step program calls it, appears essential for a solution. If so, should not government programs and government funding support such programs, neither excluding them from funding nor requiring suppression of their religious character and faith-shaped methods as a condition of eligibility for funds?

Growing Pressure to Narrow Religious Protections

As America becomes ever more diverse—religiously, philosophically, and morally—various faith-based practices that many have celebrated and nearly everyone tolerated because of their acceptance of religious freedom, in even the recent past, are now increasingly being condemned by powerful groups and officials as discriminatory and bigoted. In 2016, Martin Castro, then chairman of the U.S. Commission on Civil Rights, a federal advisory body, claimed that "religious freedom" was a "code word" for discrimination.[42] Given this view, he and many others argue that the freedom should be curtailed and should not be maintained, much less expanded. Religious beliefs and practices that he and others regard as hateful and harmful should not be shielded by the law but prohibited.

A narrow view of religion. The challenges to religious organizations are growing and multiple.[43] Sometimes the pressure to restrict institutional religious freedom is motivated by the view that only worship and prayer, not activities out in the "secular" world, are protected by the First Amendment. On multiple secular university campuses, religious student clubs that insist their leaders must be faithful to the clubs' religious beliefs have been denied official recognition, along with the related access to communications and meetings spaces, on the grounds that they are not forums for the legitimate exercise of religion but rather for hateful discrimination.[44]

World Vision, the Evangelical Christian overseas relief and development organization, had to defend its religious hiring practices in federal court against a claim that, because it was engaged in humanitarian work, not religion, and because it served all people, not just Christian believers, it must not be

---

[42] U.S. Commission on Civil Rights, *Peaceful Coexistence: Reconciling Nondiscrimination Principles with Civil Liberties*, briefing report (Washington, DC: U.S. Commission on Civil Rights, 2016). Castro's comments are on page 29. https://www.usccr.gov/pubs/docs/Peaceful-Coexistence-09-07-16.PDF.

[43] See Monsma and Carlson-Thies, *Free to Serve*.

[44] Monsma and Carlson-Thies, *Free to Serve*, chap. 2.

considered a religious organization—the only kind of organization allowed under Title VII to consider religion in employment decisions. However, the courts acknowledged that World Vision showed itself to be religious in its documents, beliefs, and practices. Further, the court held that an organization can engage in humanitarian work in a religious way: indeed, World Vision serves all, without regard to religion, precisely because the organization is sure that is what its faith requires.[45]

In 2017, Miracle Hill, a Christian child-welfare organization in South Carolina, encountered another form of opposition to religious freedom. For nearly three decades, Miracle Hill had partnered with the state government to recruit foster parents and place foster children, accounting for 15 percent of placements in the state. The funds supporting these services, although administered by the state, came from the federal government. As a Christian organization that sees fostering children as a religious ministry and not only as a secular activity, Miracle Hill has always recruited only Christian parents. That policy was sharply challenged by state officials in 2017, after the outgoing Obama administration had promulgated a new regulation for funding from the Department of Health and Human Services, the federal agency that administers federal child-welfare funding. The regulation created new categories of prohibited discrimination in the use of funds, adding, among others, discrimination on the bases of religion, sexual orientation, or gender identity.

South Carolina subsequently demanded that Miracle Hill end its practice of working only with Christian foster parents or the state would end its partnership with Miracle Hill. Fortunately for Miracle Hill, the federal regulations allowed for an appeal for an exemption, South Carolina's governor was sympathetic to Miracle Hill's plight, and the Trump administration issued the needed exemption in early 2019.[46] Although its religion-forward policies are now legally protected, Miracle Hill and the Trump administration have been subjected to strong criticism for including an allegedly improper sectarian religious requirement in services meant to contribute to the common good.

---

[45] Monsma and Carlson-Thies, *Free to Serve*, chap. 2.
[46] The exemption is announced in a letter from the Administration for Children and Families in the Department of Health and Human Services to Governor Henry McMaster, dated January 23, 2019. On the Miracle Hill story, see Bonnie Pritchett, "The Tie that Binds," *World* magazine October 30, 2018, accessed January 23, 2019, https://world.wng.org/content/the_tie_that_binds, and Jocelyn Davis, "Why It's Not Discrimination for Christian Agencies to Only Recruit Christian Foster and Adoptive Parents," TheFederalist.com, December 19, 2018, accessed January 24, 2019, http://thefederalist.com/2018/12/19/not-discrimination-christian-agencies-recruit-christian-foster-adoptive-parents/.

Conflicts about views on human sexuality. Notwithstanding incidents like these, increasingly, the opposition to religious organizations is due not to their religious character or practices but rather to religion-based beliefs and practices concerning human sexuality and marriage. The opposition, tensions, controversies, and legal pressures are legion and rapidly increasing.[47] As illustrative, consider disputes about the practices of religious higher-education institutions on the east and west coasts and the strong legal opposition to a different religious foster care organization, Catholic Social Services of Philadelphia.

Gordon College, an Evangelical liberal arts school just north of Boston, became the target of intense media and political opposition, and faced the threat of losing its accreditation—a *sine qua non* of operating as a significant educational institution—when the public suddenly, in 2014, discovered its code of conduct. That code, similar to those at many theologically conservative schools, requires professors, staff, and students to abide by a conservative set of conduct standards, which include the restriction of sexual relationships to man-woman marriages. Political authorities rushed to wash their hands of involvement with Gordon; for instance, a local school district where Gordon students had assisted low-income students for years—and received accolades, not accusations—now claimed that it was immoral for it to partner with the bigoted college. The threat to Gordon's accreditation was eventually lifted: it had, in fact, not violated any actual criterion for maintaining its accreditation.[48]

A few years later, theologically conservative colleges in California faced the severe penalty of being placed off-limits to low-income students awarded Cal Grants to help pay for higher education. The issue, here, too, was opposition to the colleges' conservative sexual standards in their community conduct codes. Such discriminatory schools, according to a bill proposed in the state

[47] Monsma and Carlson-Thies, *Free to Serve*; Douglas Laycock, Anthony R. Picarello Jr., and Robin Fretwell Wilson, *Same-Sex Marriage and Religious Liberty: Emerging Conflicts* (Lanham, MD: Rowman & Littlefield, 2008); Timothy Samuel Shah, Thomas F. Farr, and Jack Friedman, *Religious Freedom and Gay Rights: Emerging Conflicts in the United States and Europe* (New York: Oxford University Press, 2016); John Corvino, Ryan T. Anderson, and Sherif Girgis, *Debating Religious Liberty and Discrimination* (New York: Oxford University Press, 2017).

[48] Among many press accounts, see Jake New, "Keeping a Ban, Offering Support," *Inside Higher Ed*, March 17, 2015, https://www.insidehighered.com/news/2015/03/17/gordon-college-maintains-ban-homosexual-practice-creates-human-sexuality-task-force; Kate Tracy, "Gordon College Loses City Contract, Gets Accreditation Scrutiny," *Christianity Today*, July 14, 2014, accessed February 13, 2019, https://www.christianitytoday.com/news/2014/july/gordon-college-loses-city-contract-gets-accreditation-scrut.html.

legislature (SB 1146), could not be a fit place for a student to use state-government scholarship aid. Yet, these colleges were often the choice of poorer immigrant families sending their first child to higher-education institutions and seeking institutions with values aligned with their own. A public campaign pointing out the foolishness of a legal restriction that would have the effect of keeping the students the Cal Grants were meant to serve out of their preferred colleges resulted in extensive amendment of the bill before it was enacted, enabling the religious colleges to continue serving those low-income students and families.[49]

And the religious foster care provider? With odd timing, in March 2018, just weeks after the City of Philadelphia had issued an urgent call for additional foster families to cope with the flood of children needing placements, the City ended all referrals of children needing foster care to Catholic Social Services (CSS). This, after CSS in Philadelphia had been placing children in foster homes for more than a century and for fifty years in partnership with the City.[50]

The cause of the ban was the CSS policy not to place children with same-sex couples, in keeping with the church's teaching about marriage. The City called the policy discriminatory even though no such prohibition had been announced as being applicable to private foster care providers, and even though applying the prohibition would in no way expand placements with same-sex married couples: there were already far more kids needing homes than there were homes open to them.

Civic pluralism. The twin foster-care-agency cases of Miracle Hill and Catholic Social Services of Philadelphia show the continued *importance* of institutional religious freedom: this is legal protection those private religious agencies need because they maintain beliefs and practices that go against the

[49] Stanley Carlson-Thies, "California Higher Education Bill Will Undermine Faith-Based Universities," blogpost at the Institutional Religious Freedom Alliance, June 27, 2016, accessed February 13, 2019, http://www.irfalliance.org/california-higher-education-bill-will-undermine-faith-based-universities-2/; Stanley Carlson-Thies, "End of SB 1146 Threat to California Religious Colleges—For Now," blogpost at the Institutional Religious Freedom Alliance, October 7, 2016, accessed February 13, 2019, http://www.irfalliance.org/end-of-sb-1146-threat-to-california-religious-colleges-for-now/.
[50] Darel E. Paul, "Foster Care Fanaticism in Philadelphia," *First Things*, May 24, 2018, accessed January 25, 2019, https://www.firstthings.com/web-exclusives/2018/05/foster-care-fanaticism-in-philadelphia; BecketLaw, "Emergency Application for Injunction Pending Appellate Review or, in the Alternative, Petition for Writ of Certiorari and Injunction Pending Resolution" in Sharonell Fulton et al. v. City of Philadelphia, July 31, 2018, accessed January 25, 2019, https://www.kidsrightsnotfights.com/sharonell-et-al-v-philadelphia.

requirements that government officials seek to enforce on all. And the cases demonstrate the growing *opposition* to broad institutional religious freedom protections: so many powerful people and organizations are deeply opposed to those agencies' beliefs and practices and are convinced that the government ought to stop, not protect, those beliefs and practices. Yet it is possible for policy regulating private foster care and adoption services to show our society how we Americans, with our increasing differences, can nonetheless live together as good neighbors.

These child-welfare organizations are private, part of civil society, and not agencies of government. Government is required to treat everyone alike, and it acts through coercion and mandates; the institutional pattern of civil society, in sharp contrast, is characterized by voluntary, orderly, and structured diversity. Our extensive and thriving civil-society sector (and our free market, too) is the place where people and organizations that hold contrasting, even conflicting, religious beliefs, moral values, and related distinctive practices can all put their convictions and practices into action—without others being thereby compelled to forfeit their own deeply held beliefs and practices.

Consider the sharp divide in views about families and intimate relationships. Marriage equality is now the law of the land, which many regard to be right. And legally, individuals and couples may adopt or become foster parents without regard to their marital status, sexual orientation, gender identity, or religion. At the same time, many religious communities, individuals, and organizations maintain the traditional view of marriage and sexuality; this view is legally protected,[51] and people and organizations may act in accordance with it. That is, they can act on this view within limits—a chief limit being that they may not try to use the law to prohibit same-sex couples or LGBT people from becoming foster or adoptive parents.

How can the law protect both views about marriage, families, and the optimal qualifications of adoptive and foster parents? Rather than prohibiting discrimination by all private agencies based on religion, sexual orientation, and gender identity, as they recruit parents and place children for adoption or fostering, the government can permit agencies to have distinct

---

[51] From Justice Anthony Kennedy's majority opinion in the *Obergefell* case legalizing same-sex marriage across the country: "[I]t must be emphasized that religions, and those who adhere to religious doctrines, may continue to advocate with utmost, sincere conviction that, by divine precepts, same-sex marriage should not be condoned. The First Amendment ensures that religious organizations and persons are given proper protection as they seek to teach the principles that are so fulfilling and so central to their lives and faiths, and to their own deep aspirations to continue the family structure they have long revered."

policies, serving distinct communities with their varied values. And it can operate an information and referral system to help families with different values match up with appropriate agencies. Then every family and couple will be well-served by an agency or agencies that specifically welcomes them, knows best how to encourage them to engage in the challenging tasks of adoption and foster care, and can best support them through those challenges.

When, instead, it is the legal requirement that every private agency recruit families and place children without regard to religion, sexual orientation, gender identity, and marriage type, agencies committed to traditional religious and moral values are unable to be faithful to their deep convictions and will close their doors. Such a policy does not help LGBT people or others with values different than those agencies, and it results in fewer adoptions and foster care placements—just the opposite of what is needed. Moreover, such policy makes a mockery of the purported freedom of religious communities, people, and organizations to act on their convictions, for its consequence is that adoption and foster care agencies attuned to conservative beliefs cannot exist.

If respect for the varied beliefs of Americans—played out through our stated commitment to religious freedom—is to be meaningful, it must include broad institutional religious freedom; that is, the freedom to create and operate private organizations that manifest one's deep convictions, regardless of whether others in society disagree with those convictions or even regard them to be detrimental.[52]

Safeguarding Institutional Religious Freedom: Don't Leave It to the Lawyers!

What can be done to protect religious organizations and strengthen institutional religious freedom, a vital freedom that is increasingly contested as harmful?

Great lawyers and legal scholars are essential. Lawyers defend organizations facing legal trouble, while legal scholars can help construct those defenses and expand our society's understanding of what religious freedom entails. But no

---

[52] For more on this kind of civic-pluralist solution, see Stanley W. Carlson-Thies, "Why Should Washington, DC, Listen to Rome and Geneva about Public Policy for Civil Society?" in *Christianity and Civil Society: Catholic and Neo-Calvinist Perspectives*, ed. Jeanne Heffernan Schindler (Lanham, MD: Lexington Books, 2008), 165–87; Carlson-Thies, "Faith-Based Initiative," 70–85.

matter how courageous, skillful, experienced, innovative, and wise they may be, we dare not leave it to law professionals alone to uphold the religious freedom that religious organizations need. Religious leaders, staff of faith-based organizations, people of faith in business, policy advocates, elected officials and civil servants, church leaders, and citizens in general—people who understand that religious freedom is foundational, not dispensable, for a good and just America—all have roles to play.

"Upstream" Protections: Good Laws and Regulations

Better than the best courtroom defense are laws and regulations that strongly protect institutional religious freedom. As we have seen, our laws, regulations, government programs, and government processes are generally, and often very strongly, supportive of the freedom that congregations, religious nonprofits, and religion-shaped businesses need in order to be true to the religious visions to which they are committed. But, of course, laws, rules, and programs are continuously being created and modified, and increasingly, those in charge—elected officials and other civil servants—are less familiar with and sympathetic to the concerns, views, and practices of religious organizations.

Advocacy and lobbying (yes, this is legal and encouraged in the law) are vital. Communication with officials helps them better understand the religious social sector, particularly the need for and logic of religious freedom: how institutional religious freedom is indispensable for a thriving civil society and enables us to live together despite our differences. And, often, there are specific opportunities to comment on the language of proposed laws and draft regulations.

Religious freedom advocates regularly weigh in, organizing briefings, meeting with officials, and writing protest letters and technical "comments" on draft rules. All of these activities are good. But all of these activities are better—more convincing—when not just the advocates but also the leaders of the affected religious organizations speak up, even if speaking risks controversy. They know the pressures they face. They know the good that they do. They know the freedom they need to be distinctive, to be "faith-full." They can tell the persuasive stories.

Broaden the Public's Understanding of the Good of Religious Freedom

Religious freedom, like every constitutional freedom, shrivels if not spoken of, defended, and exercised. And when fewer and fewer understand and are committed to religious belief, while more and more are skeptical of or opposed to traditional religious and moral values, there is little reason to expect public sympathy for organizations with views and practices outside those valued by the majority.

In the Apostle Peter's first letter, the small bands of Christians in Roman society were admonished, because they were "foreigners and exiles," "to abstain from sinful desires, which wage war against your soul." Instead, they were to "[l]ive such good lives among the pagans that, though they accuse you of doing wrong, they may see your good deeds and glorify God on the day he visits us" (1 Peter 2:11–12).

This wisdom also applies to religious organizations in modern society, which is rapidly losing its knowledge about and appreciation for the positive value of religion and the vast amount of good done by religious organizations. Our neighbors do indeed regard some of the distinctive beliefs and practices of faith-based organizations as instances of "wrong-doing." Still, when religion-influenced companies, houses of worship, and religious nonprofits act with integrity and good intentions, and when they creatively make known to those watching them both the many good works they do and the religious beliefs that motivate and shape those good works, they give their communities a way to look past the mistrusted practices and beliefs to appreciate the genuine good that the religion has caused to grow. And as a result, critics may even come to "glorify God," or at least to support the religious freedom that these good-works organizations need.

What Religious Organizations Must Do

We have noted two of the three ways that religious organizations can, and must, act in order to protect and promote the institutional religious freedom they need. First, they must understand public policy trends and be courageous and knowledgeable enough to speak up when officials solicit guidance or take paths that will be detrimental to institutional religious freedom. And, second, they must be creative in communicating to the public not only the scope and variety and effectiveness of their good works but—and this is indispensable—how those good works, the "fruits," stem from their religious practices and commitments, the "roots." Connect those two, and the public can better understand why institutional religious freedom is good not just for religious organizations but also for the marginalized, sick, poor, and abused—good for expanding the common good and achieving social justice.

And the third action path for religious organizations? Call it organizational best practices: religious organizations should take care to align the many aspects of their operations and services with the religious values they claim to be foundational to their existence and success. Those practices and services must reflect, not conflict with, those religious commitments. Employment policy should further the mission; donors should give out of an understanding of the foundational importance of the religious vision rather than in ignorance of it; the workplace culture should be in line with the organization's stated religious values; its services should be shaped by and not ignore the ethical commitments of the faith. Otherwise, the religion will amount to mere words.[53]

What You Can Do

Institutional religious freedom is inert unless exercised: religious organizations must be courageous—and wise at the same time—to act on their religious convictions, not letting them erode out of neglect or mistaken capitulation. We've noted several ways that religious organizations can and must be active on behalf of the religious freedom they need. But what can you do—someone who sees the great gift that faith-based services are to our society? Here are six actions to take:

1. Speak up for the religious freedom of others, too. Religious freedom must be for "thee" and not only "me," or else it is not a principle but only a self-preservative strategy.

2. Speak up for the religious freedom of others even though you believe they are wrong. To be sure, religious freedom should not shield harmful actions. But beyond that, you should defend the religious freedom that others need. Suppose your views have changed, and now you support, on a religious basis, same-sex marriage. If so, your change of view is no reason for you to demand that the law should coerce others to make a change that you made by conviction.

3. Speak up for capacious religious freedom. Religion is more than worship. It also guides people in their "secular" lives: the decisions they make in business; what they regard as excellent health care; how they understand history, society, and art; how they pursue social justice; and

---

[53] See Peter Greer and Chris Horst, *Mission Drift: The Unspoken Crisis Facing Leaders, Charities, and Churches* (Bloomington, MN: Bethany House, 2014). Beginning in 2018, the Sacred Sector initiative of the Center for Public Justice began offering training to faith-based organizations and emerging leaders of such organizations, educating them on how to align their operations and services with their religious missions.

even what they understand social justice to be. Speak up for the full freedom of religion, the freedom for people to live their lives in accordance with their deep convictions; do not just defend the freedom of worship, as important as this freedom is.

4. Speak up for institutional religious freedom and not just for individual religious freedom. Institutions are means by which people put their convictions and their inspirations into practice, with others, in a durable way that can make a broad, positive impact. Defend the diversity of organizations in civil society and in the free market.

5. Speak up for other vital rights. As the United States becomes more religiously and morally diverse, more of our fellow citizens are becoming convinced that their own rights are not adequately protected; as a result, fewer people are finding legislative proposals to strengthen religious-freedom protections persuasive. We can join hands over divisions to create policies that strengthen our rights and their rights at the same time.

"When claims based on a fundamental right are in tension with other vital rights and interests, as they sometimes will be, there must be a determined effort to seek resolution through civil discussion and reasonable accommodation. . . . [R]ather than relegating competing interests and rights claims to zero-sum conflict, litigation, and judicial decrees, Americans of good will must work together to fashion reasonable accommodations for the good of all."

—American Charter of Freedom of Religion and Conscience, Article 9.

6. Speak up for civil pluralism, despite its inconveniences. It is in the best interest of everyone—employees with different values, and patients, customers, and students with varied preferences—when institutions in civil society and the marketplace are permitted to have distinctive operations, services, and goods. But there is a price: people will sometimes be turned away. They will have to look elsewhere for a desired product, drive a few extra miles to find the agency that can best serve them, apply to another employer to find a suitable workplace. That is the price of diverse institutions.[54] But diverse institutions are what we need in a diverse society.

---

[54] Monsma and Carlson-Thies, *Free to Serve*, 101–04.

The New Testament's "Religious Freedom Prayer"

Written during the reign of Nero, a notorious tyrant and persecutor of Christians, the guidance in the first letter to Timothy about how to pray for political leaders might well have recommended a plea that God convert—or else replace—the emperor of the Roman Empire. Instead, the instruction to Timothy—and now to us—is to pray for religious freedom, for the opportunity to "live peaceful and quiet lives in all godliness and holiness." Even in the midst of Nero's dissolute and brutal reign. Even in the middle of our diverse nation. May we pray for the same freedom today:

> I urge, then, first of all, that petitions, prayers, intercession and thanksgiving be made for all people—for kings and all those in authority, that we may live peaceful and quiet lives in all godliness and holiness. This is good, and pleases God our Savior, who wants all people to be saved and to come to a knowledge of the truth. (1 Tim. 2:1–4)

Conclusion

Anne R. Bradley

"I cannot accept your canon that we are to judge Pope and Kind unlike other men, with favorable presumption that they did no wrong. If there is any presumption it is the other way, against the holders of power, increasing as the power increases. Historic responsibility has to make up for the want of legal responsibility. Power tends to corrupt, and absolute power corrupts absolutely. Great men are almost always bad men, even they exercise the influence and not authority, still more when you superadd the tendency or the certainty of corruption by authority."

—John Emerich Edward Dalberg-Acton

"From Oriental despotism to American hegemony, the state has never failed to attract, with its power and pelf, those who would fabricate apologia. But their litany of claims—that our rulers are wise and their rule is beneficent, that our rulers protect us from horrible dangers, that our rulers uphold the glorious tradition of our ancestors, that our rulers embody the interests of society, that our rulers are appointed by God, that our rulers bring science and reason to society, and so on—never explain how such claims turn hegemony into voluntary association, murder into defense, kidnapping into voluntary association, and taxation into free-will offering."

—Jeffrey Herbener

This book is about freedom of conscience, a biblical idea that is grounded in the pursuit of truth, the desire for which is steeped in human anthropology. This book is about liberty, spiritual individualism, peaceful cooperation, and voluntarism. Religious freedom is freedom to pursue truth in one's life. It is the natural extension of human reason and purpose. The freedom to understand or reject the divine is necessary for human beings to experience true personal flourishing. The state has no moral role in mitigating one's conscience, and a "legitimate" state is one that protects rather than directs, engineers, or constrains these freedoms. The state can neither assign nor legitimately restrict rights; it can only protect. The United States has largely been an experiment in religious, political, economic, and overall human freedom.

The Growth of the State as a Threat to Religious Freedom

The past one hundred years, however, have witnessed expansive increases in both the size and scope of the government (or *state*), in the United States in particular.[1] In 1913, U.S. government spending as a percentage of gross domestic product (GDP) was 7.5.[2] Today, it is 38 percent. This trend is true not only in the United States but in all industrialized economies: government spending for early industrialized economies has grown significantly and is largely explained by two factors: health care and education.[3]

With the increased size (what the government spends) and scope (what the government can influence) of government affairs, the battle over where the government is or is not "sovereign"[4] continues to be fought—over all spheres of culture. In early twentieth-century America, the government occupied a small percentage of overall national income, which meant that the government was necessarily limited in its domain. It had a relatively small budget with which to carry out what some might call "necessary services," like the protection of property and national defense.

With the growth in government expenditures (the *size* of the government), "necessary services" have necessarily increased, quite beyond what the government is capable of and intended for. The onset of the federal income tax allowed the government a constant stream of cash, which it previously did not have. This created an incentive to spend more, which increases power and creates government agencies with greater control—also an aspect of power. The government necessarily grows, and special interests form that encourage that

---

[1] Robert Higgs, "The Growth of Government," The Library of Economics and Liberty, accessed March 30, 2019, https://www.econlib.org/library/Enc/GovernmentGrowth.html.

[2] Vito Tanzi and Ludger Schuknecht, *Public Spending in the 20th Century: A Global Perspective* (New York: Cambridge University Press, 2000), 6.

[3] Esteban Ortiz-Ospina and Max Roser, "Government Spending," Our World in Data, accessed March 27, 2019, https://ourworldindata.org/government-spending.

[4] Abraham Kuyper, *Abraham Kuyper: Lectures on Calvinism: Six Lectures from the Stone Foundation Lectures Delivered at Princeton University* (Cedar Lake, MI: Readaclassic.com, 2010), 57–81.

growth for their own benefit. The costs are spread out over the tax base, and we are left with a winner-loser environment. So, the goal posts of state "sovereignty" have moved as federal income tax has increased, and with that come predictable power struggles.

The *scope* of the government has also necessarily expanded. The government desires to control and influence who we trade and associate with, what we value, and what we buy. It has a built-in incentive to expand its reach, and with that come divisions and struggles over what the government *should* do. This incentive is endemic to government institutions because they operate on the basis of coercion, rather than on the basis of profit and loss. Lord Acton's famous remark, "Power tends to corrupt and absolute power corrupts absolutely," reflects both the sinful nature of man and the institutions of government. Acton continues with the insight that "great men are almost always bad men;"[5] his indictment on the powerful. Therefore, Christians need to be worried about the expanding role and size of the U.S. government at all levels. As the scope of power increases, the taste for power among the powerful increases—at the expense of personal liberty, spiritual individualism, and free choice and agency.

The growth of the government invites more people in to determine the rules of state action, so we find ourselves in the twenty-first century wondering what the terms of employee-provided health care should be, what employees can wear to work, what the government forces firms to sell, or what it may force consumers to buy. Outside the government and inside the context of economic freedom, the market, undergirded by a morality of individual liberty and personal responsibility, and checked and supported by the bulwark of civil society, works this out without need of the government. What freedom implies is not a release from sin and the Fall, but rather the freedom to exit; the right to say, "No, thank you."[6] The "No, thank you" axiom is key for any possibility of peaceful coexistence among people holding different views and spiritual practices.

Human Anthropology as the Foundation for Freedom

Human anthropology, properly understood, directs us away from the wrong questions and into the right ones. We are made in the image of God, and our human anthropology, grounded in Scripture, demonstrates that we are finite,

---

[5] Lord Acton, "Acton-Creighton Correspondence [1887]."
[6] Jim Otteson, *Honorable Business: A Framework for Business in a Just and Humane Economy* (New York: Oxford University Press, 2019), 9.

that we live in a world of scarcity, that we are self-interested, and that we need to cooperate. We need each other. We must come into community with one another for civil society and economic thriving. However, we are all fallen images, and no matter how perfect we may think our own theology is, we are not perfected in the here and now. Humans are humans. We all sin, seek our own gain at the expense of others, and are easily corruptible. Thus, creating a flourishing society is not about finding good people, immune to sin, to oversee it. But rather, the task of political economy is to find institutions that take men as they are and induce them to cooperate in ways that help one another.

Market economies buttressed by the ethos of property rights, discovery, and service are the way we bring about more flourishing. There are no "angels" who can govern the halls of Congress, the pulpits of churches, or the offices of Wall Street. The task of human flourishing is to provide people a space to be free, to learn, to pursue truth through reason and discovery, and to voluntarily adopt and abide by principles that suit them—and people must be free to do that to the extent that they don't inhibit the rights of others. All of this requires a small and limited government focused on protecting freedom—religious, economic, and political.

The growth of the government over the past century brings with it the quest for power, not just among current politicians but also among groups who think they can benefit by using the government for their own purposes at the expense of others. This growth of the government is bad for religious freedom, and it corrupts religious organizations by distorting incentives and creating an environment for them to use the government as their weapon against other religions, beliefs, or values. This bargaining by religious groups to appropriate the government for their own interests induces the element of coercion into the expression of religion and conscience, and this tears at the fabric of civil society, crowds out church and religious organizations, and distorts economic and political freedoms. Those who "win" acquire the government's privilege through coercion, then use that power of coercion to limit others in their pursuit of conscience and reason: it is an environment that creates winners and losers. No one wants to be the loser, so the political battles over what constitutes permissible activities have no foreseeable end. The battle should not be over which faith is coerced on individuals by the government; rather, the battle should be to keep the coercive and corruptible government powers constrained to the sphere of "legitimate" government affairs, such as providing the rule of law. Any person from any faith community or nonfaith community, such as an atheist, should be free to live as his or her conscience directs and to live by and advocate for those beliefs in the public square.

These debates regarding the "proper role of government" dominate American culture today, from the news media, to the pulpit, to the family dinner table. Yet, without a theological understanding of human anthropology and purpose, and of the economic realities of what the government is capable of, these debates turn into nothing but shrill armchair theorizing; and the republic hangs in the balance—with one of its cornerstone virtues up for debate: religious freedom. This book provides a needed biblical defense of religious freedom that stems from a biblical understanding of human anthropology and purpose. We are created free. It is always moving to reflect on the profound reality that God did not *need* us but created us and the universe because he *wanted* us. God is the master architect of humanity and desires an intimate relationship with each of us.

Christian theology teaches us that sin entered the world through the disobedience of Adam and Eve. This fall from grace explains why not all will desire God (Rom. 1:18–23), and while those who do not will be held accountable for their decisions, they must be free to navigate their own pursuit of truth and meaning. Freedom is part of our creation and necessary for our journey in seeking the truth. In this respect, we are made free—not a freedom without boundaries, but a freedom where the boundaries must be discerned through reason and the application of conscience to the realities in which we find ourselves. We cannot let the government coerce citizens into believing in any religion because, in fact, the government cannot force a person to believe. They may force a statement or confession of belief, but true belief can come only from the human heart. Religious freedom is an inalienable right of every individual and exists beyond the reach of the civil magistrate. Religious freedom protects each person's pursuit of the truth, even if one ultimately rejects God. Thus, religious freedom is not for Evangelicals only—on the contrary. For religious freedom to operate as it is supposed to, and for it to allow us to fully experience the quest of being human, it is required for all.

The Priesthood of All Believers

We live in amazing and rare times. Globally, people are freer and richer than ever before. The long story of human history has not been a story of religious, economic, political, or other freedoms. Prior to 1750, no society had ever experienced sustained growth in per-capita income. Colonial America in 1750 was almost identical to China at the time.[7] Most of human history is a story of

---

[7] Robert E. Lucas Jr., "Industrial Revolution: Past and Future: 2003 Annual Report Essay," Minneapolis Fed, May 2004, accessed March 27, 2019, https://www.minneapolisfed.org/publications/the-region/the-industrial-revolution-past-and-future.

antifreedom—both religious and otherwise. After 1750, in many countries, sustainable economic growth became something we could count on if the rules, laws, and incentives were appropriate, but there was an unleashing of religious and political freedom. Religious freedom, economic freedom, and political freedom are symbiotic. They need each other. Religious freedom provides an environment of personal agency and free will to discern truth, which encourages and is encouraged by the individual spirit of hard work and entrepreneurship so necessary for economic growth. Christianity predates the Industrial Revolution and what Deirdre McCloskey calls the "Great Enrichment," which is descriptive of a sustained period of not only economic growth but also personal freedom, which is predated by a revolution in ideas and rhetoric.[8] If the theology of Scripture, which includes the notions of property rights, stewardship, free will, prudence, hard work, integrity, trade, and community, is so ancient, why is the spread of religious freedom over the scope of human history such a new phenomenon?

These ideas in Scripture must be adopted and lived out by ordinary people. Prior to the Protestant Reformation, the notion that ordinary Christians could have a nonhierarchical relationship with God that was individual, spiritual, and direct was radical. After the Reformation, the important notion that we are a priesthood of believers had an important impact on the rise of both religious freedom and economic freedom. It is the ideas of religious freedom and economic freedom working in concert that brings about the incredible rise in the standard of living that we have seen over the last two hundred years. The church, which had been tightly bound to the government, was no longer the paternalistic institution with political hegemony that stood between people and God. Now, ordinary folks had direct access to God and were empowered to use it. This idea sparked a need for a new political economy—one where the church and the government did not hold sway on all of economic and civic life but where, instead, people needed to be free to discover truth and live by it. This requires a *true* environment of religious freedom, one in which your neighbor may fiercely disagree with you on religious doctrine, but that disagreement is acceptable and, in fact, peaceful.

U.S. citizens live in one of the freest, richest, and most tolerant places on earth. There are, and always have been, threats to personal freedoms, and religious freedom is no exception. To win the war, which requires a long-term view,

---

[8] Deirdre Nansen McCloskey, *Bourgeois Equality: How Ideas, Not Capital or Institutions, Enriched the World* (Chicago: University of Chicago Press, 2016), Exordium xv.

we must stand up for religious freedom for everyone. We must understand how symbiotic religious freedom is with the other freedoms that we hold so dear: economic and political freedom. We must fight for the freedom of all people to live out their beliefs as they see fit, so long as they do not truncate the rights of others. To do any of this, we must recognize the proper role of the government. With its power of coercion, it will always be an institution that special interests seek to use to their own gain, at the expense of others. For religious freedom to reign, we must follow God's primary commandments: "Love the Lord your God with all your heart and with all your soul and with all your mind. This is the first and greatest commandment. And the second is like it: 'Love your neighbor as yourself'" (Matt. 22:37–39).

In Jer. 29:13, God says, "You will seek me and find me when you seek me with all your heart." When Christians are free to worship and live out their faith in every dimension of life, God will use the testimony of their lives and work to bring all those who truly seek him to himself. Those who do not know God will be able to seek him (or not, if they so choose) when they have the freedom to do so. The best the government can do is protect this environment of religious freedom, and the government must seek to do only that. The rest is up to God working through us.

Contributors

Anne R. Bradley
Dr. Anne R. Bradley is the George and Sally Mayer Fellow for Economic Education and academic director at The Fund for American Studies where she teaches economics at George Mason University. Dr. Bradley is also the vice president of Economic Initiatives at the Institute for Faith, Work & Economics (IFWE). Dr. Bradley is coeditor of and contributor to IFWE's *Counting the Cost: Christian Perspectives on Capitalism* and *For the Least of These: A Biblical Answer to Poverty*. She is a professor at the Institute for World Politics and adjunct professor at Grove City College. She is an affiliate scholar for the Acton Institute and a member of the Faculty Network at The Foundation for Economic Education. Previously, she taught at Charles University, Prague, and served as the associate director for the program in economics, politics, and the law at the James M. Buchanan Center at George Mason University. Dr. Bradley received her PhD in economics from George Mason University in 2006, during which time she was a James M. Buchanan Scholar.

Stanley W. Carlson-Thies
Stanley W. Carlson-Thies is founder and senior director of the Institutional Religious Freedom Alliance, a division of the Center for Public Justice, which promotes the religious freedoms that enable faith-based organizations to make their uncommon contributions to the common good. Carlson-Thies served on the initial staff of President Bush's White House faith-based office (2001–2002) and in 2009–2010 served on the church-state taskforce of President Obama's faith-based Advisory Council. He has advised federal departments and states on how to construct productive and respectful relationships with faith-based and secular community organizations. He is the organizer and long-time host of a monthly nonpartisan and multifaith gathering of religious freedom advocates and leaders of faith-based organizations, the Coalition to Preserve Religious Freedom, which monitors and educates Congress and the executive branch.

Joseph Connors

Joseph Connors is an assistant professor of economics in the Barney Barnett School of Business and Free Enterprise at Florida Southern College where he is also a fellow of the Center for Free Enterprise. He teaches microeconomics, micro theory, and the philosophy of business. His research interests are how economic and political institutions impact the poor in the developing world and the political economy of rent-seeking. Dr. Connors is a research fellow for The Institute for Faith, Work & Economics. Before his career in economics, Dr. Connors was an electrical engineer and worked for various firms in Silicon Valley.

Daniel L. Dreisbach

Daniel L. Dreisbach is a professor of Legal Studies at American University in Washington, DC. He earned a doctor of philosophy degree from Oxford University, where he studied as a Rhodes Scholar, and a juris doctor degree from the University of Virginia. His research interests include constitutional law and history and the intersection of religion, politics, and law in American public life. He has authored or edited ten books, including *Thomas Jefferson and the Wall of Separation between Church and State* (New York University Press, 2002) and *Reading the Bible with the Founding Fathers* (Oxford University Press, 2017). He is a past recipient of American University's highest faculty award, "Scholar/Teacher of the Year."

Barrett Duke

Barrett Duke is the executive director and treasurer of the Montana Southern Baptist Convention. Prior to his current position, Dr. Duke was vice president for Public Policy and Research in the Washington, DC office of the Southern Baptist Ethics & Religious Liberty Commission. Duke has worked with legislators and various government agencies on many legislative and public policy issues, including religious liberty. He speaks regularly on Christian worldview and related topics in many religious and civic settings. Duke earned his PhD in religious and theological studies from the joint PhD program of the University of Denver and the Iliff School of Theology, where he studied biblical interpretation.

Os Guinness

Os Guinness is an author and social critic. He is the great-great-great grandson of Arthur Guinness, the Dublin brewer, and was born in China in World War Two where his parents were medical missionaries. A witness to the climax of the Chinese revolution in 1949, he was expelled with many other foreigners in 1951 and returned to Europe where he was educated in England. He completed his undergraduate degree at the University of London and his D.Phil in the social sciences from Oriel College, Oxford. Os has written or edited more than thirty books, including *The Call, Time for Truth, Unspeakable, A Free People's Suicide,* and *The Global Public Square*. His latest book, *Last Call for Liberty: How America's Genius for Freedom Has Become Its Greatest Threat,* was published in 2018. Since moving to the United States in 1984, Os has been a guest scholar at the Woodrow Wilson Center for International Studies, a guest scholar and visiting fellow at the Brookings Institution, and senior fellow at the Trinity Forum and the EastWest Institute in New York. He was the lead drafter of the Williamsburg Charter in 1988, a celebration of the bicentennial of the U.S. Constitution, and later of "The Global Charter of Conscience," which was published at the European Union Parliament in 2012.

Mark David Hall

Mark David Hall is Herbert Hoover Distinguished Professor of Politics and Faculty Fellow in the William Penn Honors Program at George Fox University. He is also associated faculty at the Center for the Study of Law and Religion at Emory University and a senior fellow at Baylor University's Institute for Studies of Religion. Hall has written, edited, or co-edited a dozen books, including *Did America Have a Christian Founding?: Separating Modern Myth from Historical Truth* (Nelson Books, 2019); *Great Christian Jurists in American History* (Cambridge University Press, 2019); *Faith and the Founders of the American Republic* (Oxford University Press, 2014); *The Forgotten Founders on Religion and Public Life* (University of Notre Dame Press, 2009); and *The Sacred Rights of Conscience: Selected Readings on Religious Liberty and Church-State Relations in the American Founding* (Liberty Fund Press, 2009).

Art Lindsley

Rev. Dr. Art Lindsley is the vice president of Theological Initiatives at IFWE, where he oversees the development of a theology that integrates faith, work, and economics. He joined the C.S. Lewis Institute as president in 1987 and remains a senior fellow there. Dr. Lindsley is coeditor of and contributor to IFWE's *Counting the Cost: Christian Perspectives on Capitalism* and *For the Least of These: A Biblical Answer to Poverty*. Dr. Lindsley also authored *C.S. Lewis's Case for Christ, True Truth, Love: The Ultimate Apologetic,* and IFWE booklets *Free Indeed* and *Be Transformed* (in English and Spanish). He has been a frequent guest on radio talk shows across the country, his articles have been featured in publications such as *The Daily Signal* and *The Gospel Coalition,* and his op-eds published nationwide by *The Washington Times, Christianity Today, The Christian Post,* and others. He is on the board of the Geneva Institute for Leadership and Public Policy and leads government outreach for Transform World 2020. Rev. Dr. Lindsley earned an MDiv from Pittsburgh Theological Seminary and a PhD from the University of Pittsburgh.

Jennifer Marshall Patterson

Jennifer Marshall Patterson is a senior visiting fellow for the Institute for Family, Community, and Opportunity at The Heritage Foundation. She is also a visiting lecturer and directs the Institute of Theology and Public Life at Reformed Theological Seminary in Washington, DC. She holds a master's degree in religion from Reformed Theological Seminary, a master's degree in statecraft and world politics from the Washington-based Institute of World Politics, and a bachelor's degree in French from Wheaton College in Wheaton, Illinois. She is pursuing doctoral studies in moral theology and ethics at the Catholic University of America.

John S. Redd Jr.

John S. Redd Jr. is the president and associate professor of Old Testament at Reformed Theological Seminary (RTS) in Washington, DC, as well as an ordained minister in the Evangelical Presbyterian Church. He began his career in media consultation but left the business world to pursue a Master of Divinity at RTS Orlando. Dr. Redd completed his doctoral dissertation in the Department of Semitic Language and Egyptian Languages and Literatures at the Catholic University of America. Over the years, Dr. Redd has served in churches located in Washington, DC, Raleigh, NC, and Orlando, FL. He has also taught at Catholic University of America, the Augustine Theological Institute in Malta, the International Training Institute in the Mediterranean basin, and for Third Millennium Ministries. Dr. Redd has served as dean of students at RTS Orlando. His interests include literary approaches to the Bible, linguistics and biblical languages, ancient Near Eastern backgrounds to Scripture, and Old Testament theology.

E. Gregory Wallace

As a professor of law at Campbell University School of Law, Wallace teaches constitutional law with an emphasis on religious freedom and the right to arms. He holds LLM and SJD degrees from the University of Virginia School of Law, a JD degree from the University of Arkansas (Little Rock) School of Law, and an MA degree from Dallas Theological Seminary. Professor Wallace's doctoral dissertation is entitled "Higher Call: Foundations of Religious Freedom in American Constitutionalism." He has taught on religious freedom at law schools in China and South Korea and was a discussant at the Federalist Society/Templeton Foundation 2016 colloquium on The Past and Future of Free Exercise. Wallace has published several academic articles on religious freedom, the right to arms, and cultural issues involving law and religion.

Hugh C. Whelchel

Hugh C. Whelchel is the executive director of the Institute for Faith, Work & Economics (IFWE), a Christian research organization advancing a free and flourishing society by revolutionizing the way people view their work. Previously, Hugh served as director of Reformed Theological Seminary's (RTS) Washington, DC, campus. Whelchel has been published by a variety of media outlets from *The Washington Post* to *Christianity Today*, *The Gospel Coalition*, and *ByFaith* magazine. He has also been a guest on Moody Radio Network's "In the Market with Janet Parshall," Salem Radio Network, IRN/USA Radio Network, and Truth in Action Ministries' "Truth That Transforms," and the "Jack Riccardi Show," among other shows. Additionally, Hugh has over thirty years of experience in the business world. He graduated from the University of Florida, earned a master's in theology from RTS, and is completing his Doctor of Ministry at Gordon Conwell Theological Seminary. Hugh authored *How Then Should We Work? Rediscovering the Biblical Doctrine of Work*. He sits on several nonprofit boards, including The Fellows Initiative, an umbrella organization supporting and establishing church-based fellows programs designed to help young adults understand God's vocational calling on their lives as they enter their careers. He also serves as an elder at McLean Presbyterian Church (PCA).

Index

Index

Index

Index

Grudem, Wayne, 141
Gutiérrez, Gustavo, 128

Hagner, Donald, 46n9
Halo effect. *See* economic halo effect
Hamilton, Marci, 189
Hayek, F. A., 145, 149–150, 151, 156, 160, 162, 166
Health insurance, 170
Helwys, Thomas, 102
Henry, Patrick, 127, 199
Henry III, 149
Herbener, Jeffrey, 241
Hercules Industries, 79
"Here I Stand" speech (Luther), 69–70
Heritage Freedom Index, 139
Hill, Austin, 141
Hindus, 128
Hirono, Mazie, 173–174
Hitchens, Christopher, 19
Hitler, Adolf, 151
Hobby Lobby, 170, 206, 225
Hodge, A. A., 69
Holy Spirit, 52
Hope Center, 179
Hubmaier, Balthasar, 100
Hu Jintao, 17
Human anthropology, 148, 243–245

Idolatry, 37
Image of God, 27–31
Imago Dei, 27–28
Immanent frame, 29
Immunizations, 203. *See also* vaccinations
Individual sphere, 44–50
Industrial Revolution, 246
"In Europe God Is (Not) Dead," 140–141
Inner freedom, 129, 134–135
Institute for Faith, Work & Economics (IFWE), 1
Institutional Profiles Database (IPD), 156–157
Institutional religious freedom, 223–224
  extensive protections, 226–230
  indicators of importance of, 211–212
  laws and regulations protecting, 236
  operational policies, 225–226
  safeguarding, 235–236

Internet, 14–15
Intolerance, 95–96
Islam, 158
"Is Progress Possible?", 137
Israel, 37–39, 55–56

Jackson, James, 192
Jackson, Robert H., 200–201
James, Charles Fenton, 115n18
Jefferson, Thomas, 61n1
  election of 1800, 122, 123
  Notes on the State of Virginia, 76–77
Jehovah's Witnesses, 200
Jesus Christ, 52, 56, 80, 101. *See also* New Testament; Old Testament
  biblical view of freedom, 128–129
  body of, 134
  on church and state, 85–88
  as a creator, 38–39
  heretics, 101
  hypocrites and false believers, 36
  inner freedom, 134
  kingdom, 38–39, 86, 101
  persecution, 86–87
  rejecting lordship of, 56
Jews, 23, 37, 56n22, 57, 68n22, 131
  discrimination against, 16
  forced conversion of, 12
  human rights, 16
  Nazi Germany, 151, 165
John of England, King, 149
Johnson, Byron, 216
Judaism, 130
Judeo-Christian origins, 148
Judeo-Christian political tradition, 159

Kavanaugh, Brett, 174
Kennedy, Anthony, 183, 186n3, 234n51
King & Spalding, 178
Kistemaker, Simon, 47n12
Kittel, G., 68n20
Knights of Columbus, 173–174
Knowledge, 68n21
Knox, John, 70
Kreeft, Peter, 142

Lactantius, 12, 66, 93–95
Langston, Chelsea, 214n7

Index

Index

Index

Index

Index